THE NATURE
OF SEXUAL DESIRE

THE NATURE
OF SEXUAL DESIRE

JAMES GILES

PRAEGER

Westport, Connecticut
London

Library of Congress Cataloging-in-Publication Data

Giles, James, 1958–
    The nature of sexual desire / James Giles.
        p. cm.—(Critical perspectives on culture and society, ISSN 1097–5020)
    Includes bibliographical references and index.
    ISBN 0–275–95995–3 (alk. paper)
    1. Sex. 2. Love. I. Title. II. Series
    HQ21.G538 2004
    306.7—dc22   2004049562

British Library Cataloguing in Publication Data is available.

Library of Congress Catalog Card Number: 2004049562
ISBN: 0–275–95995–3
ISSN: 1097–5020

First published in 2004

An imprint of Greenwood Publishing Group, Inc.
www.praeger.com

Printed in the United States of America

The paper used in this book complies with the
Permanent Paper Standard issued by the National
Information Standards Organization (Z39.48-1984).

10 9 8 7 6 5 4 3 2 1

Copyright Acknowledgment

Some of the material in Chapters 3 and 5 was previously published in James Giles,
"A theory of love and sexual desire," *Journal for the Theory of Sexual Behaviour*. I
therefore thank Blackwell Publishing for allowing me to reprint it here. I also thank
Hong Kong University Press for granting permission to reprint the extracts from
page 78 and page 128 of *Cantonese Love Songs: An English Translation of Jiu
Ji-yung's Cantonese Songs of Early 19th Century*, translated by Peter T. Morris.

To Karen

The sexual impulse is the most vehement of cravings, the desire of desires, the concentration of all our willing. Accordingly, its satisfaction, corresponding exactly to the individual desire of anyone, thus a desire directed to a definite individual, is the summit and crown of his happiness, the ultimate goal of his natural endeavours, with whose attainment everything seems to him attained, and the missing of which everything seems to have been missed.

SCHOPENHAUER

Contents

Preface

Anyone who studies sexual desire will learn that no particular discipline has exclusive claim on this topic. Thus, philosophers, psychologists, biologists, and poets all have much to say about this most pressing of human desires. To try, therefore, to approach sexual desire within the confines of only one traditional discipline is to miss out on what has been gained here by other disciplines: it is to see sexual desire from only one angle.

It seems to be this awareness of the multifaceted aspects of not only sexual desire but also of various sexual phenomena that has given rise to the interdisciplinary subject of sexology. For sexology is just the attempt to cross traditional boundaries and see sexuality and thus sexual desire, which lies at its core, in all its dimensions. Although my training is mainly in philosophy and psychology, it is in this interdisciplinary spirit of sexology that I have undertaken the present study. This means that those readers coming from a strictly, say, psychological background might be taken aback to see discussions of contemporary psychological research and ancient Indian erotology taking place side by side. However, drawing on such diverse sources not only enables us to form a more well-rounded view of sexual desire but also helps us to disentangle the universal aspects of sexual desire from its merely culturally specific features. Further, it serves as a check on the various biases, such as ethnocentrism, that are wont to plague such discussions.

The ideas in this book have been developed through my teaching of courses in human sexuality, philosophy, psychology, and social anthropology and through my supervision of student projects and theses. This work has been done at various universities in different countries and so has given me the chance to engage people's ideas about sexual desire from within a cross-cultural perspective. While teaching at the Hawaii campus of Kansai Gaidai University, for example, my students were primarily Japanese females. Their candid discussions about their views of sexuality gave me, a Western male, the opportunity to explore the idea of sexual desire from both a female and an East Asian perspective. Likewise, while teaching in Denmark, my students gave me access to a Scandinavian perspective on sexual desire. On the other hand, teaching in the International Programme at the University of Cambridge gave me a kaleidoscope of views from students from all over the world.

If being able to use materials from sources other than one's personal background is important in most of the human sciences, it is particularly important in sexology. This is because, as one sexologist put it, "writing about sex is seen as writing about oneself" (Manderson, 1992, p. 451). Drawing upon such materials to develop one's own ideas should help take the force out of this standard criticism. The cultures of the various students I have taught differ, of course, in numerous ways, as does the gender of males and females. Yet a comparison of the views of sexual desire held by my students, along with the study of a wide range of both ancient texts and modern research, has convinced me that there is an essential core to sexual desire that cuts across epochs, cultures, and genders. It is part of our common human condition.

I have also benefited from discussions of sexual desire with many of my colleagues and friends, both male and female. To all these people I express my gratitude for their openness in discussing what is still, all these years after Freud, a subject surrounded with taboo and anxiety. Although the people who helped with this book are too numerous to thank individually, I must nevertheless give special thanks to Cherry Ekins, Jane Garry, and Ross Hughes, all of whom took the time to read the manuscript and offer their insightful comments.

The Problem of Sexual Desire

AN UNSETTLING STATE OF AFFAIRS

Of all the desires that make up human yearnings, sexual desire holds a unique place. For although it is a desire that affects us in powerful ways and whose fulfillment is of the utmost significance to us, it is nevertheless a desire whose ultimate goal seems shrouded in obscurity. For what is it exactly we desire? Although there are many quick replies that can be given here, a careful examination of most of them will show that they fail to capture the essence of the longing in our hearts.

It thus turns out that, in an important sense, we are not completely clear about the ultimate object of our own desire. This is a problem because to be hard pressed by a desire, the goal of which is unclear, cannot help but be an unsettling state of affairs. In such a situation, one can feel left behind, so to speak, by one's own desires. Here sexual desire seems to take on a life of its own, rushing through us toward its secret goal, dragging us with it like a broken tether behind a runaway horse. In this sense, the problem of sexual desire is an existential problem. That is, it is a problem rooted in a central feature of human existence.

It is possible, of course, to disagree with this view in various ways. Someone might argue, for example, that there is nothing especially powerful about sexual desire or significant about its fulfillment and that sexual desire is but one more of our many desires. Such a view, however, flies in the face of everyday experience. It does not take particularly great powers of observation to see that sexual matters are everywhere, that sexual meanings infiltrate and imbue our daily interactions, that sexual glances are forever being made, that sexual fantasies quietly attend our dealings with numerous people (and also our moments alone), that a person's gender and sexual attractiveness fundamentally determine how we react to him or her, and that most people are particularly, and many even desperately, concerned over finding and keeping an appropriate sexual partner.

But what is it that ultimately fuels this profusion of sexual awareness? The answer is sexual desire: for to glance at someone in a sexual way is to betray the stirrings, however faint, of sexual desire, just as to fantasize sexually about someone is to be moved by sexual desire to imagine the fulfillment of one's desires. In the same way, it is because sexual desire aims fundamentally at persons of a desired gender, and from there to sexually attractive persons of that gender, that gender and sexual attractiveness cast their nets over us, enabling sexual desire to pull us in its distinctive way, even if ever so slightly, toward those who would most fulfill our desires. Further, it is this same sexual desire that, gathering force from its first stirrings, moves beyond the realm of the imagination and leads us actively to search for an attractive person of the longed-for gender. There are, of course, other desires, intentions, and concerns that blend themselves with such instances of sexual awareness, but this does not change the fact that what ultimately lies at the core of such instances of awareness is sexual desire.

To this it could be protested that sexual desire is not something that appears in such everyday occurrences as brief moments of eye contact or in fantasies about other persons. Sexual desire, it could be said, is rather an intense experience that occurs only in overtly sexual interactions that provoke a sense of urgency, as, for example, when a passionately involved couple are on the verge of sexual intercourse. A person holding this view might feel that the experience that takes place outside of such encounters is best described as merely sexual interest, or some such thing, rather than as sexual desire. But if this is the case, one immediately wants to know what it means to have sexual interest in someone: for to be sexually interested in someone *is* to be interested in that person in a sexual way. But what is the reason for being interested in someone in a sexual way? Plainly, it is because one has sexual desire, be it strong or barely there, toward that person. The reason that someone wakens my sexual interest is because I notice that she is sexually attractive. But to notice that she is sexually attractive is, at the same time, to notice that she rouses my desire. Moreover, to hold that sexual desire is necessarily intense is tantamount to disallowing the idea that sexual desire is something that can happen with varying degrees of urgency. That is, it is to assert that when the intensity of sexual desire begins to lessen, it is no longer sexual desire.

Yet it is obvious that sexual desire is something that occurs in all variety of degrees and does not simply disappear when it is no longer urgent. Thus, although I might feel intense sexual desire in the moment of an intimate embrace with a person whom I find sexually attractive, it is evident that the same though less urgent experience can occur when I merely see the same person sitting across from me in a restaurant or walking past me in the street. In each of these cases, what I feel is a sense of motion toward the person with her attractiveness taking hold of me and pulling my awareness toward her. In the first case, the sense of motion toward her is unrelenting and the grip of her attraction firm and overpowering. In the second case, things are milder. Here the motion is felt to be gentle and more stable, with her attractiveness softly calling out to me and encouraging my awareness to linger. Yet my desirous orientation toward her is the same in each situation. What is different is the degree of urgency.

Or, again, sexual desire can vary in degrees according to how sexually desirable one finds a particular person. Thus, I might find one person to be exceedingly attractive, while another person might appear as only mildly so. In the first case, it is understandable that my sexual desire toward the person would be more powerful than in the second case. Further, it is obvious that people themselves differ according to the strength of sexual desire they tend to experience. Some persons have high amounts of sexual desire and are forever fantasizing about and seeking out sexual interaction. At the other end of the spectrum are those who have relatively lower amounts of sexual desire and have less of an urge to fantasize about and search for such interactions—which is not to say that such persons' sexual desire is not a pressing affair for them, only that it is less so than for those with higher amounts of sexual desire. Between these two extremes stretch a range of persons with different amounts of sexual desire. All this points toward the idea that sexual desire is something that exists in various degrees.

But now we come to the question of why sexual desire should exert such an influence on us. The obvious answer is that it works the way it does because of the momentous significance that most of us give to its fulfillment. This significance is well expressed in the Indian erotic poem "*Smaradipika,*" or "Light of Love." Here the poet Rudra says that "the joy of love-play, manifested in so many attractive forms, makes the human condition blessed" such that "he who has lived one year with the Love God's favour has lived for all time and counts all else as nothing" (Rudra, 1964, p. 85). The god that Rudra is referring to here is Kama, the ancient Indian god of love and erotic pleasure.[1] But that Kama has at least this seemingly dual designation raises another question. For if Kama is the god of both love and erotic pleasure, could it not be that it is really love rather than sexual desire whose favor we so devotedly court? Thus, although it might be

---

[1]Although the terms "erotic pleasure" and "sexual pleasure" are basically synonymous, the word "erotic" seems to refer to the occurrence of enjoyment in the way that the word "sexual" need not. For this reason I prefer to use the term "erotic pleasure."

true that finding an appropriate sexual partner is of the greatest importance to most people, this, it could be argued, is simply because those with whom we are in love also tend to be the main persons toward whom we have sexual desire. Consequently, it is the finding of someone to love that is of prime importance to us, not the finding of a sexual partner. The finding of a sexual partner is simply an incidental outcome of finding a love partner.

Although this seems a common view, it depends on the debatable assumption that there is an essential difference between being in love and having sexual desire, such that one can be in love with a person without, at the same time, also having sexual desire toward that person. Such an idea is debatable because it appears to go contrary to the way in which romantic love is experienced. For it is evident that most people do sexually desire the person with whom they are in love. This is not to deny that there are genuine love relationships where one or both of the lovers avoid sexual contact with the other or appear to lack sexual desire toward their partner. In such cases, however, the lack of sexual desire tends to be only apparent. For evidence suggests that sexual desire in such genuine love relationships is not really absent but only overridden or suppressed by anxieties or other stronger and countervailing desires (see, e.g., Kaplan, 1987, 1995). In those situations where there really is no sexual desire between the partners, then it is more than likely that the relationship is not one that is based on genuine romantic love.

Although we will explore the bond between love and sexual desire more fully in Chapter 5, for now it can be asked why it is that persons who are sexually orientated to the opposite sex, that is, heterosexuals, also seek their romantic love partners among the opposite sex, whereas persons who are sexually orientated to persons of the same sex, that is, homosexuals, likewise seek their romantic love partners among the same sex. The most probable answer would be that romantic love has embedded within it the elements of sexual desire. And were, for example, a man who claimed to be exclusively heterosexual—that is, to desire only females as sexual partners—to announce that he had fallen romantically in love with another man, most people would either not accept his claim that he was exclusively heterosexual or not believe that he had actually fallen in love with a man. Why is this? Because most of us feel that romantic love must imply sexual desire. And if sexual desire is such a decisive part of romantic love, then one cannot live in the love god's favor without living in sexual desire. In other words, one cannot court romantic love without at the same time courting sexual desire. Indeed, as I shall try to show, love has its very basis in sexual desire.

But this still leaves us with the question of why we impart such significance to the fulfillment of our sexual desires. Such a question, however, is one whose answer must wait until the conclusion of this study. For only after we have inquired into the nature of sexual desire can the existential situation that gives birth to sexual desire, and thus to the significance that we invest in its fulfillment, be made fully clear.

Another way to disagree that there is a problem about sexual desire is to question the idea that there is anything obscure about the goal or object of sexual desire. Someone taking this position might try to argue that what we desire when we have sexual desire is something that is eminently clear. The trouble, however, is that people seem in much disagreement over what exactly sexual desire is desire for. Thus, one variously hears that sexual desire is the desire for sexual intercourse, erotic pleasure, orgasm, companionship, emotional intimacy, love, self-esteem, power, propagation of the species, or immortality through one's progeny. But how is it that there could arise such disagreement if the goal of sexual desire were so obvious? Perhaps it might be felt that sexual desire is the desire for all these things and that people are not really in disagreement but simply emphasizing the different aspects of sexual desire. But this maneuver will not work because one can easily imagine instances of sexual desire that do not contain the desire for any of these things and yet, for all that, are still instances of sexual desire. This does not mean, however, that the desires for such things do not frequently accompany and even become blended with sexual desire, only that they cannot be what lies at the heart of sexual desire.

Another reply that might be given here is that there is no one thing that we all sexually desire. For everyone, it might be argued, has his or her own particular object of sexual desire. At one level—the level of what might be called sexual taste—this is certainly true. Thus, one person's sexual tastes might be primarily focused on sexual intercourse in a particular position, while another person's tastes might focus on being masturbated by a partner. Plainly, both these sexual activities differ in many ways. Yet their difference is hardly enough for us to be completely at a loss to understand why people refer to both of them as the same sort of activity, namely, as *sexual* activity. Consequently, within the desires that underlie the diverse elements that make up different person's sexual tastes, there would seem to be a common feature that gives each desire its sexual quality. This is something we will deal with in Chapter 3.

But how could it be that something whose presence is everywhere, woven through our daily existence, is nevertheless hidden in obscurity? The answer here could not be better put than in a statement made by the ancient Greek philosopher Heraclitus (fifth to sixth century BCE). For, Heraclitus tells us, "many people do not understand the sorts of things they encounter! Nor do they recognize them even after they have had experience of them—though they themselves think they recognize them" (1987, p. 19; punctuation amended). Although there is much disagreement as to what sorts of things Heraclitus has in mind here, applying his claim to the issue of sexual desire seems to capture the problem before us. For here we could say that although we both encounter and experience sexual desire, we nevertheless fail to understand and recognize it, even though we think we recognize it. Thus, although we frequently experience sexual desire, we might nevertheless mistakenly think that its nature is to seek out sexual intercourse, erotic pleasure, or orgasm. Or again, because people often hold such views, they may not recognize sexual desire when it wells up within them. In this sense, they are, as Heraclitus also puts it, "separated from that with which they are in most continuous contact" (p. 45).

Yet, in another way, to encounter, experience, and be in most continuous contact with something is to have its essence laid bare before us. For to undergo something in this way is nothing other than to have it presented directly to us. This is evident with sexual desire because even though at one level we might not be fully aware what it is that our desire is striving for, at another level it is also clear to us that we are in collusion with sexual desire. Here we are aware that it gets its force only because its object, which is clear to us, is something that we want so badly. In fact, sexual desire is nothing more than our wanting of this object. Thus, as we move forward with our sexual desire, as we reach out to its fulfillment, there is, somewhere within us, also an awareness of what it is we want. After all, the actions that our sexual desire gives rise to are those that are executed with the purposeful awareness that it is just these actions that will serve to fulfill our desire. It is as though in addition to being dragged behind a horse that seems out of our control, we are also somehow firmly in the saddle, guiding it to where we long to go.

Thus, even though the essence of sexual desire may seem to escape us, it is in fact fully within our gaze, or at least very close to our gaze. Here one is naturally reminded of Freud's claim concerning a person's knowledge of the meaning of his or her own dreams. According to Freud, the person who has had a dream knows exactly what his dream means, "only he does not know that he knows it and for that reason thinks he does not know it" (1916, p. 101; italics removed). In Freud's view, this conundrum is explained by seeing that the mind has both conscious and unconscious levels. Thus, although the dreamer does not know that he knows the meaning of his dream, this is only at the conscious level, for at the unconscious level, he does know the meaning of his dream. In Freud's technique of dream interpretation, then, the process involves bringing the meaning of the dream from the unconscious to the conscious level.

Such a picture, however, does not represent the essence of the problem of sexual desire. For here it is not that we lack conscious knowledge of what we desire, but nevertheless know it unconsciously. For although it may be that unconscious desires often attach themselves to and become blended with sexual desire—especially since sexual desire is something that some people experience with anxiety—sexual desire itself is not an unconscious phenomenon. And this remains true despite the fact that a person's sexual desire might have taken the form it has because of long-forgotten and now unconsciously repressed events from childhood. For although these events may have caused, and even continue to cause, a person's sexual desire to take a particular form, the desire itself is still something that presents itself to awareness. This is not to claim, however, that particular sexual desires are always consciously experienced. For plainly certain types of sexual desires are disturbing enough to the person who has them that, as a defense against being aware of them, they are unconsciously repressed. For example, as pointed out by Freud, among a person's earliest sexual desires are those directed toward his or her family members. Here a boy may have sexual desires directed toward his mother or sister, while a girl may have such desires toward her father or brother. However, because of the powerful taboos against incest in most cultures, people often feel immense guilt or disgust over having such desires. Nevertheless, such desires frequently continue into later life and thus are often unconsciously repressed. Here sexual desire exists beyond the person's full awareness.

When, however, no such guilt or disgust is experienced with sexual desire, then there is no need for sexual desire to be relegated to the realms of the unconscious. Here sexual desire presents itself to us in all its detailed fullness. The difficulty, however, is that such sexual desire is typically experienced in concert with numerous other desires and concerns. These other elements, which are extrinsic to the nature of sexual desire, then overlay sexual desire like camouflage netting and thus obscure—though do not remove—the awareness of the object of sexual desire. Consequently, the task of giving an account of sexual desire involves the task of seeing through this netting in order to locate sexual desire itself. What is required, then, in order to make our way through this problem is a method that enables us to see through the various extrinsic elements and to direct our gaze on sexual desire itself. The means for such gazing is what I will call phenomenology, a method that has been employed by both philosophers and psychologists (e.g., Churchill, 1990; Dossett, 2002; Kvale, 1983) and one that will be used throughout this study.

This method is a technique of inquiry that was first systematically expounded by the German philosopher Edmund Husserl. For Husserl (1913), phenomenology is a way of uncovering the nature of reality by an examination of ideas or how things present themselves to us. By turning to this presentation—"to the things themselves," as Husserl puts it—we free ourselves from anticipatory ideas and other prejudices that obscure our perception of reality. This is the basis of Husserl's concept of *epoché,* or setting to one side the question of what exists beyond our immediate experience.

Thus, in turning to the examination of a particular idea or experience, Husserl sets to one side or suspends the question of whether the experience reflects or is caused by something beyond itself and attempts to describe only the experience as it exists, in all its meaningfulness, in awareness. This investigation of meaning is one of the crucial differences between the phenomenological method and the introspective techniques used by Wundt and others, techniques that depend on the assumption—rejected by phenomenologists—that experience can be reduced to conscious elements and attributes that are devoid of meaning. This focus on experience, however, does not imply that things like theoretical discussion have no place in a phenomenological inquiry, for such discussions can often help to support or integrate the findings of phenomenology. Still, the results of such a discussion can be of only secondary importance to the phenomenologist.

A consideration of the phenomenological method, however, makes it evident that many thinkers before Husserl and from very different cultures than Husserl's also used a similar approach. Thus, Dogen, the medieval Japanese Zen master, argues that only through the observation of experience, or "the flow of life," as he puts it, can we come to know the nature of reality. That is, reality is that which presents itself to us. This is the basis of his claiming that "nothing throughout the entire universe has ever been concealed" (Dogen, 1994, p. 3; translation amended). This does not mean that the world in its entirety is always presenting itself to us: for the world is vast and unlimited, and what we experience is forever shifting according to our point of view. It does mean, however, that within the moment of experience, there is no element of reality that is integral to the experience but remains somehow concealed beyond it. For Dogen, the phenomenologist—or Zen yogin, as he would put it—must attempt to cultivate a receptive state of awareness in which anticipatory ideas and so forth are disengaged and an openness to experience is brought to the fore. Dogen refers to this state of awareness as the place within from which one undergoes the presence of things as they are:

To be sure, having once realized the place within, you must not analyze it in order to understand it through discriminatory thought and, thereby reduce it to fit your opinions. When you have bored through to certainty, it all at once manifests before your very eyes, yet that which is the most intimate will not necessarily take some visible form: 'manifesting before your very eyes' may or may not have a literal meaning. (Dogen, 1996, p. 59; translation amended)

Being a Buddhist philosopher, Dogen's concerns are ultimately with the experience of enlightenment, or what he calls authentication (*sho* in Japanese). Yet the state of authentication is not at all dissimilar from the receptive awareness of phenomenological inquiry. In both cases, what is cultivated is an openness to experience that allows phenomena to present themselves as they are.

THE NATURE OF DESIRE

Having presented the problem of sexual desire, I must now turn to the problem of the nature of desire. For in order to come to an understanding of the nature of sexual desire, one must first come to an understanding of desire itself. This is simply because an intrinsic feature of sexual desire is that it is a desire. Although this is an area that has received a fair amount of attention from both philosophers and psychologists, most of the work here has tended to focus on the function that desire plays in motivation rather than on the experiential features of desire. Thus, scholars working in this area will often point out that in order for desire to motivate a person to act, it must occur together with certain beliefs: beliefs about the way things are, about which actions are possible given the way things are, and about which actions are likely to bring about the desired change. This preoccupation with the role of desire in action has led to various attempts to define desire in terms of its function in bringing about action. The problem, however, is that although such discussions are useful in their own right, they seek to give an account of desire from the outside, as it were, not from the perspective of the person having the desire and the way in which desire presents itself to his or her own awareness. This is a problem because it neglects a fundamental dimension of desire, namely, the dimension from which we live out our desires.

A similar sort of problem can occur when, rather than focusing on the effects of desire, one focuses on the causes of desire. For here too desire itself is all but ignored. A good example of this latter sort of neglect can be found in the social psychologist McDougall's (1908) definition of desire. Here we are told that "desire is the general name for that peculiar experience which arises in every mind (sufficiently developed intellectually to hold before itself the idea of an end) whenever any strong impulse or conative tendency cannot immediately attain or actively progress to its natural end" (p. 367). But this definition is unsatisfactory because, whether desire arises in the way suggested or whether it is only sufficiently developed minds that enable it to occur, the definition tells us nothing about the nature of desire itself. All we are told here is that it is "that peculiar experience." But obviously, to know the nature of desire itself—rather than what causes it or who can have it—we must know about the experience of desire. Being told merely that it is a "peculiar experience" is of no help.

To get at this experience of desire, a person must therefore direct his or her gaze to desire as it is delivered to awareness in the moment that the desire appears. Here desire presents itself as none other than a motion of awareness that presses awareness in the direction of the object that is desired. This motion weaves into all corners of awareness while, at the same time, racing out toward its object. In this racing toward its object, while at the same time being woven into awareness, desire pulls the general state of awareness with it. Thus, although other aspects of a person's awareness—thoughts, feelings, sensations, and so forth—might strive to present themselves independently, they too are under the pull of the outreaching desire and therefore find themselves caught up in its motion. It is as if the desire were a current within awareness that gradually draws the other elements of awareness along with it.

This is why when I desire something, especially when I desire it strongly, my thoughts, feelings, and daydreams keep returning to the object desired. This is not, however, because desire is a foreign element that enters my awareness and takes control, for this weaving through and pulling of awareness is none other than awareness acting on itself. Desire just *is* my awareness when it is thrown into this configuration. The degree to which this swaying of other aspects of awareness occurs will depend much on both the strength of the desire that is pulling in one direction and the strength of the other aspects of awareness that are pulling in another. In some cases when the desire is weak, other aspects of awareness will be able to hold themselves relatively free from its influence, especially if they themselves are of a high intensity. However, in other cases where desire is forceful, then they will easily be swept along (and even away) by the sheer power of the desire, especially if they themselves are of a weak intensity.

This reaching out of desire, however, is not the only instance of motion in desire, for there is also the attraction of the object of desire itself. Here the object of desire seems to exert its own pull on the different elements of my awareness. This is the sense in which the object of desire is felt as desirable. Thus, such an object does not come to my awareness as a neutral entity that my awareness then reaches out toward. Rather, it presents itself as something that is in itself desirable. This quality then radiates from the object attracting my attention like a lamp in the night. This attraction of the object of desire, however, is not the reason for my awareness reaching out to it, for the awareness, which the desirability of the object shines upon, is already in the configuration of desire toward the object. Indeed, it is just my desiring of the object that imparts to it the sense of desirability that it then sends sparkling back to my awareness. If it is allowed that what is desirable might also in some sense be experienced as good, then this is in essence the same point made by 17th-century Dutch philosopher Spinoza. As Spinoza (1955) puts it, "In no case do we strive for, wish for, long for, or desire anything, because we deem it to be good, but on the other hand, we deem a thing to be good, because we strive for it, wish for it, long for it, or desire it" (p. 137).

To this it could be objected that there are numerous instances of desire in which such a direction or pull toward the object of desire never appears. Thus, it might be argued, when I desire to turn the page of a book that I am reading, there is no sense of my awareness being pressed or reaching out toward a specific object: here I simply turn the page as part of the process of reading. And this might well be true. But then the question arises as to whether the word "desire" has the same sense here as it has when it is used to describe those instances where there is a genuine motion toward the object. Since cases like those involved in turning a page while reading are distinct enough from those in which I do experience the pulling of my awareness in the direction of the object I desire, there seems little phenomenological grounds for claiming that both involve desires in the same sense. Only in the case in which I feel my awareness being directed in this way does any phenomenon appear to which we might apply the word "desire."

It is in response to this experiential distinction between these two sorts of cases that various philosophers (e.g., Locke, 1982) have pointed out two distinct senses of the word "desire," namely, one that refers to genuine desires and another that merely indicates that a person has acted intentionally. Here the term "desire" is logically tied to the idea of acting intentionally. In this sense, "I desired to turn the page" just means "I intentionally turned the page." Employing this distinction and using "desire" in its genuine sense, one could then say that although I intentionally turned the page, I had no desire to do so. Although this might seem paradoxical, this is so only, I suggest, if we use the term "desire" in its formal sense. If, however, the word is used in the sense that clearly refers to a movement or feeling within awareness, which is how we often speak about desire, then it does sound false to say, "I had a desire to turn the page," for in the moment of my turning the page, no such configuration of awareness occurs that could reasonably be called desire.

In addition to this motion of awareness, desire also presents itself as imbued with various meanings. These meanings, which take turns coming to the fore, follow the pattern of a network of implications, hints, and suggestions that trigger each other at various points in the unfolding of the desire. As each one is thus brought forth, it cuts a path through consciousness, as it were, throwing new light on various aspects of the desire, now showing one way of seeing the desire, now showing another. It is as if a meteor shower were taking place in which each meaning makes its appearance like a separate shooting star: each one carrying my gaze in a different direction as I traced its path across the evening sky. The direction of my gaze then brings me to see the next shooting star, which has its beginning where the earlier one ends, while numerous other such stars are forever coming and going on the periphery of my vision. Here, the following through of one meaning immediately leads me to see another, while various other meanings make brief appearances on the perimeter of my awareness. The central meanings of each desire will, however, be determined to a large extent by the object of the desire, for although the general structure of a desire will include the motions discussed so far, all these motions center around, strive toward, or emanate from the object of desire. Consequently, in the structure of desire, the object ascends to a prominent position from where it secures its role in the central meanings attached to the desire.

Related to these central or intrinsic meanings, however, will be extrinsic meanings that likewise attach to the desire. These extrinsic meanings, being based as they are primarily on character or cultural traits, are only contingently related to the desire. That is, their role in the structure of the desire is non-essential. Thus, for example, Menaker (1979) gives the case of a man whose idea of sexual intercourse inevitably carried with it the meaning that the male was being "serviced" by the female. Moreover, this meaning was so powerful for him and filled him with so much guilt, that he often avoided sexual intercourse. Nevertheless, this meaning is not a central or intrinsic feature of the desire for sexual intercourse, for an examination of the awareness of this desire will show that such a meaning need not appear and that, if it does, it can be disengaged from the desire without altering the desire's basic structure. This is also supported by the fact that many persons who have desire for sexual intercourse have no awareness of being serviced or servicing as part of the meaning of their desire for sexual intercourse. Consequently, the meaning of the female servicing the male is one that is extrinsic to the structure of the desire for sexual intercourse.

But what can be said about the object of desire that I find my awareness reaching out toward? Obviously, the crucial features that press me toward making it an object of desire will differ markedly in each case. For nearly anything can be an object of desire. This is why a central part of any phenomenological inquiry into the nature of a specific desire will be an investigation of the object of the specific desire. For it is the revealing of the distinctive structure of the object of desire that will reveal the distinctive nature of the desire.

Still, some thinkers argue that there are basic features that all objects of desire must share in common. Descartes, for example, argues that for anything to be an object of desire, it must at least be a future state of affairs or situation. That is, whenever we desire something, it is always something that has not yet occurred, and it must also be something that, when it happens, is an occurrence rather than, say, a material object. On this second point it seems Descartes is right. This is simply because of the structure of desire. For as just shown, desire consists of a motion and directedness toward an object. But the movement here is the movement toward a situation in which the object can take place, and "taking place" is a situation, not a material object. Thus, although I might think, for example, that I desire a plum (that is, a material object), if I examine my desire more closely I will see that what I really desire is the occurrence of a situation in which I am perhaps eating, holding, or smelling a plum. That is, my desire here aims at a situation in which a plum is involved. This point is one that will become clearer when we come to the object of sexual desire.

With the other point, however—namely, that the object of desire must lay in the future—Descartes is on less certain ground. For why can I not desire something that is already taking place? Consider the example of desiring to embrace someone, and imagine that my desire is fulfilled and I am in this moment now embracing her. In this moment when I feel her body pressing into mine, I might well have the thought, "This is what I desire!" And were I to examine my awareness in that moment, it is possible I would see that, despite the sense of fulfillment, all the motions and pullings of awareness that make up my desire were continuing just as they were before my embrace. This point is well-made by Levinas (1961) when he says that the desire that animates the caress is reborn in its satisfaction. Consequently, there is nothing in the fulfillment or satisfaction of my desire that need bring about the cessation of desire. This is because there is nothing in the nature of desire itself that implies it must cease simply because it is fulfilled. It is true that some desires cease with their fulfillment. Thus, in the case of the desire that constitutes hunger, the fulfillment of one's desire leads to the cessation of the desire. That is, upon consuming the appropriate food, my hunger is terminated (if it is not, then, I would argue, the desire for food here is not really motivated by hunger but rather by a desire for something that the food or eating symbolizes, such as, for example, comfort, happiness, or even sexual interaction). Of course, after a certain amount of time I will be hungry again. But for the time being the desire for food has ceased. In the case of a desire that need not cease with its fulfillment—like the desire to be embraced—the desire merely takes its fulfillment in stride and persists undaunted. In some cases the fulfillment of a desire even seems to strengthen the desire, thus ensuring its continuation throughout and after the fulfillment. Just how this occurs will, in each case, depend much on the specific object of the desire.

Of course, someone might try to argue here that what one desires in such a case is really the *continuation* of the object of desire. Thus, it might be claimed that what I desire in the example just given is the continuation of the embrace and that the idea of continuation is something that points to the future. Consequently, here too the object of desire is something that lies in the future.

But such an argument has no basis in experience. For although I might in this instant have a desire to continue the embrace, nothing in this example implies this must be so. Turning to my awareness, what I see is that I want the embrace simply as it is and so persist in desiring the embrace. Concerns about the future or hopes for continuation are foreign to my desire here. The thought "This is what I desire!" gazes neither to the past nor to the future but merely focuses on what is taking place in the moment.

Another thing that Descartes thinks about desire—something with which many people seem to agree—is that it is a passion or emotion. Now although the movements of consciousness I have been discussing can be forceful enough to lead to the physiological changes that many people, including Descartes, see as being definitive of emotions—increased heart and breathing rate, perspiration, and so on—it is noteworthy that there is no implication in the given observations that such disturbances must occur. All such changes in consciousness can occur with or without the occurrence of the physiological changes associated with emotion and therefore with or without the sensations that such changes bring to aware-ness.Therefore, even though it may be true that the alterations in con-sciousness brought about by desire frequently and even usually do give rise to the experience of such bodily sensations, and thus that desire is often accompanied by emotion, this is merely a contingent and therefore extrin-sic feature of desire. Consequently, if one wants to define emotion in terms of physiological arousal or perception of that arousal, then it must follow that desire is not, as is often thought, an emotion.

Some people, however, do not feel that emotion need necessarily involve physiological changes. Taylor (1986), for example, argues that what he calls calm emotions need not involve any of the bodily sensations associ-ated with the more excitable emotions (his example here is the calm enjoy-ment of gardening). In trying then to characterize what is involved in such calm emotions, Taylor says that the nearest he can come to giving a char-acterization is to say it is natural to describe such emotions with the metaphors of "'uplifting' and 'exalting' which imply some sort of change from a uniform state" (p. 229).

But again it seems that such experiences are not intrinsic to the nature of desire. For although one might find some desires to be accompanied by a sense of being uplifted or exalted, plainly there are other desires—such as the desire for a cup of tea—that need not have anything uplifting or exalt-ing about them. The conclusion, then, must be that although emotions and desires often come together, they are different phenomena. It might well be that, as Taylor argues, every emotion carries with it the element of desire, but, as phenomenological investigation shows, the converse is not true. That is, desire need not carry with it the element of emotion.

But if desires are not emotions, what are they? This is a question whose answer will depend much on which aspects of desire one chooses to emphasize. Some scholars here have suggested that desires are best seen as volitional or conative states and for this reason choose to emphasize desire's similarity to things like inclinations, intentions, and other psycho-logical states that lead to or are intimately connected with action. This is reasonable enough. But, here too, it must be noted that doing so serves to remove the focus from the internal structure of desire and looks more to its effects. If, however, we look to the internal structure, then there are ways in which desire is similar to imagination. For an important part of desiring something is holding, however vaguely, the object of desire in mind. This holding in mind seems to have much in common with imagina-tion. In this way, then, desire is quite dissimilar to something like an incli-nation or mere intentional activity where one seems to act without such an object in mind. Here, desire's cognitive aspects (constructing a mental object) and ideational features (envisaging the mental object) are empha-sized over desire's conative features. But this classification then misses out on the aspect of desire that pulls us toward its object, for there is nothing, or very little, in imagination *per se* that pulls us toward the object that is imagined: one can be either uninterested in the object one is imagining or even afraid of it.

With this it seems that any attempt to classify desire will miss out on one or another of its central features. It is perhaps this distinctiveness of desire that leads some scholars to see desire as playing a central role in our psychology. Some scholars, for example, see desires as the basic fundament around which other psychological states turn—a view that, though not at odds with other accounts, at the same time places desire in a category unto itself. The 17th-century philosopher Thomas Hobbes says, "Thoughts, are to the Desires, as Scouts, and Spies, to range abroad, and find the way to Things Desired: all Stedinesse of the mind's motion and all quicknesse of the same, proceeding from thence. For as to have no Desire, is to be Dead" (1974, p. 139). Likewise, various Buddhist thinkers have pointed to the tendency of desire to generate numerous other psychological states that obscure awareness. However, a correct understanding and acceptance of this aspect of desire allows desire to become the instant of full self-awareness. Here, in the words of the 13th-century Japanese Buddhist Nichiren (1990), earthly desires are enlightenment. If this is so, and if *sexual* desire holds a distinctive place among our desires, then here too we have an indication of why we attach such consequence to the fulfillment of sexual desire.

2

The Sexual Process

THE IDEA OF A SEXUAL PROCESS

Sexual desire bears several intimate relations to other sexual phenomena. In order to proceed with this study, it will be helpful to see how the element of sexual desire ties in with these other events. Here then I will turn to the notion of what I will call the sexual process; that is, the sequence of various experiential, behavioral, and physiological events that often give rise to and accompany human sexual activity.

The notion of a sexual process is one that has been addressed in different ways by different people, with the earliest accounts going back at least to the time of ancient China. Early Taoist thinkers put much weight on the knowledge and practice of sexual activity, considering it essential for health and spiritual satisfaction. They thus produced manuals of sexual guidance that were based on the events of the sexual process. In one manual known as *Talk on Supreme Guidance for the World* (second century BCE), we are told how breathing during sexual activity proceeds from normal to rapid breathing during the feeling of urgency, to sighing after vaginal penetration, rough breathing during climax, with heavy breathing indicating ecstasy. This process is accompanied by further processes in which, for example, the woman's nipples become erect, tongues become "sweet and slippery," the woman's thighs become wet with vaginal secretions, and her throat gets dry. Here we are told that "nibbling and vibration of the body indicate that a woman wants her man to continue" while "signs of the final finish are the woman's nose running and lips becoming pale, hands and feet trembling, buttocks rising off the bed" (Cleary, 1999, pp. 29–31).

This alone should be enough to lay to rest Foucault's (1979) claim that modern Western civilization is "undoubtedly" the only to practice a science of sexuality. Plainly, the ancient Chinese were also interested in producing such a science. Indeed, there are several instances of fascinating agreement between ancient Chinese sexologists and those of modern Western sexologists.

In this chapter, I shall examine some of the more important views of the sexual process. This will not only provide us with a vantage point from which to see where sexual desire lies on the landscape of sexual phenomena but also help clear the way for a purely phenomenological account of the sexual process. Such an account will then enable us to locate more precisely sexual desire by helping to disentangle it from related phenomena.

ELLIS AND THE MECHANISM OF DETUMESCENCE

One early modern account of the sexual process is given by Havelock Ellis in his six-volume work *Studies in the Psychology of Sex* (1897–1910). In this work, particularly in the sections titled "Analysis of the Sexual Impulse" (1903) and "The Mechanism of Detumescence" (1905), Ellis analyzes the sexual process in terms of the two stages of tumescence and detumescence. Although these terms normally refer to the processes of congestion and decongestion, Ellis points out that he is using them also to refer to the equally important processes of nervous charging and discharging. Although the two stages may appear to be distinct, says Ellis, they are intimately related as two stages of the same unified process: "a first stage in which—usually under the parallel influence of internal and external stimuli—Images, desires, and ideals grow up within the mind, while the organism generally is charged with energy and the sexual apparatus congested with blood; and a second stage in which the sexual apparatus is discharged amid profound sexual excitement, followed by deep organic relief. By the first process is constituted the tension which the second process relieves" (1903, pp. 54–55).

Tumescence begins with the first appearance of sexual excitement and is slowly built up through what Ellis calls an abbreviated courtship, the main causal mechanism here being the tactile stimulation of the erotogenic zones. Although Ellis feels that any part of the surface of the body can be erotically sensitive, there are, he says, primary erotogenic regions for each sex. For the male, the one primary erotogenic region tends to be the penis, while for the female, whose sensuality is more diffuse, there are three primary regions, namely, the clitoris, the entire vaginal tract (including the vaginal portion of the uterus), and the nipples, though he also says that, for the female, the entire genital region, including the anus, is sensitive to erotic contact (it was Freud who later argued that the anus and the rest of the genital region in the male should also be included). Outside of the zones he mentions, Ellis feels that the lips are normally the most erotically sensitive regions of the body.

As sexual excitement increases, tumescence of various organs takes place. This involves the erection of the penis in the male and the engorgement of vaginal walls and the uterus. This is accompanied in the female by vaginal lubrication and a dilation of the vaginal entrance. The lubricating process can also take the form of a "real ejaculation," says Ellis, in which the fluid is spurt out from the glands at the vaginal entrance. In addition to the vasocongestion of the sex organs, there is also a surface congestion of the skin that spreads over various parts of the body. There is further an increase in the heart rate, and breathing becomes rapid and shallower as orgasm approaches. Also, muscle tensions begin to spread over the entire body.

What changes the process of tumescence to that of detumescence is the sudden "convulsion" of orgasm. In the male, this involves the rhythmic contractions of muscles at the base of the penis along with those surrounding the urethra. This causes ejaculation. In the female, whose muscular process here is less visible and more complex, the walls of the vagina, which had contracted rhythmically at intervals prior to orgasm, now break loose in a series of well-marked rhythmic contractions. In both sexes, "with the onset of muscular action, which is mainly involuntary, even when it affects the voluntary muscles, detumescence proper begins to take place. Henceforward purposeful psychic action, except by an effort, is virtually abolished. The individual, as a separate person, tends to disappear. He becomes one with the other person, as nearly one as the conditions of existence ever permit" (Ellis, 1905, p. 149).

With the passing of the physiological explosion of orgasm, as Ellis calls it, the person enters a state of deep relaxation. In men there is normally a sense of profound satisfaction and mental liberation. And under "reasonably happy circumstances," the man will not feel that the woman has lost her "charm." In women there is often a sensation of repose, free and joyous energy, and even intoxication that may last for several hours. Although one can find many descriptions of the state that Ellis is here referring to, a particularly appropriate one is given by a woman who says, "the sensation is one of laziness, euphoria—sort of a floating, drifting, luxurious feeling. It is probably the happiest time of the day. I feel very secure, time seems suspended, and I feel as if I have no cares" (Fisher, 1973, p. 204).

By describing the sexual process as a two-stage integrated physiological and psychological process of rising tumescence and falling detumescence, Ellis presents a simple and elegant account that provides a useful framework in which to organize various events of the sexual process. One of the problems, however, is that it might be too simple. For it seems as though Ellis wants the term "detumescence" to cover at least two rather distinct events. That is, he seems to use the term to refer both to orgasm (which is itself a complex phenomenon) and to the process immediately following orgasm in which the various organs begin to lose their tumescence.

Although Ellis is aware of his shift of the meaning of the term "detumescence" to a discharge of energy, he does not seem aware that he has also shifted the meaning to include orgasm. And this is a further shift in meaning. For the usual meaning of "detumescence" does not include orgasm. This makes sense because when something detumesces, it simply loses what it gained when it tumesced. And although orgasm might be the trigger that starts the process of detumescence, orgasm itself is not an instance of detumescence. Rather, it is clear that the sexual and other organs hold their full tumescence until orgasm is finished (Master and Johnson's observations suggest that detumescence sets in with the last muscle contractions of orgasm [1966, pp. 30, 86, 185, 209]).

Because of this lack of clarity and the obvious distinction between orgasm and the process of detumescence, it seems that Ellis' account of the sexual process would have been more understandable if he had at least allowed for this distinction. Therefore, instead of presenting a two-stage theory of tumescence and detumescence, he could instead present a three-stage theory, namely, one that included tumescence, orgasm, and detumescence. Orgasm would then be the stage in which built-up nervous energy discharges, and detumescence would be the following stage in which vasocongestion dissipates. Since both energy charge and discharge and vasocongestion are basic to Ellis' account, this would be a natural development of Ellis' view of the sexual process. To be fully accurate, however, such an account would have to also draw further distinctions, both physiological and experiential. What these distinctions are will become clear shortly.

FREUD AND THE PLEASURES OF EXCITATION

Freud gives another view of the sexual process. In *Three Essays on Sexuality* (1905), Freud tells us that the sexual apparatus is set in motion by stimuli from three different sources, namely, excitations of the erotogenic zones by the external world, excitations by the interior of the body, and those caused by fantasy. All three of these types of stimuli produce sexual excitation both mentally and somatically, with the mental excitations consisting of an awareness of a tension "of an extremely compelling character" (p. 208) and the somatic excitations consisting of, among other things, the erection of the penis and lubrication of the vagina. All these stimulations have the effect of increasing the pleasure experienced in the sexual excitation, which in turn increases the demand for more pleasure, which in turn increases the tension of the sexual excitation. This increased tension is the basis for extra energy that can be used to bring the sex act to its conclusion. If the demand for increased pleasure is not met here, there immediately appears an experience of unpleasure.

This escalation of tension together with the stimulation of the appropriate erotogenic zone by the appropriate object (Freud's example is the penis by the vagina and the vagina by the penis) sets in motion a reflex path that suddenly discharges the tensions in orgasm. "This last pleasure," says Freud, "is the highest in intensity, and its mechanism differs from that of the earlier pleasure. It is brought about entirely by discharge: it is wholly a pleasure of satisfaction and with it the tension of the libido is for the time being extinguished" (1905, p. 210). Thus, while the earlier erotic pleasure is one that is built upon increasing excitation, a pleasure that demands more pleasure through increasing tension, the second pleasure is based on the release of all such tension. This release of tension is often what is referred to as orgasm.

Because of the fundamental differences in the mechanisms on which these two types of pleasure are based, Freud gives them different names, calling the first type fore-pleasure and the second type end-pleasure. Although Freud does not refer to the idea of stages, it is plain that what he is presenting here is in fact a two-stage model of the sexual process: an earlier stage of fore-pleasure that involves a cycle of increasing pleasure through rising tension and mental excitations and a second stage in which a new and more intense sort of pleasure is suddenly achieved through a discharge of the accumulated tensions. On the point of there being two stages, he is thus in agreement with Ellis, though Freud presents his view more in terms of a phenomenological account of stages of pleasure.

Freud also points here to various gender differences in terms of the sexual process, differences that have their origin in sexual development. For while the leading erotogenic zone of the male—namely, the penis—typically remains the same from childhood through the transformations of puberty, the female's leading erotogenic zone changes from the clitoris in childhood to the vaginal entrance at puberty. This is not to say that in such post-puberty sexual acts the clitoris plays no role, for "it still retains a function: the task, namely, of transmitting the excitation to the adjacent female sexual parts, just as—to use a simile—pine shavings can be kindled in order to set a log of harder wood on fire" (1905, p. 221).

One of the problems that Freud discusses here is the connection between sexual excitation and fore-pleasure. It is understandable, he argues, that end-pleasure can be pleasurable, for it is simply a discharge of high levels of tension, and such a release from tension is clearly pleasurable. But fore-pleasure involves the escalation of tension, and tension, says Freud, is inherently unpleasurable. So how is it that an unpleasurable state of affairs can also be experienced as pleasurable? Although in *Three Essays on Sexuality* Freud merely acknowledges this problem and declines to deal with it there, in his paper "The Economic Problem of Masochism" (1924) he returns to this issue. Here Freud argues that even though pleasure is intimately connected with the release of tension and pain or unpleasure to the increase of tension, there are nevertheless examples of pleasurable increases in tension and unpleasurable relaxations of tension. Consequently, he says, pleasure and unpleasure cannot be solely dependent on quantities of tension. Perhaps, he suggests, it has more to do with a qualitative factor: "the rhythm, the temporal sequence of changes, rises and falls in the quantity of stimulus" (1924, p. 160). He does not, however, pursue this further, adding merely, "we do not know."

Although Freud's account is not as detailed as Ellis', he nevertheless presents the groundwork for an overview of the sexual process. There are, however, various problems with his view. First, it is not clear that the phases of pleasure he refers to can simply be divided into fore-pleasure and end-pleasure. For it seems evident that in the sexual process there are other sorts of pleasure that belong neither to fore-pleasure nor to end-pleasure. Consider here the remark by Rollo May (1969):

The moment of greatest significance in love-making, as judged by what people remember in the experience and what patients dream about, is not the moment of orgasm. It is rather the moment of entrance, the moment of penetration of the erection of the man into the vagina of the woman. This is the moment that shakes us, that has within it great wonder, tremendous and tremulous as it may be—or disappointing and despairing, which says the same thing from the opposite point of view. This is the moment when persons' reactions to the love-making experience are most original, most individual, most truly their own. This and not orgasm, is the moment of union and the realization that we have won the other. (p. 74)

This point is one that, for some reason, has been all but ignored in discussions of the sexual process. And yet it is obvious that the moment of penetration is something completely unto itself. For here, two distinct bodies have at last, typically after much expectant yearning, come together. And they have come together in a seemingly mysterious way, a way in which the surfaces of one body seem to cross and descend below the surfaces of the other, one enfolding the incursion of the other while this other moves into the containment of the first one. Here the surface of the male's body is drawn into the interior of the female's body and surrounded and held by hers as though his body were being integrated into hers. At the same moment the female's body is pushed open and drawn back around the male's body as though her body were being spread over and thus blended with his body. Here their distinction as two separate bodies and two separate genders is fundamentally called into question. It is this peculiar partaking of the other person's body and thus gender, I suggest, that lies at the core of the great wonder to which May refers and the idea that we have "won the other."

The significance of the moment of penetration is underscored, I would argue, by a wholly distinct form of pleasure. In contrast to fore-pleasure, which pulls us forward to increase the pleasure by increasing the tension, the pleasure associated with penetration is one that beckons us to abide in the tensions, momentarily subduing or relieving the urges of fore-pleasure. Here the entrance-pleasure, as it might be called, seems to spread itself out over the rising tensions (much like the woman's body spreads itself out over the man's), dampening their energy while balancing, as it were, on their peaks. Here the pleasure is gentle, persistent, and radiating (much like the man's body seems persistently to radiate into the woman's). It is a pleasure that is associated neither with the increasing tensions of fore-pleasure nor with the release of tensions in end-pleasure. Although entrance-pleasure seems usually to be momentary, dissipating shortly after the moment of penetration, and is thus lost on many people, this seems to depend much on the activity following penetration. If the persons involved immediately begin pelvic thrusting, then the distinct pleasure of penetration is quickly lost and supplanted by fore-pleasure. If, however, both partners remain still in a silent embrace, then it seems entrance-pleasure can easily continue.

Further, although this form of pleasure is typically associated with penile penetration of the vagina, this is not the only sexual activity that gives rise to such pleasure. For there is also the moment of the genitals being brought into contact with the mouth or hand, the intermolding of the lips in a deep kiss, or simply the moment of warm intertwining of bodies in a naked embrace. In each instance, the two persons can also achieve their yearned-for bodily joining. Here the pleasure, though not necessarily associated with the genitals, can also take the form of something that radiates throughout the body, riding the tensions, and yet suspending the urge to increase the tensions.

In addition to entrance-pleasure, it also seems there is another form of pleasure that is neither a form of fore-pleasure nor a form of end-pleasure. This is the pinnacle of orgasm that appears at the juncture where fore-pleasure stops and end-pleasure starts. Whether one sees this as the actual moment of orgasm or whether one feels that orgasm includes the subsequent episode of end-pleasure will depend on how broadly or exclusively one wants to define orgasm. My impression is that people tend to use the word indiscriminately to refer to either or both.

Phenomenologically, however, it is clear from people's descriptions that this peak-pleasure, as it might be called, differs fundamentally from both fore-pleasure and end-pleasure. While fore-pleasure results from a gradual and more or less voluntary increase in sexual tensions and is a pleasure that urges one on actively to pursue it (by further increasing such tension), peak-pleasure is the sudden and involuntary ascension of pleasure to a point where it seems to shatter the barrier against which all the increasing

tensions of fore-pleasure were straining. It does so, however, not by a
release of tension but by giving an autonomy to the sudden escalation or
acceleration of tension. At this point all tensions, which seem to have collected into a concentrated point of intensity, suddenly rush upward,
streaming into every corner of consciousness: the awareness of time, space,
self, other, and so on are scattered and left behind in this wild dash to an
unknown destination.

An aspect of the distinctiveness of this peak-pleasure is that while it
maintains the tensions of fore-pleasure, though concentrating them in a
way that they become barely recognizable, these tensions nevertheless proceed in a completely involuntary way. Here there is no effort or straining
or feeling of compulsion as there is in fore-pleasure. Part of the pleasure
here seems to be that one is involuntarily and thus relaxingly swept forward, and yet powerfully so, on a sea of tensions.

Not only does this differ from fore-pleasure, but it also differs fundamentally from end-pleasure. For on Freud's definition, end-pleasure is the pleas-
ure that results from a release of the tensions that have accumulated in fore-
pleasure. However, by the point at which end-pleasure sets in, peak-pleasure
has already come and gone. Biologically, end-pleasure appears with the
onset of muscle contractions, contractions that, with the male, typically
coincide with ejaculation. Ejaculation is thus an event that usually takes
place during the phase of end-pleasure, not peak-pleasure. With the female
these contractions tend not, like with the male, to be concentrated, or at
least have their origin, in the genitals. End-pleasure is felt as an immense
release of tension that sends waves of pulsation rippling throughout the
entire body, receding into the distant corners of bodily awareness. These
waves, though quick and firm at first, gradually dissipate as the contractions weaken. Here, like in peak-pleasure, one feels oneself being swept
involuntarily along by the events taking place. However, unlike in peak-
pleasure, it is not the sudden escalation of tension that sweeps one along;
rather, it is the release of tension that does so. Further, in end-pleasure one
undergoes the pleasure as pulsations or waves spreading outward, whereas
in peak-pleasure the pleasure appears as a sudden racing upward.

Part of the problem with making the distinction between fore-pleasure,
entrance-pleasure, peak-pleasure, and end-pleasure seems to be that in the
moments in which fore-pleasure or entrance-pleasure changes into peak-
pleasure and peak-pleasure into end-pleasure, consciousness is often drastically altered. Consequently, it is difficult to be fully aware of the differences between the sorts of pleasure. This is reflected by the fact that our
word "orgasm" seems to cover at least peak-pleasure and end-pleasure. In
Male Sexuality, Zilbergeld (1978), however, points out that "some men,
who have trained themselves carefully to tune into their sensations during
sex, say that they sometimes notice very high peaks of feeling long before
ejaculation. Were they not so indoctrinated into the idea that orgasm

occurs only with pelvic contractions and ejaculation, they would be inclined to call these peaks orgasm" (p. 106).

Further, it is also possible to find this distinction in some personal descriptions of the experiences of erotic pleasure, those given by both men and women. This can be seen in the following description of a masturbation experience given by a woman:

As I feel this energy building up in me, I start rocking and pumping from the pelvis. Instead of letting go, I build the energy up more. I imagine looping the energy around and around through my body so that it builds up a reservoir. I breathe with it. I work with this energy, squeezing my pelvic muscles as I let my breath out. When the energy starts to feel locked in my genitals, I touch myself there to let the energy out and help it move through me. As the energy builds, my breathing intensifies. I open my throat and let sounds emerge. My voice changes as I get deeper into orgasmic sounds. I keep the energy looping the energy around and around through my body until I feel the orgasm moving up from my pelvis and my G-spot, into my heart. When the orgasm reaches my throat, my body arches and the energy finally explodes in me. The sounds I make echo what I'm feeling throughout my body. My voice wavers and soars like the call of a wild jungle bird. (Maltz and Boss, 1997, pp. 45–46)

In this description it is possible to discern the mechanisms of fore-pleasure, peak-pleasure, and end-pleasure (entrance-pleasure seems absent because of the lack of penetration or interaction with a partner). The mechanism of fore-pleasure is evident in the woman's account of building up energy by "rocking and pumping her pelvis" by "not letting go" and by "squeezing my pelvic muscles." All this seems to refer to the increasing tensions of fore-pleasure. The onset of peak-pleasure seems to be when she feels "the orgasm moving up from my pelvis and G-spot, into my heart" (the G-spot, which will be discussed later, is located in the vagina), and finally into her throat. End-pleasure comes at the point when she says, "the energy finally explodes in me."

Another difficulty with Freud's account lies in the notion that erotic pleasure is brought to conclusion with end-pleasure. There is a difficulty with this for two reasons. First, there are either cases in which people can experience multiple orgasms or cases in which the orgasm is not experienced as the end of erotic pleasure. In this latter case a person might desire to continue with sexual activity and even proceed through new instances of fore-pleasure to another orgasm. Secondly, there are other sorts of pleasures that are part of the sexual process—for example, Ellis' account of feeling of liberation—but that nevertheless come after the end-pleasure of orgasm. It is interesting to note here that in the ancient Indian treatise on love and sex, the *Kama Sutra* (about CE 400), sex (*rata* in Sanskrit) is not considered to have ended until well after orgasm has taken place. Thus, Vatsyayana, the sutra's author, describes how after sexual intercourse the couple should relax in each other's company drinking "sweet liquors, while chewing from time to time sweet or tart things." Then, "climbing to the terrace on top of the house to take advantage of the moonlight, they give themselves over to pleasant conversation. She lays her head on the boy's knees to look at the moon. He explains the figures of the constellations to her: Arundhati the faithful, Dhruva the polestar, the garland of the seven Rishi. Thus sex comes to an end" (Vatsyayana, 1994, p. 200; translation amended).

One can, of course, wonder what looking at constellations has to do with the sexual process, but when one considers the peculiar blend of excitement and relaxation that can flow between a couple who have sexually engaged each other, and when one considers the subtle erotic sensations that often ensue simply by being in the presence of someone with whom one has just shared the intimacy of sexual penetration or orgasm, then it does not seem wholly unreasonable to see joint activities taken thereafter—like drinking sweet liquors and stargazing—as a form of continuation of the sexual activity, which contains its own diffuse form of erotic pleasure.

As for the question of how fore-pleasure can be pleasureful, this is a problem for Freud because he sees tension, upon which fore-pleasure is based, as inherently unpleasant. But why hold such a view when it is clear that tension can produce pleasure? Perhaps Freud is influenced by a consideration of the intensity of pleasure that appears in the release of tension in end-pleasure. But if the account just given is correct, the most intense pleasure appears at the moment of peak-pleasure, that is, in the moment of the sudden escalation to the highest increment of tension. Moreover, even end-pleasure is not completely a pleasure of tension release. For although the accumulated tensions of fore-pleasure and peak-pleasure are finally released in the process of end-pleasure, the release of tension is here carried out through a series of muscle contractions, that is, through an alternating series of both increases and releases in tension.

Likewise, in the process of fore-pleasure, which is overall one of an increase of tension, the pleasure does not seem to be one based purely on a uniform increase in tension but also on an alternation between increase and slight release of tension. This would appear to be the basis of the rhythmic or thrusting motions characteristic of many forms of sexual activity. No doubt, it is a consideration of these sorts of alternations that leads Freud to speculate that pleasure might also have something to do with the rhythm, sequence of changes, or rises and falls in the quantity of stimulus rather than merely tension release.

REICH'S ORGASTICALLY SATISFYING SEX ACT

Further development of the idea of the sexual process was left to Wilhelm Reich, who was a student of Freud's. Reich takes a particular interest in the sexual process, especially in the orgasmic phase because, as a therapist, he sees it as being a crucial factor in psychological well-being. In his *The Function of the Orgasm* (1941), Reich presents his account of the sexual process in terms of what he calls the "orgastically satisfying sex act," which is a more specific version of his "orgasm formula." He also presents variations of this more specific account that occur in "unsatisfying acts" like premature or retarded ejaculation.

As the term "orgastically satisfying sex act" makes clear, Reich's interest here is in giving a description of the sexual process, which is experienced as fully satisfying by the person involved, that is, a sexual process that demonstrates what Reich calls "orgastic potency." Reich contrasts this concept with mere "erective" or "ejaculative" potency in the male. For it is possible for a male to have both erections and ejaculations but yet not experience pleasure or satisfaction in the sex act. Reich is saying two things here. First, he is pointing to the fact that ejaculation is not to be equated with orgasm—for ejaculation can occur without orgasm—and, secondly, that not all orgasms are experienced as pleasurable. Likewise, just as a male can have erections and orgasms that bring no pleasure, so can a female have vaginal lubrications and orgasms and still not find the sex act pleasurable. Orgastic potency consequently refers to the ability to have orgasms that are experienced as fully satisfying. Consequently, and in line with his therapeutic interests, Reich presents his account through a comparison with orgastically unsatisfying or impotent acts. In the orgastically satisfying sex act, Reich delineates 10 substages that occur within a four-phase framework of fore-pleasure, penetration, acme, and relaxation (because Reich distinguishes fore-pleasure from penetration, it is clear that he is here using the term in a different way than Freud).

The first phase begins for the male with erection, which is experienced as pleasurable. Here is where the urge for penetration makes its appearance. For the female this beginning is marked by the genitals becoming engorged and the onset of the natural lubrication of the vagina.

In the beginning of the penetration phase, the pleasurable excitations suddenly increase when the penis penetrates the vagina. Here the male experiences a sensation of being sucked into the vagina, while the female experiences the complimentary sensation of sucking in the penis (this would seem to be Reich's way of referring to the distinctness of the moment of penetration). The male then experiences the urge to penetrate deeper into the vagina, but without the sadistic desire to pierce or hurt the female. The sensation that typically occurs in the male immediately prior to ejaculation is completely absent, and both the male's and the female's awareness is spontaneously concentrated on the pleasurable sensations caused by the slow and rhythmic movements of the penis within the vagina.

At the beginning of this phase the excitations remain in the genitals. By the end, however, they begin to spread outward to the rest of the body. Because of the mounting tensions of this phase, voluntary control of the excitation finally becomes no longer possible. Here the excitation begins to overwhelm the person. This is accompanied by a melting sensation that, says Reich, "can best be described as a radiation of excitation from the genitals to the rest of the body" (1941, p. 83).

Entering the acme phase, the excitations suddenly increase dramatically and move quickly toward orgasm. In the male the onset of this phase usually coincides with the first ejaculatory contraction, an involuntary contraction that is followed by a momentary subsidence before the other involuntary contractions of orgasm set in. The same sequence of contractions occurs for the female, and in both cases there is "a more or less clouding of consciousness." For the male the urge to "penetrate completely" intensifies with each ejaculatory contraction, while for the female this is experienced as the urge to "receive completely." The accompanying contractions, which start in the genitals, quickly spread throughout the entire body as there occurs at the point of acme a sudden release of sexual tension. Up to the point of acme, there had been the experience of excitation flowing toward the genitals from the body. However, with the release of tension at the point of acme, the direction of the flow suddenly changes and then heads back to the body from the genitals. It is this complete flowing back of excitation that, on Reich's view, constitutes the intense pleasure of orgasm.

In the relaxation phase, the excitation gradually subsides in a gentle curve and is at the same time replaced by pleasant bodily and psychic relaxation. Although the sensual excitations are gone, there continues "a grateful tender attitude towards the partner" (Reich, 1941, p. 84). Here we see that Reich paints a post-orgasmic picture that is much in agreement with both Ellis' account and that given in the *Kama Sutra*. All three stress the pleasantness, lack of exhaustion, and positive feelings toward the partner. For Reich, this is in contrast to "orgastically impotent" persons, who at this stage may feel exhaustion, disgust, indifference, or hatred toward the partner. Such feelings are often a reaction to the post-orgasmic disappearance of the fantasy that enabled the orgastically impotent person to maintain his or her sexual excitation. With the fantasizing over, the person is often painfully aware of the disparity between the fantasized object and his or her actual partner. Reich feels that the use of conscious fantasy during sexual acts shows an inability to spontaneously concentrate on the sexual exchange and is therefore indicative of orgasmic impotency.

Despite the careful and detailed analysis of the sexual process given by Reich, there are, nevertheless, some difficulties with his position. One such difficulty is that, for Reich, the onset of the acme phase coincides with the first contraction of ejaculatory or vaginal contraction. Yet, as previously mentioned, it is evident that the rapid movement toward the release of tension has little to do with the contractions that accompany ejaculation and the vaginal counterpart. The movement of this phase is rather a sudden and autonomous escalation of intensity that ends by bursting through the tensions and thus setting off the first of the rhythmic contractions. We will see how this occurs shortly.

Another problem here comes from Reich's account of the pleasure associated with this phase. For Reich, the intense pleasure of the orgasm comes from the flowing back of excitation from the genitals to the rest of the body. But as Reich himself is aware, the flowing back of blood from the tumesced sex organs does not occur until after the last contractions of orgasm have taken place, that is, until both peak-pleasure and the most intense moments of end-pleasure have come and gone. No doubt the sort of flowing that Reich describes does give rise to a certain pleasure, but having occurred after orgasm has taken place, it cannot be said to constitute the intense pleasure of orgasm.

A more general complaint one might want to register here is that it is unclear why an orgastically satisfying act has to take the specific form that Reich describes. Here the process is given exclusively in terms of heterosexual intercourse between a loving, or at least mutually caring, couple. And yet it is obvious that other types of sexual acts, such as cunnilingus, group sex, or lesbian tribadism, can also be orgastically satisfying for those who prefer them or are at least are open to them. The orgastically satisfying act, however, seems to rule out such acts.

Part of the problem seems to be that in describing the orgastically satisfying act, Reich is concerned primarily with providing a baseline of comparison for orgastically impotent acts, or what might be called sexually dysfunctional acts or variations that are often experienced within the context of one-to-one heterosexual intercourse—with the term "dysfunctional" here referring to a chronic lack of sexual satisfaction. As a result, he refers by way of comparison to such things as premature ejaculation, priapism, vaginismus, and sadomasochism, all of which, he argues, diminish the satisfaction of heterosexual intercourse. He refers, for example, to "phallic-narcissistic" males whose "excessive erective potency" is a defense against unconscious homosexual fantasies and who use the penis as a piercing instrument against the woman in sadistic fantasies. Not only is such sexual behavior typically dissatisfying for the male—a man engaging in such behavior is incapable of complete surrender to the sexual act—but also, says Reich, it leaves women with much disgust for sexual intercourse.

If the idea of an orgastically satisfying act is thus understood as a baseline for such comparisons, then the fact that it refers only to heterosexual intercourse need not be such a problem. It is just that the term "orgastically satisfying sex act" should be understood to mean "orgastically satisfying act of one-to-one heterosexual intercourse." Once this is clear, Reich's account need not be seen as implying that other (non-dysfunctional) sexual acts cannot be equally orgastically satisfying. Consequently, it is quite consistent with Reich's account, though he does not discuss this, that there could also exist an orgastically satisfying act of cunnilingus, digital penetration of the vagina, or tribadism. Of course, not all such acts would involve the mutual orgasmic satisfaction that Reich describes in his account, for in some cases one partner might be focusing on giving the other person orgasmic satisfaction rather than attaining his or her own satisfaction. This would particularly seem to be the case in certain instances (though not all; see Bruijn, 1982b) of oral sex or masturbation of one's partner but might also be the case in heterosexual intercourse. However, nothing inherent in such activities seems to warrant the claim that they must be orgastically dissatisfying for the person who is receiving the erotic pleasure. The important thing is that for these other acts to be orgastically satisfying, the persons engaging in them must also be free from dysfunctions like premature or retarded ejaculation, painful vaginal spasms, sadistic or masochistic elements, and other such things that might hinder their full enjoyment of and abandonment to the sexual act. That the crucial element is full enjoyment and abandonment is made clear by Reich when he says that "the involuntary contractions of the organism and the complete discharge of excitation are the most important criteria for orgasmic potency" and also that the "ability to concentrate oneself with one's whole personality on the orgasmic experience, in spite of possible conflicts, is a further criterion of orgasmic potency" (1941, p. 85; italics removed).

MASTERS AND JOHNSON'S SEXUAL RESPONSE CYCLE

Let us now move on to the account of William Masters and Virginia Johnson (1966), two sexologists whose views have been highly influential. Masters and Johnson's account owes much not only to the work of Ellis, Freud, and Reich but also to that of Kinsey and his colleagues (1948; 1953), who explored similar issues in the sexual process. However, Kinsey did so with interviews rather than with Masters and Johnson's technique of direct observation. It is this use of direct observation that is often felt to give a special weight to the account of Masters and Johnson.

According to these sexologists, the sexual response cycle, as they call it, is a series of psychological and physiological responses that occur to sexual stimulation. This stimulation can be either psychological or physical. In the latter case, the stimulation can be "exteroceptive," that is, stimulation from the surface of the body by external objects, or "proprioceptive," that is, stimulation from the tissues within the body. These three forms of stimulation are none other than Freud's distinction between excitations caused by fantasy, the external world, and the interior of the body.

In Masters and Johnson's account, sexual stimulation gives rise to two physiological responses that are distributed throughout the body. These are vasocongestion (congestion of the blood vessels) and myotonia (muscle tension). These responses are essentially Reich's notions of mechanical

tension and bioelectric charge given in his orgasm formula, with the difference that while Reich focuses on the neural charge that leads to muscle
tension, Masters and Johnson focus on the muscle tension itself. These,
along with other responses of the sexual response cycle, are presented in
terms of the excitation phase, the plateau phase, the orgasm phase, and the
resolution phase. Because there are numerous things wrong with Masters
and Johnson's account, and because it is nevertheless so widely accepted, it
will be worthwhile to take some time to examine closely their position.

The excitement phase begins with the first responses to psychological or
physical sexual stimulation. Here vasocongestion and myotonia make their
first appearance. In the female these are accompanied by vaginal lubrication and lengthening, distention of the inner vaginal barrel, increase in size
of the clitoris, nipple erection, engorgement of the breasts, and elevation of
the uterus. In the male there occurs erection of the penis, constriction of
the scrotum, and elevation of the testes.

In the plateau phase the tensions continue to build before leveling off at
their highest point before orgasm. In the female the changes include a red
coloring of the labia minora, retraction of the clitoris, further elevation of
the uterus, and engorgement of the outer third of the vaginal barrel, creating
the "orgasmic platform." In the male plateau phase changes are said to
involve the penis undergoing a minor diameter increase as orgasm
approaches, in some cases a deepening of color of the glans, and a continued
elevation of the testes. In both the female and male there appears hyperventi-
lation, an increase in heart rate and blood pressure, and mottling of the skin.

With the orgasm phase the built-up tensions suddenly release. This
release, in the female, typically begins with rapid muscle contractions in
the orgasmic platform section of the vagina, immediately followed by contractions of the uterus and, in some cases, by contractions of the rectal and
urethral sphincters. All this is accompanied both by involuntary spasms in
the limbs and by various voluntary muscle tensions. Simultaneously with
the last orgasmic contraction, detumescence usually sets in. Here, however,
some females, though not males, are capable of rapidly returning to
orgasm or maintaining an orgasm or possibly a series of orgasms.

Further, Masters and Johnson assure us that all female orgasms are cli-
torally based. That is, there is no such thing as a female orgasm that is due
to vaginal stimulation alone. They allow that women do have orgasms
during vaginal stimulation, but only because of indirect stimulation of the
clitoris. Moreover, although one of the subjects whom Masters and Johnson studied was able to have orgasms through having only her breasts fon-
dled, Masters and Johnson argue that such an orgasm is still clitoral
because it also involves an indirect stimulation of the clitoris.

Psychological factors are said to involve three stages. These are a feeling
of "suspension or stoppage," an intense awareness thrusting upward from
the clitoris into the pelvis and a loss of sensory acuity; then a suffusion of

warmth; and then a feeling of involuntary contraction and of throbbing. As for the so-called sociological factors, Masters and Johnson have little to say. Their main point here seems to be that although orgasm is something most women are capable of, the female's achievement of orgasm seems also to depend on our culture's acceptance of female sexuality, whatever that means.

The male orgasm, which they also term ejaculation, is divided into two stages. Physiologically the first stage involves the expulsion of seminal fluid from the seminal vesicles and other secondary reproductive organs into the prostatic urethra, while the second stage is the expulsion of the fluid from there through the penis. Psychologically this sequence is paralleled by the sensation of "ejaculatory inevitability," where the upcoming ejaculation is experienced as inevitable and then a sensation of urethral contractions and a further sensation of the expulsion of semen. Sociological factors, say Masters and Johnson, have little influence on the male orgasm but are more relevant in the male's ability to have or maintain an erection.

The resolution phase of both genders is marked primarily by the rapid loss of myotonia and vasocongestion. In the clitoris and the penis, detumescence tends to occur more quickly than in the rest of the body. With both the male and female, however, this loss of vasocongestion and myotonia need not fully take place if sexual stimulation continues. When it does take place, the male immediately enters a "refractory period" during which he cannot respond to sexual stimulation. This period continues until his remaining sexual tensions have fallen to low excitement-phase levels of response. With the female, no such refractory period exists. and she continues throughout the resolution phase to be able to respond to sexual stimulation.

One of the odd things about Masters and Johnson's theory of a sexual response cycle is that although it received early and extensive criticism from many quarters (e.g., Bentler and Peeler, 1979; Kaplan, 1977; Robinson, 1976; Singer and Singer, 1972; Zilbergeld, 1978), it still seems to be routinely accepted in the sexological literature (see, e.g., Byer and Shainberg, 1991; Marrow, 1997; Milsten and Slowinski, 1999). Even those who disagree with it still frequently accept the term "sexual response cycle," even though such a term forces us to see the sexual process (my preferred term) in a highly limited way. For there is little about the sexual process that indicates it must occur in a "cyclical" fashion: phases can be skipped, take varying amounts of time, or occur in different orders.

In addition, although the notion of a cycle implies a degree of regularity of occurrence (as in the menstrual cycle or the cycles of the moon), nothing about the sexual process implies that it must take place at regular intervals. Moreover, in both physiology and psychology, the term "response" implies a reaction to a stimulus. In this sense the term "sexual response cycle" suggests that what happens in human sexual activity are merely passive and automatic reactions to stimuli. Yet such a view presents a distorted picture by failing to acknowledge the active role played by the individual.

For my purposes, however, the most serious shortcoming is that although Masters and Johnson repeatedly assure us that the sexual response is as much a psychological event as a physiological event, they say next to nothing about the psychology or experience of the sexual response. And what they do say under this heading are merely brief descriptions of some sensations. Consequently, the entire realm of meanings that imbue and seem to lie at the heart of the sexual process are lost to them.

A good example of this neglect of the experiential component of the sexual process can be found in their discussion of the issue of vaginal versus clitoral orgasms. Here they say that although there has been much written about clitoral as opposed to vaginal orgasms, biologically or anatomically there is "absolutely no difference." Their reason for asserting this is that their observations have included women undergoing orgasms through breast stimulation, sexual intercourse, direct clitoral manipulation, and mons area manipulation, and, in each case, "when any woman experiences orgasmic response to effective stimulation, the vagina and the clitoris react in consistent physiologic patterns. Thus the clitoral and vaginal orgasms are not separate biological entities" (1966, p. 67).

The peculiar thing about this remark is that although Masters and Johnson start off by referring to when a woman "experiences" orgasm, they end up referring to orgasms as "biological entities." It is almost like they want us to believe that if the biology of the two orgasms is the same, the experience of the two must be the same. But rather than making such an assumption, why do not Masters and Johnson simply ask their female subjects if they experience the two types of orgasms in the same way? The answer, it would seem, is because Masters and Johnson are probably well aware that women do experience the two sorts of orgasms in different ways (Chesser, 1969; Fisher 1973; Singer and Singer 1972). Not only do women experience vaginal and clitoral orgasms differently, but different women also show preferences for one or the other form of stimulation. Here are some descriptions given by women of vaginal versus clitoral stimulation:

With vaginal stimulation I have a rather cool sweat all over my body. It is a very long and lingering feeling. It can even become a sleeping feeling. There is no great intensity, only consistency of the mood and feeling. It can even become a sleeping feeling with no desire to continue. Clitoral is much more intense. It is a hot, sweating feeling all over. It is more demanding and brings forth much better results. (Fisher, 1973, pp. 195–196)

Vaginal stimulation is more gratifying than clitoral stimulation because it gives me a more whole and complete feeling. It is deeper than clitoral stimulation and I respond better. Clitoral stimulation does tend to aggravate me after a while. (Fisher, 1973, p. 196)

Fisher, who collected these and other descriptions, concludes that words like "warm," "ticklish," "sharp," and "electrical" tend to be used by women to describe clitoral stimulation, while words like "soothing," "deep," and "comfortable" tend to be reserved for describing vaginal stimulation. Fisher's view is that although for many women orgasms result from an indistinguishable blend of vaginal and clitoral elements, there are nevertheless experientially unique qualities to those orgasms that tend to be more one than the other. In their later work, Masters et al., (1993) briefly acknowledge these findings of Fisher, Singer and Singer, and others but have no reply and quickly pass them over.

It consequently appears that if Masters and Johnson had asked their subjects about their experiences of vaginal versus clitoral orgasm, then they would have data on their hands that contradict their anti-Freudian stance. The better strategy would thus be to avoid making definite statements about the experiential element of the two sorts of orgasm and instead imply that there is no experiential difference by asserting that there is no difference at the physiological level.

The problem, however, is even if this implication were valid, it would still not be true because it is simply false that there are no physiological differences between clitoral and vaginal orgasms. First, there has been evidence for some time that the vagina and not just the clitoris is also endowed with nerve centers, the stimulation of which can lead to orgasm. Probably the best-known evidence here comes from Grafenberg (1950), who located a particularly sensitive area that is known as the Grafenberg-spot, or G-spot. Since then, other sexologists have found support for similar areas within the vagina (Alzate, 1985; Alzate and Londoño, 1984; Heath, 1984; Hoch, 1980, 1983). Masters and Johnson deal with these findings by simply ignoring them or denying them (Masters et al., 1993).

It does not seem, however, that a refutation of Masters and Johnson's claim that physiologically there is absolutely no difference depends on this sort of evidence. For the simple anatomical differences between vaginal intercourse and clitoral stimulation without intercourse make it plainly untrue that the vagina and the clitoris react in consistent physiological patterns regardless of the way in which female orgasm is achieved. If, for example, a woman is having an orgasm through sexual intercourse, then her vagina is distended to accommodate the erect penis and is being continually moved about by her partner's or her own thrusting. Further, if the thrusting is deep enough, the penis will be coming into continual contact with the cervix, in turn creating further rhythmic stretching and movement of not only the walls of the vagina but also the uterus and other proximal organs.

This extensive movement of the female's vagina and displacement of her other internal organs due to penile penetration has been documented both by Riley et al., (1992) with the use of ultrasound during sexual intercourse

and by Faix et al., (2001) with magnetic resonance imaging of sexual intercourse. This is physiologically and anatomically a very different reaction of
the vagina from that in which orgasm is achieved only through clitoral
stimulation. In the case of clitoral stimulation, although the upper two-
thirds of the vagina shows some distension as an expression of sexual
excitement, the lower section of the vagina remains closed with the anterior and posterior walls in contact. Nor are the walls of the vagina being
stroked and shifted about as they are in the case of vaginal intromission.

Similar things could be said about the reaction of the clitoris to orgasm
reached through the different forms of sexual stimulation. The firm pressure and vigorous movement that the clitoris undergoes during an orgasm
achieved through direct stimulation is also a different anatomical situation
than the minimal pressure and movement that it receives during orgasm
achieved through, say, rear-entry sexual intercourse.

It is therefore simply false to assert that physiologically there is
absolutely no difference between a vaginal and a clitoral orgasm. Because
of all this, it is some cause for wonder that there are still sexologists (e.g.,
Lips, 1997) who cling to the idea that Masters and Johnson have somehow
proved there to be no such thing as a vaginal orgasm.

THE PLACE OF SEXUAL DESIRE IN THE SEXUAL PROCESS

By failing to take seriously the experiential element of the sexual process,
Masters and Johnson pass over in silence one of the most basic elements in
the sexual process, namely, sexual desire. Although the idea of sexual
desire did not receive extended treatment in the works of earlier sexologists, they seem at least to show an awareness of its place in the sexual
process. Thus, Ellis refers to a first stage in the sexual process in which
"images, desires, and ideals grow up within the mind." Also, for Freud one
of the three causal factors in the sexual process are fantasy and mental
excitations consisting of an awareness of a tension of a compelling character. Likewise, for Reich an important element in the sexual process is the
male's urge to penetrate completely and the female's urge to receive completely. Even in the *Kama Sutra*, Vatsyayana's discussion of the sexual
process includes reference to sexual desire and its varying degrees of force.

One of the first sexologists to point to this deficiency in Masters and
Johnson's account of the sexual process was Helen Singer Kaplan (1977).
Because Kaplan's interest in the sexual process is primarily from the view-
point of sex therapy, her main concern is to be able to locate the points in
the sexual process where her patients experience difficulties. And, according to Kaplan, although people can experience difficulties in the excitement and orgasm phases—for example, showing an inability to sustain the
excitement phase or an inability to have orgasms—the majority of sexual
problems have little to do with the phases as described by Masters and

Johnson but rather have to do with a person's having too little sexual desire, a condition she terms "hypoactive sexual desire." Kaplan therefore proposes her own model of the sexual process, a model that involves the three sequential phases of sexual desire, excitement, and orgasm. Thus, in addition to adding the phase of sexual desire, she also eliminates both the plateau and the resolution phases on the grounds that the idea of a plateau and resolution phase have little therapeutic utility.

Because Kaplan's orientation is primarily therapeutic, it is difficult to judge her full reconstruction of the sexual process on purely phenomenological grounds. Clearly, however, she is right not only for therapeutic reasons to reject the idea of a plateau phase, for, as Robinson (1976) has shown, such a phase does not exist. Her dismissal of the resolution phase (Reich's relaxation stage) is, however, even on therapeutic grounds, more problematic. David M. Reed (in Stayton, 1989), for example, argues that the post-orgasmic stage—one that he calls "reflection"—is a decisive element in the sexual process because it is here where the person reflects over and evaluates the sexual encounter that just occurred. And such reflection will have important consequences for future occurrences of the sexual process.

Still, whether focusing on this phase will have any therapeutic value remains an empirical question that only research can answer. From a phenomenological point of view, however, it is obvious that there are distinct events immediately after the final orgasm in which one experiences a gradual detumescence and enters, to use Reich's words, into a pleasant bodily and psychic relaxation. I will have more to say about this phase shortly.

For the present discussion, a more crucial difficulty with Kaplan's model is that she seems to conceive of sexual desire as though it were a phase that occurs prior to both of the other phases, much like she thinks (also incorrectly) that the excitement phase occurs only prior to the orgasm phase. However, judging from people's descriptions of the sexual process, it is clear that sexual desire is not something that occurs in a discrete phase only to disappear and be replaced by another phase. Consequently, although sexual desire makes its appearance before the "excitement phase," the appearance of the this phase does not extinguish sexual desire. On the contrary, sexual desire seems to be something that persists throughout the excitement phase and indeed seems to be an integral part of that phase.

Likewise, sexual desire does not suddenly terminate with the onset of the orgasm phase. Rather, it seems that it is the persisting element of sexual desire that gives orgasm its intensity. This is, of course, a difficult moment to analyze because, as Reich says, there is a clouding of consciousness. But, as Reich also says, there occurs in orgasm the urge to receive completely on the part of the female and the urge to penetrate completely on the part of the male, the latter point foreshadowing Masters and

Johnson's observation that during orgasm many men plunge their penis as deep as possible into the vagina. (Although Reich uses these descriptions in referring to the occurrence of orgasm in sexual intercourse, one can imagine similar urges in the instance of orgasm achieved in other forms of sexual activity.) Consequently, it seems that sexual desire persists into and during orgasm.

But if this is true, we are then left with the question of when in the sexual process does sexual desire terminate. One reply that suggests itself is that it terminates with the end of orgasm. But various considerations go against such an idea. First, there is the phenomenon of multiple orgasms. Here a person undergoes a series of distinct orgasms that follow one another in rapid succession. In such cases a person's sexual desire is not completely relieved by the first or even subsequent orgasms. Since it seems still a common belief that it is only females who have multiple orgasms (a view that Masters and Johnson seem to be responsible for), it is important to note that males can also undergo multiple orgasms (Arora and Solursh, 1991; Dunn and Trost 1989). Listening to many personal accounts of the sexual process has also made me suspicious of the idea that, after orgasm and a pause in sexual stimulation, males must undergo a refractory period before being susceptible to further sexual stimulation.

Part of the confusion here probably results from Masters and Johnson's equating male orgasm with ejaculation and failing to notice the pinnacle of orgasm is really the peak-pleasure that typically takes place well before ejaculation. For although the series of rhythmic expulsions of semen that occur in the male's sexual process tend to occur only once, the sudden escalation of peak pleasure, which occurs apart from ejaculation, can easily occur more than once. In their later work, Masters et al. (1993) refer to some of these findings but attempt to dismiss them as "unsubstantiated" or only occurring in a "small number" of men.

There is also the situation in which a person does not have multiple orgasms but does not feel like stopping after his or her first orgasm and thus continues with sexual activity, sometimes to a further orgasm. Thus, one woman describes her sexual interactions with her husband by saying, "what happens many times is that I'll reach orgasm in one position and then we'll shift and I'll reach it again, etc., until my husband reaches a climax which in turn makes me climax again" (Fisher, 1973, p. 204). Sometimes, the further orgasms are felt to be more satisfying than the first, as shown by a woman in Kaplan's (1995) case studies who says, "my second orgasm is really much better than the first. After I have one I'm all wet and aroused and I enjoy it so much more" (p. 82).

It might be argued that such cases are not common and that sexual desire usually terminates with the end of orgasm, or at least with the end of the final orgasm (whenever that is). This is the view that Kaplan takes. According to her, "after the reproductive act is completed, most adult men feel 'sated' and are refractory to further sexual stimulation. The female satiation point is more variable, and while some women are satisfied after one orgasm, others want more, but eventually even the sexiest women become sated" (1995, p. 18). To this passage she adds the footnote that "some adolescent or very young men do not feel sated until they have come more than once." What Kaplan means by "sated" and its exact relation to the "end of the reproductive act," however, is not at all clear, and it is suggestive that she feels the need to put the word "sated" in quotation marks, which here hints at some kind of uncertainty.

Simone de Beauvoir also pursues this problem of the termination of sexual desire, but here we get a slightly different picture. According to Beauvoir,

there is no doubt that for the man coition has a definite biological conclusion: ejaculation. And certainly many other quite complex intentions are involved in aiming at this goal; but once attained, it seems a definite result, and *if not the full satisfaction of desire,* at least its termination for the time being. In woman, on the contrary, the goal is uncertain from the start, and more psychological in nature than physiological; she desires sex excitement and pleasure in general, but her body promises no precise conclusion to the act of love; and this is why coition is never quite terminated for her: it admits of no end. (1949, p. 395; italics added)

Beauvoir is thus in agreement with Kaplan about the idea that the male's sexual desire is typically brought to more of a termination with orgasm than the female's desire is, but she is in disagreement with Kaplan concerning the finality of the termination in the female case. For Beauvoir, the female never reaches a definite conclusion in her sexual activity, and her sexual desire is thus never really terminated. Although Beauvoir here makes her point in terms of coition or sexual intercourse, her general discussion makes it clear that she is not making a specific point about the shortcomings of sexual intercourse as opposed to other female sexual activities, say, masturbation or cunnilingus. Rather, she is making a general point about the nature of female sexual desire and its lack of termination in any type of sexual activity.

In arguing for her point about female sexual desire being interminable, Beauvoir tries to contrast it with male sexual desire by pointing to ejaculation as the conclusion of the sexual act for the male and suggests that this somehow terminates his desire in a way that the female's desire is not terminated. However, just as with Kaplan, here too one notices a hesitancy and uncertainty. For ejaculation is put forward as being "a definite *biological* conclusion," not a definite psychological or phenomenological conclusion of desire. And a few lines later we are told that ejaculation is, "*if not the full satisfaction of desire,* at least its termination for the time being" (italics added in the last two quotations). But how could someone's sexual desire not be fully satisfied and yet be terminated for the time being?

One way of dealing with this problem is by recalling what was noted in the first chapter, namely, that the fulfillment or satisfaction of desire need not bring about the cessation of desire. Part of the difficulty, however, in getting clear about such a view is that when words like "fulfillment," "satisfaction," "satiation," "termination," and "cessation" are used in reference to desire, they are often used interchangeably. (Beauvoir uses the French terms *l'assouvissement du desir* and *suppression,* translated above as "satisfaction of desire" and "termination," respectively. She also makes no clear distinction between such terms, even though her discussion points in such a direction). This usage obscures an important distinction between what is perhaps best called the satiation, satisfaction, or fulfillment of desire and the termination or cessation of desire. Bringing this distinction to Beauvoir's discussion, one could then say that although ejaculation might signal the satisfaction of a male's sexual desire, it need not thereby bring about its termination.

However, even once this distinction is clearly made, there still remains a problem with Beauvoir's account. This involves her blending of the biological and psychological. Thus, although she might be right that ejaculation is a definite *biological* conclusion, it does not thereby follow, as Beauvoir seems to think, that the male's sexual desire as an *experience* is thereby terminated. Perhaps it is the awareness of this that makes her qualify her claim with the clause "if not the full satisfaction of desire," a clause that refers to the psychological rather than the biological aspect of the completion of the male's sex behavior.

On this interpretation, one could say that although ejaculation might signal the end of a male's participation in active sexual intercourse, it need not mean that his sexual desire is thus terminated or even satisfied. This would then give rise to the question of why the sex act might draw to a close after ejaculation if sexual desire were not terminated or satisfied. The obvious answer to this question is given by Beauvoir herself in her discussion of the interminableness of female desire. Here she says, "it is often nervous or cardiac fatigue or psychic satiety that limits woman's erotic possibilities, rather than specific gratification; even when overwhelmed, exhausted, she may never find full deliverance" (1949, p. 396).

Without denying possible differences between the female and male sexual process here, could it not be that a similar account might also be applied to the male? That is, it is not so much the satisfaction of his desire that limits his erotic possibilities but rather simply that after the "physiological explosion" of orgasm and ejaculation, the body and sexual apparatus are fatigued or have their energy spent. On this account sexual desire might well continue but, because of physical fatigue, continuation of a sexual activity is rendered difficult: ejaculation, discharge of built-up energy and subsequent loss of myotonia, and loss of erection along with a general detumescence might all contribute to render the pursuit of further sexual tension and excitement problematic and therefore impracticable.

To get an idea of what would be involved in this situation, consider the following example. A woman and man, because of sexual desire toward each other, have just had sexual intercourse. After lying some time together, the woman gets up and starts to dress while the man continues to lie in bed in a state of pleasant bodily and psychic relaxation and watches her. In such a case it might easily happen that, despite his state of relaxation, he notices her extreme sexual attractiveness: the curve of her hips, the smoothness of her skin, the way she moves as she slips into her clothing. All this fills him with an awareness of the sexual desire he continues to bear toward her, and yet because he has just had a sexual encounter with her and has already ejaculated, begun to lose his erection, and so on, he might not want to try to engage her sexually again.

What is limiting his erotic possibilities here is simply the physical fatigue of his sexual system, not a loss of sexual desire. Something like this seems to be what Ellis is getting at when he says that, in happy circumstances, even after orgasm the male will not feel that the female has lost any of her charm. "Charm" is a good way of putting it because a male's attributing such a quality to a female does not imply outright the idea of an immediate desire to engage her in a sexual act, but it does carry the meaning that such a female is attractive and thus seems to have the undertone that he still entertains sexual desire toward her. And this example—which seems nothing out of the ordinary—is one that can admit of numerous variations, all of which might equally demonstrate the persistence of sexual desire beyond orgasm. Because of this it seems that there must be a sense in which male sexual desire is also, like female sexual desire, at some level interminable.

Therefore, when Beauvoir, trying to be more definite about the male sexual process, says that "male sex feeling rises like an arrow; when it reaches a certain height or threshold, it is fulfilled and dies abruptly in the orgasm," she is clearly wrong if her term "sex feeling" (*plaisir* in French) is to be equated with "sexual desire" (If *plaisir* is translated as "erotic pleasure," then here too she is also wrong.) If, however, her term is meant to refer to biological phenomena like muscle tension, organ tumescence, and the buildup of energy, then her account is perhaps more acceptable, though even here it is not fully correct. As Masters and Johnson (1966, p. 186) point out, when the erect penis has been contained in the vagina for many minutes during prolonged intercourse, then, even after ejaculation, the onset of the loss of erection may be postponed indefinitely. The reason for the infrequent occurrence of this form of persisting erection would then simply be the extremely short duration of intercourse that seems to be the Western cultural norm. Kinsey, for example, estimated that most married males tend to ejaculate within two minutes of having entered the vagina, with many ejaculating even more quickly. And not much has changed here since the Kinsey reports: sex therapists McCarthy and McCarthy (1998) suggest that the average length of intercourse is between two and seven minutes.

Further, even if there is an initial slight detumescence of the penis after ejaculation, full loss of erection after orgasm depends much on the male's post-coitus behavior. If, after orgasm, he moves away from his partner—a behavior that the psychoanalyst Stoller (1975) suggests is fairly widespread— or gets up and walks around, then his erection tends to be quickly lost. If, however, he remains close to the female or does not withdraw his penis from her vagina, then the duration of his erection may be quite prolonged. The reason for this persistence of erection is clearly that, by lying close to his partner or having his penis remain inside her after ejaculation, the male is continuing to receive powerful sexual stimulation. Also, especially in the case where there has been prolonged vaginal penetration prior to ejaculation, it seems likely that the male senses a clear continuity with earlier pre-ejaculation levels of sexual excitement. Consequently, despite his sexual fatigue, he is still being sexually excited—which shows the error of seeing excitement as a phase in the sexual process that occurs only before the orgasm phase.

Looking to the biological aspects of the sexual process, it can be seen that the female and male processes operate in distinctive enough ways that, if one was not careful to distinguish such aspects from the element of desire, one might end up holding that male desire terminates in a way that female desire might not. This is because, it would seem, that when one thinks of the biological aspect of male sexual desire, one typically thinks of the erect penis. An erect penis is something that unmistakably presents itself as such and is something that neither the male who has it nor the female who sees it or is penetrated by it can fail to notice.

Likewise, the male's ejaculation, which is frequently associated with erection, is also a clearly public and unmistakable event, not something that is hidden within his body. Of course, ejaculation often occurs out of sight when the penis is in the vagina or other bodily orifices, but even here, because of the distinct sensation of the expulsion of a volume of semen, the male is usually in no doubt about its occurrence. Nor is the event lost on the female who, if not directly aware of the ejaculation when it occurs within her, is soon aware of the extra fluid in her vagina that quickly begins to run out of her. This, taken together with the fact that upon ejaculation many males in Western culture stop their thrusting motions, withdraw from the vagina, and begin to lose erection, suggests the termination of something.

However, when one thinks of the biological aspect of female sexual desire, there is no one unmistakable and public event that suggests itself. Although the biological events in the female sexual process include observable events like the parting of the labia majora, engorgement of the clitoris, and erection of the nipples and engorgement of the breasts, none of these presents itself to awareness as the definitive indication of female sexual desire. Neither the opening of the labia majora nor the engorgement of the clitoris is unmistakably evident to either the female or her partner. As Masters and Johnson point out, clitoral tumescence is usually observable only with magnification, and even then many women do not show clitoral tumescence. Moreover, if it does occur, it does so only in the latter stages of sexual excitement. Likewise, the opening of the labia major is but a slight movement that occurs only after the female has been sexually excited for some time. As for breast and nipple changes, these again are variable, depending on both the female and the shape and size of her breasts and nipples, and may occur earlier or later in the sexual process. Nipples can easily become erect for reasons other than sexual excitement, and some women's nipples show no erection despite sexual stimulation.

If there were one physiological event that is most associated in awareness with female sexual desire, it would probably be the lubrication of the vagina. Like the male erection, the lubrication of the vagina is one of the first physiological events in the sexual process and also has a clear sexual function, namely, to prepare the vagina for sexual intercourse. But even here it is neither an unmistakable event nor an unmistakably sexual event: both the female and her partner can fail to notice the moistening of the vagina, and the vagina can easily become moist for reasons other than sexual excitement. Likewise, there is no readily observable event, like the male's ejaculation, that might serve to indicate the female has had an orgasm. This is why a female can quite effectively pretend to have an orgasm (see Darling and Davidson, 1986)—something that the male cannot do quite as well.

It is true that there has been some discussion of the possible existence of a female ejaculation that might be analogous to the male ejaculation. Ellis points to the phenomenon of a spurt of fluid during female sexual excitement that, he thinks, comes from glands at the entrance to the vagina. There is, however, much disagreement about the nature, incidence, and even existence of a female ejaculation that might be analogous to the male's. Although some sexologists (e.g., Grafenberg, 1950; Ladas et al., 1982) have argued that evidence supports the idea of a distinct ejaculatory phenomenon that occurs in some (but not all) women, others (e.g., Freese and Levitt, 1984; Masters et al., 1993) have argued that such an event is typically an expulsion of urine during orgasm and is thus best understood as an instance of urinary stress incontinence. Moreover, chemical analyses of the ejaculated fluid have proved inconsistent. For while some findings suggest that the ejaculated fluid has a different appearance from urine (Goldberg et al., 1983) or even that there might be low amounts of chemicals in the urine that distinguish it from pure urine (Addiego et al., 1981), others suggest that the fluid is indistinguishable from urine (Alzate, 1985; Alzate and Londoño, 1984).

Interestingly, and as one might expect, this lack of clarity surrounding the biological question of female ejaculation is also reflected at the experiential level. In a large study by Darling et al., (1990), only 40 percent of the women questioned claimed to have a fluid release during orgasm. And even here "those reporting having ejaculated were [like researchers in this area] also confused. Many were either unable to perceive or verbalize the exact location of the spurt of fluid, how it is released, or the differences between lubrication and the spurt of fluid" (p. 44). So even if there might exist an ejaculation with some women, it seems to be neither a universal, a definite, nor a clearly observable event that could serve to demarcate the occurrence of the female orgasm.

There are, it is true, vaginal contractions associated with female orgasms, but again these do not always seem to be clearly evident to the male or even the female. In Beauvoir's words, they appear as a "system of waves that rhythmically arise, disappear, and re-form, attain from time to time a paroxysmal condition, become vague, and sink down without ever quite dying out" (1949, p. 396). Beauvoir might here be referring to what Singer and Singer (1972) call a uterine orgasm or perhaps to what they call a blended orgasm. According to Singer and Singer, the uterine orgasm is one that depends on (typically penile) stimulation of the cervix and that involves deep orgasmic sensations in the uterus that spread to other areas of the body. In such an orgasm there are no definite vaginal contractions. A blended orgasm is one that blends aspects of both the uterine orgasm and vaginal contractions. (Masters and Johnson's failure to notice these sorts of orgasms, suggest Singer and Singer, is probably due to their laboratory setting that would not be conducive to the intimate emotional atmosphere required for such orgasms.)

It thus is clear that, in both genders, sexual desire is something that persists beyond the biological events of the sexual process. Indeed, it is something that is forever infiltrating our daily existence. As one woman put it, "I guess with every beautiful person you see, there is like a hint of sexual stuff, but it's not. . . . It's not the same as like 'Hey baby, I want to do you' or anything like that. It's just this real little, small little, hint of sexual that's going on" (Dossett, 2002, p. 91; ellipsis in the original). When such a hint of sexual desire appears, it need not do so with any form of accompanying physiological arousal. Here one merely notices the slight movements of awareness that, I have argued, have no essential connection to emotional arousal.

What is needed, therefore, is an account of the sexual process that shows how sexual desire intermingles with the sexual process in such a way that it sets the other elements of the sexual process in motion and yet can persist into and even beyond their occurrence. Such an account, however, it should be clear, must be given in phenomenological terms. This is because sexual desire is related to the events of the sexual process, not in terms of what those events are as purely biological events but rather in terms of what meaning they have for the person undergoing them.

Consequently, any account of the sexual process that hopes adequately to integrate the fundamental element of sexual desire must look to the way in which the events of the sexual process present themselves to our awareness. This does not mean that the biological elements in the sexual process will not in themselves play an important role, for a special feature of sexual desire is its unique relation to the bodily events of the sexual process. Consequently, the mainly biological accounts that we have so far examined will prove useful in providing us with knowledge of the biological substratum, as it were, upon which awareness in the sexual process takes a point of view.

THE PHENOMENOLOGY OF THE SEXUAL PROCESS

In presenting a phenomenological account, it will help to start by asking, Why is it that particular regions of the body—the penis, vagina, and so on—are typically the primary erotogenic regions? A possible answer here is that it is these areas of the body that are innervated by a particular type of erotic nerve. Unfortunately, though, we know very little about the nature of the nerves that innervate the primary erotogenic regions (Levine, 2002). Since, however, the entire body has the potential to be erotically sensitive, it is doubtful that the erotic aspects of these areas have much to do with their particular type of nerve endings. Rather, when the way in which these areas of the body are seen to differ from other areas, it becomes clear that they share a common feature; namely, they are all entrances or areas surrounding or nearby entrances into the body. Thus, the penis is the cite of the urethral opening, while the female's genital region surrounds not only the urethral opening but also the vaginal tract, which itself leads up to and surrounds the cervical opening (another erotogenic zone). Likewise, the nipples in the female and the anus and lips in both sexes all present themselves as pathways to the interior of the body.

Further, other typical erotogenic regions, such as the testicles in the male or the insides of the thighs in both the male and female, also lie close to both the genital and anal apertures. (The testicles, it should also be seen, are connected to the interior of the body by the spermatic cord. This connection also allows external stimulations to penetrate easily into the depths of the body.) Here it is worth noting that the ears, a further entrance to the body, are, for many people, also highly erotogenic regions—which might also explain why the sides of the neck under the ears are typically sensitive to erotic stimulation. The main exception here would seem to be the nostrils, whose immediate and vital function of breath control along with the closely related sneezing reflex might well limit their potential to be also deployed as erotogenic zones (though even in this case, many people see similarities between sneezing and orgasm).

But why is it particularly the entrances to the body that should function as erotogenic regions? The answer, I want to suggest, has to do with the meaning that such regions hold for us. For it is these regions that are seen to provide the other person with pathways into our bodies or, like the penis and nipples, protrusions that can penetrate the other person's body and that, at the same time, offer pathways from our own body into the body of the other person. Likewise, in the other person, these apertures offer themselves as channels into the interior of his or her body.

This awareness of the primary erotogenic regions as pathways between the interior of my and the desired person's body is an awareness that exists as a phenomenological layer within the sexual process. It is a layer that extends beyond the elements of pure bodily awareness and encompasses the awareness of my body's relation to the desired person's body. As such it is an awareness whose full meaning will become apparent only once we have explored the place of gender in sexual desire. However, within the layer of bodily awareness—a phenomenological layer that is not fully distinct from the one just referred to but within which distinct elements can nevertheless be discerned—the erotogenic zones often exist as focal points of bodily awareness during the unfolding of the sexual process.

It is not, however, that this aspect of the erotogenic zones exists in full clarity in our awareness, for in the bodily awareness that accompanies sexual activity we never experience the erotogenic zones as isolated or disconnected elements but rather experience them as integral aspects of the entire body. Consequently, the erotogenic zones as bodily entrances exist in awareness as indistinct hubs around which our bodily awareness circulates during the sexual process. Therefore, as sexual desire pulls me toward the other person, within the layer of bodily awareness the erotogenic zones typically act as vague focal points that, being entrances, seem to open the body in preparation to receive the other person's body. It is within this movement toward the other person's body that the unfolding of the sexual process takes place.

This view of sexual desire as a sense of motion toward another person—or rather toward an activity with another person, as I shall argue shortly—is one that enables us to get an idea of what a phenomenological account of the sexual process must look like. Although the phases of this process—phases that I will call the ascending, entering, rushing upward, bursting, descending, and floating phases—tend to come in a specific order, it is important to remember that the phases here, like the ones just discussed, can, for numerous reasons, be broken off at any point or even skipped. The process starts, however, when the rising of the urgency of sexual desire gives birth to an excited sense of a gradual but directed ascending. In this phase, I experience my desire as slowly collecting and intensifying my awareness of the other person (in reality or in fantasy) and moving me forward gradually to ascend toward some distant peak where the desired person's body and mine will somehow have fully received one another (here is where I feel the mutual pull of our primary or other erotogenic zones). It is worth noting here that this sense of rising and intensification is paralleled at the physiological level by the rising of tumescence and the intensification of muscle tension. Here is where the mechanism of fore-pleasure sets in, or at least can set in if the sexual activity (real or fanta-sized) is one that is highly desired.

Thus, the relation of the movement of sexual desire to the elements of the sexual process is such that, in its urgent appearance, sexual desire is like a wind that sweeps through the various elements of that process, tum-bling them, as it were, like leaves down a street. And similarly, just as a gentle wind need not disturb the leaves, so a non-urgent sexual desire need not set the sexual process in motion. Here the "small little, hint of sexual that's going on" wafts its way through our daily lives gently, nearly unno-ticeably, drifting toward "every beautiful person" we see. It is this subtle sexual desire that directs our awareness to the scent of a perfume, the tone of a laugh, the sway of a hip, causing our glance to linger, however briefly, before turning away. It is also this same sexual desire that, maintaining and sharpening its focus, eventually both surrounds and bathes the rest of the sexual process in its motion, transmitting its urgency to the events of that process.

The wind, however, is not the only thing capable of transmitting its motion to the leaves: a passerby, for example, might similarly disturb them as he walks down the street. In just this same way, sexual desire need not be the only thing that causes or even sustains the sexual process. For as pointed out by Freud, both internal and external excitations of the eroto-genic zones can also set things in motion (were the excitations to be caused by fantasy—Freud's other source—then it would seem that sexual desire had already made its appearance). An unexpected stroking of or pressure on, say, the genitals might well lead to the beginnings of the ascending phase. When this occurs, then it is altogether possible that such events might stir the beginnings of sexual desire, much like the movement of the leaves disturbed by the passerby might itself create a gentle wind. Whether this occurs will depend on how one chooses to interpret the excitations, a choice that in turn will be influenced by such things as personality factors, expectations, various situational cues, and the norms of the culture in which one lives. Thus, the causal relation between sexual desire and the other events of the sexual process is a two-way relation. And as the sexual process begins to unfold, it is more than likely that both will mutually affect one another, giving more and more force to the entire process itself.

This, however, is only one possible sequence of events. Another is that, due to the lack of sexual desire, the ascending phase draws quickly to a close without proceeding to the later phases. Yet another is that the ascending phase, even without the influence of sexual desire, continues on to the other phases. This is so because the physical event of excitation of the erotogenic zones is quite enough in itself, even without sexual desire, to cause organ tumescence and muscle tensions that can also be sufficient to lead to the physiological event of orgasm and its aftermath.

A dramatic example of this is given in Burgess' (1981) study of 16 female patients who had been sexually abused by a particular gynecologist during vaginal examinations. Here, although none of these women had or developed any sexual desire toward the physician, 10 of the abused women patients had feelings of sexual arousal during the exam, while eight even had orgasms (the gynecologist, who allowed the sessions to go on for 20 to 30 minutes—far longer than is usual for such exams—pretended to be examining each woman all the while moving his fingers in and out of her vagina and rubbing her clitoris). The noteworthy thing, however, was that none of these women had any feelings of erotic pleasure during their sexual arousal or orgasms, events that they rather described as being simply warm, weird, and even painful.

This situation in which the sexual process takes place with neither erotic pleasure nor sexual desire is one that seems similar to that of Reich's orgastically impotent patients who were able to have both erections and ejaculations but without the accompanying experience of erotic pleasure, having what Reik (1940) appropriately calls a "flat orgasm." The reason for this lack of erotic pleasure, I would argue, is that in both cases there is a lack of sexual desire—the difference being that the lack in the case of the abused women is determined merely situationally (none of them had any desire toward the gynecologist), and the lack in the case of orgastically impotency is determined by the person's character (each of them had a chronic lack of sexual desire that cut across situations and partners).

At any point in this ascending phase, the entering phase can suddenly take place. This happens when the person feels he or she has somehow entered or been entered by the other person's body. Here a breach in the barriers between the two bodies makes its first appearance. Typically, this is the moment of the penetration of the vagina by the penis (see e.g., Laumann et al., 1994), though it can just as easily take place in the act of kissing or other forms of embrace. To what extent such penetration is attended by the gentle and radiating sense of entrance-pleasure will, in a like fashion, typically depend on both how quickly other actions supplant the moment of penetration and the intensity of the desires that surround the act of penetration.

The entering phase, however, is not a necessary phase in the sexual process. Just as it is an event that can occur and thereafter terminate at any place in the sexual process, so is it an event that might equally well not occur: for its non-appearance does not hinder the progression of events. The ascending phase can, with or without the entering phase, proceed to its highest point where the phase of rushing upward suddenly takes over.

Or again, the ascending phase, with or without the entering phase, may or may not proceed to such a rushing upward.

When it does, the sudden upward surge takes over as the sense of directed effort gets left behind and various conceptual awarenesses are scattered by the force of an overwhelming sexual desire. At this point sexual desire seems to move along with this surge, overtaking our sense of control and hurling us upward into the realms of peak-pleasure like an object sent whirling into the air by a windstorm. Numerous variations in this experience will be possible, especially for the female with her possibilities of clitoral, vaginal, or uterine orgasms. In the first case the upward rushing may have more of an intense or sharp sensation to it, while in the second it may be more soothing and warm. Also, the fact that both the vaginal and uterine orgasms will typically take place during penile penetration—with the uterine orgasm even possibly depending on penile or penile-like stimulation of the cervix—means that deeper bodily sensations and movement of organs will add their kinesthetic coloring to the sense of rushing upward.

This phase comes swiftly to an end as its accumulated intensity reaches a summit that seems to burst through any remaining tensions. In this moment of the bursting phase there is an instantaneous sense of liberation in which all forms of withholding are suddenly released and left far behind, disappearing into the distance like a stage falling back to earth from a climbing rocket. (Although calling this phase the bursting phase might be thought to reflect a male point of view—alluding to the burst of ejaculation that is about to follow—it is important to note that many women use just this word to describe their experiences at this point in the sexual process [Fisher, 1973]). In this instant sexual desire becomes momentarily obscured, as the force of its movement seems to scatter it in numerous directions, leaving the desire or, rather, its fragments dispersed among the horizons of consciousness. Here this racing upward of peak-pleasure seems to teeter on its highest point. Thus, peak-pleasure attends both the rushing upward phase and the bursting phase, with the difference that in the bursting phase it has attained its highest limit.

However, no sooner has this point been gained than it is in the same instant suddenly lost. This loss, and thus the start of the descending phase, is signaled by the first of a rhythmic succession of powerful contractions that, along with end-pleasure, instantly break into awareness. It is here typically that the first deep contraction immediately preceding the male's ejaculation takes place. This is why Reich is mistaken to locate the first contraction of the sexual process in the onset of his acme phase. For the first contraction occurs well after the acme phase of the sexual process— what I call the rushing upward phase—has begun. Indeed, with the first contraction the upward movement of this part of the sexual process has already finished and the bursting phase has taken over. Here existence itself seems to pulse as everything suddenly collapses inward, abruptly halts, releases, and expands, only to immediately collapse inward again and so on in a succession of gradually softening waves. Oddly enough, the tensions that seemed forever lost in the pinnacle of the rushing upward phase here again reassert themselves. Here they are revealed as the sense of tightening that pulsates through the experience of collapsing inward. They are, however, strangely altered. For here they appear rhythmically and effortlessly of their own accord, doing so each time with a sense of gradual dissipation.

This dissipation is something that itself can have but a brief existence. That is, in some cases this dissipation can suddenly reverse direction and once again revert to a rushing upward, a phase that is similarly followed by another bursting phase. This reversion seems intimately linked to the fact that even though the descending phase is overall one of a gradual release, it is nevertheless filled with the pulsating tensions of inward collapsing. Consequently, surges of intensity, and thus fleeting moments of rushing upward, are no strangers to this phase. When a reversion takes place, what happens is that, rather than releasing, one of the inward movements (usually the first) continues to hold, transforming itself, as it were, into what seems similar to the final tensions of the ascending phase. This brings forth another surge of intensity that moves everything forward once again into the rushing upward phase. Here is what is often referred to as multiple orgasms.

When, however, the tensions continue to release, there comes a point when the final inward pull of tension subsides. This is where the floating phase takes over. This happens when the length of time following the last inward collapsing is such that it is evident that no more such motions are to come. At this point one neither descends nor ascends but rather seems to float on a sea of sparkling pinnacles, suspended in time, as the woman referred to earlier puts it. Here a heightened awareness imparts a gentle excitement to what is also, at the same time, a deep sense of relaxation. It seems significant to note here that the element of excitement is not a new element in the sexual process that makes its entrance at this stage. Rather, it is a residual feature from the first stirrings of the ascending phase that has, in more or less degrees, persisted throughout the process. This shows the unhelpfulness of trying to portray any particular phase in the process as "the excitement phase." It is, however, this fascinating blend of arousal and relaxation that is the hallmark of the floating phase.

Although it might seem paradoxical that the tensions of arousal and the softness of relaxation could exist simultaneously in the same awareness, those who practice hatha yoga often describe such a state. Here the yogin sinks into her *asana* (or posture), which, because of the persistent stress on the body, sends tensions rippling throughout her awareness. Yet at the same time, her use of *pranayama* (or breath regulation), her familiarity with the *asana*, her non-attachment to the tensions, and her ability to exist in between them, as it were, gives rise to a deep sense of repose.

As for the erotic pleasure of the floating phase, this is something that is not as distinct as that of the earlier phases but, because of the sense of arousal, is nevertheless present. It is much like fore-pleasure shorn of its compelling character. This compelling character is gone because of the present-looking quality of the floating phase. With fore-pleasure the gaze is essentially forward as the pleasure presses one on to increase or hold the tensions. In the pleasure of the floating phase, one allows the tensions to subside or hold of their own accord, observing them as from a distance. In this instance the sense of erotic pleasure seems to drift throughout the body, no doubt reflecting Reich's "flowing back" of blood from the genitals to the rest of the body. Here the gripping aspects of erotic pleasure are held in check by the simultaneous pull of relaxation. Here, also because of the relaxation, sexual desire loses its urgency.

This phase, it must be mentioned, can just as easily appear after the sexual process has reached its highest point of the ascending phase. In such a case the sexual process skips over the rushing upward, bursting, and descending phases and moves directly into the suspension of the floating phase. Here there is also a remaining sense of tension carried over from the descending phase while at the same time a sense of deepening relaxation imparted by a lull in the urgency of sexual desire. However, the persisting sense of attraction to the other person indicates it has not disappeared. Rather, it continues to move gently through awareness, keeping its direction toward the other person. The sense of relaxation will, however, tend to inhibit the excitement from imparting urgency to sexual desire.

Although some people seem to think that sexual activity that does not lead to orgasm must be inherently unpleasant and thus could not lead to the pleasantness of the floating phase, this is a view that is ungrounded. Some people, typically males, it seems (McCarthy and McCarthy, 1998), might well sense frustration if a sexual encounter has not led to orgasm, but one cannot help but wonder how much of this stems from a cultural indoctrination that prescribes orgasm as the goal of all sexual activity. As will be seen in the next chapter, orgasm is not always a sought-after outcome of sexual interaction. Here the compelling character of fore-pleasure is something that eventually abates, leaving the person with that special mixing of euphoria and suspension that is characteristic of the final phase of the sexual process. It should be seen, however, that because of this blend of two elements, a person could end the floating phase by focusing more and more on one rather than the other. In the case of focusing on the excitement element, one might well try to start the sexual exchange again or, like Vatsayana's lovers, to head up to the roof and gaze at the stars. In the case of focusing on the relaxation, one might simply fall asleep.

3

The Object of Sexual Desire

SEXUAL DESIRE AND REPRODUCTION

Having explored both the nature of desire and the relation of sexual desire to the sexual process, I have surrounded but not yet captured the decisive element in this inquiry, namely, the object of sexual desire. This element is decisive because it is the object that both distinguishes sexual desire from other desires and gives it membership in the sexual process. To move forward, the question that now needs to be asked is, What is the object of sexual desire, or, in other words, what is it that we desire when we have sexual desire? Although to many people the answer to this question might seem immediately obvious, there is much disagreement over what it is we really desire. One of the main reasons for such disagreement seems to be that sexual desire is a phenomenon that operates within a complex network of biological, social, experiential, and existential concerns. Consequently, it is always possible that what one takes to be an element essential in the nature of sexual desire, say, its essential object, is in reality only part of the contingent network in which sexual desire exists.

To see how such difficulties arise, and by way of finding an answer to this question, we can begin by noting that sexual desire has an obvious connection to the process of biological reproduction. That is, sexual desire can be a causal factor leading to sexual intercourse, which in turn can lead to pregnancy and from there to childbirth. Consequently, although sexual desire might seem to be directed to various objects, activities, or experiences, it nevertheless remains true that sexual desire has a basic connection to human reproduction. Because of this, someone might well be led to argue that reproduction is, in some sense, the real goal or object of sexual desire.

Such a position was first clearly articulated by Schopenhauer, the 19th-century idealist philosopher. Schopenhauer's view is based on a metaphysics in which human beings are seen to consist of an intellectual and volitional faculty. This volitional faculty, which he calls "the will to live," is one that operates within us independently of the intellectual faculty and consequently is beyond our reason and control. It does this because the will to live is something that transcends our individuality. It is an impersonal phenomenon of which each individual is merely a separate avatar. Here we see where Schopenhauer is under the influence of the ancient Upanishadic *rishis* or seers of India. For according to these thinkers, the apparently individual self, something they called *Atman,* is merely part of a greater ultimate reality, something they called *Brahman.* For Schopenhauer, *Brahman* becomes the will to live, and *Atman* becomes each individual expression of this will.

Because of its freedom from the constraints of the intellect, this will to live does not care about what form it takes but strives at all costs simply to continue. Consequently, the will to live cares not for individuals in themselves but only for individuals sofar as they enable the will to live to pursue it its path. Since individuals die, the important thing for the will to live is that the individual reproduces itself. For in doing so, the will to live is able to persist in another avatar. In other words, individuals are dispensable; the chain of life is not. Individuals come and go, and life continues, but when the chain is gone, life is gone. And when life is gone, the will to live is gone.

Here, then, the relation between the will to live and sexual desire becomes evident. For sexual desire is nothing more than the will to live. Indeed, for Schopenhauer, it is the ultimate expression of the will to live: it is this desire that leads to reproduction and thus to the survival of the will to live. Consequently, although we may think that the object of our sexual desires is love, erotic pleasure, or some other such personal concern, this is merely a delusion of the intellect. For the real object of sexual desire—an object chosen not by us but by the impersonal will to live—is reproduction.

Despite it highly metaphysical content, Schopenhauer's view concerning the object of sexual desire is essentially the same as the view put forward by modern and supposedly non-metaphysical disciplines like sociobiology and evolutionary psychology. What researchers in these disciplines would find objectionable about Schopenhauer's theory would thus not be his conclusion but rather his teleological views that underlie that conclusion. For in arguing that reproduction is the desired object of a will to live, Schopenhauer seems to be introducing the teleological element of a purposeful goal. He is thus giving a pre-Darwinian view about how the desire that leads to reproduction operates. Strangely enough, however, this is just what sociobiologists and evolutionary psychologists are themselves forced to do. For if one wants to argue that reproduction is the object of sexual desire, then clearly there must somewhere exist a desire—that is, a purposeful teleological wanting—whose aim is to reproduce. The difficulty, however, is that such a view goes against the non-teleological idea of natural selection that supposedly lies at the basis of sociobiology and evolutionary psychology.

To see the problems that this leads to, let us have a look at a well-known account of one of these disciplines. In *The Evolution of Desire: Strategies of Human Mating* (2003), evolutionary psychologist David M. Buss argues that sexual desire, preferences, and choices are the results of millions of years of natural selection. What have been selected are sexual desires that pick out reproductive capacity in potential mates. Thus, men sexually desire women who have youth, a feminine figure, and health and beauty because these are good indications of a female's capacity to reproduce the man's child. Similarly, women sexually desire men who have strength, status, industriousness, and commitment because these features indicate a male's ability to sustain a steady flow of resources to the woman and her child. Schopenhauer says the same thing.

Although Buss does not directly raise the question of the object of desire, it is clear from his discussion that the object of sexual desire is supposed to be reproduction. But in what sense could this be true? This question needs to be raised because in the most obvious sense it is plainly false. When someone has sexual desire, it seems that what the person desires is something that transpires in the moment of sexual activity, not progeny, which may or may not appear long after one's sexual desire has been satisfied.

This is not to say, however, that people do not, on various occasions, have a desire to reproduce. Nevertheless, such a desire is one that operates independently of sexual desire. For one need not experience sexual desire when one experiences the desire to reproduce, nor need one experience the desire to reproduce when one experiences sexual desire. People can, of course, desire to engage in sexual intercourse with the goal of reproducing in mind, but then they can also desire to engage in sexual intercourse without such a goal in mind and even engage in sexual intercourse while taking definite precautions not to reproduce.

The obvious response to this criticism would be to claim that a person need not be aware of the real object of his or her desire. Therefore, even though we might not be aware of desiring reproduction when we have sexual desire, at another level, this is what we really desire. That Buss seems to hold such a view is indicated by his remarks about what he calls "sexual strategies" or "psychological mechanisms such as preferences for a particular mate, feelings of love, desire for sex, or jealousy." Here he tells us that

although the term *sexual strategies* is a useful metaphor for thinking about solutions to mating problems, it is misleading in the sense of connoting conscious intent. Sexual strategies do not require conscious planning or awareness. Our sweat glands are "strategies" for accomplishing the goal of thermal regulation, but they require neither conscious planning nor awareness of the goal. Indeed, just as a piano player's sudden awareness of her hands may impede performance, most human sexual strategies are best carried out without the awareness of the actor. (2003, p. 6)

Thus, although sexual desire might well be something we experience consciously, since it is a sexual strategy there is no reason why it requires an awareness of its goal.

The problem with this explanation, however, is that it confuses two incompatible analogies. Consequently, it is difficult to see exactly what is meant by saying that a sexual strategy does not require "awareness of the goal." The first analogy is that of a sweat gland's being a "strategy" for thermal regulation. If a sexual strategy, like sexual desire, is a strategy in this sense, then clearly it is a mechanism that has nothing to do with awareness of the goal. It is, like the activity of a sweat gland, merely a biologically evolved process that occurs automatically without any awareness. Indeed, it is doubtful whether it is even correct to speak of a goal here at all. For the notion of a goal seems to imply a purpose or some intended result, in other words, a teleology. But thermal regulation is not the "intended result" of a sweat gland's activity, for sweat glands have no intentions. Therefore, unless one wants to hold a pre-Darwinian view of evolution in which organisms or their biology somehow evolve in a purposeful goal-directed way, then the activities of things like sweat glands are merely the unintended result of millions of years of natural selection.

The second analogy, however—that of the movement of a piano player's hands during a performance—is fundamentally different than the sweat gland analogy. Supposedly, this analogy refers to a strategy about how to best execute a piano performance. But if a sexual strategy is a strategy in this sense, then it plainly is not an automatic and naturally evolved mechanism that operates beyond our awareness. It is true that if a pianist wants to perform well, then she should not focus intense awareness on her hands during a performance, especially if such awareness involves observing her hands from an external point of view. Obviously, such a type of awareness—what one might call spectatoring—would impede her performance. But this has little to do with the fact that, even though the pianist is not intensely observing her hands, she still, with full awareness, chooses to give the performance, chooses to perform one piece rather than another, and chooses to continue playing the piece and to play it, say, quickly rather than slowly, loudly rather than softly, and so on. Clearly, there is an overall and consciously intended goal behind her piano performance. If sexual strategies operate in this way, then they are events that, unlike glandular thermal regulation, require awareness of their goal.

Buss' account here thus betrays a fundamental inconsistency in the notion of a sexual strategy. On the one hand Buss wants a sexual strategy to be an automatic mechanism that has nothing to do with an awareness of its goal, but on the other hand he wants it to be something that depends on such awareness. But why does he want it both ways? Why does he not, for example, simply dispense with the second analogy and hold that a sexual strategy is a strategy in precisely the sense that a sweat gland is a strategy for thermal regulation? The answer, it seems, is that were he to do so, then his account would lack all credibility. This is because it is obvious to anyone that a sexual strategy like sexual desire is, in some sense, intimately connected to and dependent on awareness of a goal. As a result, to account for this feature of sexual desire, Buss is forced to bring in a further analogy where awareness does play a role.

It should be remembered, however, that in this second analogy—that of a piano performance—the awareness is of a peculiar sort. It is an awareness that is not sharply focused on the movement of hands and is one that, in one sense, seems to let the hands move in a semiconscious way, even though, in another sense, they are clearly operating according to one's fully conscious desires. It is this peculiar feature of the awareness that might appear to make the analogy compatible with the strategy of sexual desire, for sexual desire also seems to involve various levels of awareness. But if this is the case, then why does not Buss simply stick to this analogy and dispense with the sweat gland analogy? The answer here would seem to be that the piano performance analogy implies nothing about the evolution of an automatic process that lacks an awareness of its goal. For piano performances are not biologically evolved processes; they are events that depend on conscious intent, practice, and awareness of a goal.

Here then we can also see the similarities between Schopenhauer's view and that of Buss. For like Buss, Schopenhauer is also sensitive to the fact that in people's awareness sexual desire has nothing to do with the desire for reproduction. Schopenhauer's solution is to place the desire for reproduction, as the object of sexual desire, beyond our awareness and within the will to live. In doing so he remains true to the idea that if something (here reproduction) is to be the object of a desire, then there at least must be a desire that aims at it. The desire that aims at it is the desire of the will to live. With this he avoids Buss' problem of having to blend two inconsistent views and talk about sexual desire as a blindly evolved automatic process that nonetheless is, like the piano player's performance, also, at some level of awareness, a consciously chosen and desired activity.

The difficulty for Schopenhauer, however, is that even if there were an impersonal will to live that operates within us—and the Buddha had some fairly decisive arguments against such a Brahmanic view of reality—he is still left with the problem of bringing our conscious sexual desires into relation to the reproductive desire of the will to live. For again, a careful examination of the experience of sexual desire will reveal that, in its intrinsic elements, it lacks any reference to the idea of reproduction and in fact aims consciously and powerfully at another object. Consequently, there is no grounds for insisting that reproduction is the real goal of sexual desire.

However, rejecting this position does not force one to hold that all the elements of sexual desire must take place at a fully conscious level of awareness. We know from psychoanalytic research that conscious sexual desires often incorporate various unconscious elements. But this is a different story from the workings of a sweat gland. For unconscious psychological processes that operate in this way were once conscious and have become unconscious only through psychological mechanisms like repression. Moreover, they also have the possibility—through free association, self-analysis, dream interpretation, and so forth—of becoming conscious again. None of this, however, applies to biologically evolved mechanisms like thermal regulation by sweat glands. For these mechanisms are not *un*conscious mechanisms in the psychoanalytic sense, for unconscious mechanisms are psychological mechanisms. Thermal regulation by a sweat gland is, however, like photosynthesis, a process whose essential operations have nothing to do with psychological mechanisms.

This should not be taken to mean, however, that sexual desire did not evolve out of or have its beginnings in a primitive motivational state that, over millions of years, was selected because it led to reproduction. This seems the likely phylogenic history of sexual desire. However, with the emergence of human consciousness and its decisive features of self-awareness and imagination, sexual desire as we know it also emerged. When it thus appeared, it seems probable that it would have taken over the role of the pre-human reproductive motivational state. This motivational state would then have disappeared from our constitution because with the emergence of sexual desire it was made redundant. It thus was no longer selected. This is because, with its close relation to sexual intercourse, sexual desire led to essentially the same result as its ancestral motivational state, namely, reproduction.

This would also explain the existence of sexual desires like homosexuality that clearly have nothing to do with reproduction—something that sends evolutionary psychology into groundless speculations about the homosexual keeping his or her own supposedly unfit genes out of the gene pool or about mitochondrial DNA—which exists in both sexes but is passed on only through females—attempting to "disable" the reproductivity of male fetuses by turning them into homosexuals (Sykes, 2003). Since, on the view just given, sexual desire is liberated from its (or its ancestral motivational state's) original ties to reproduction, it is now free to seek out modes of satisfaction that do not lead to reproduction. That is, it has acquired a plasticity that was lacking in the primitive motivational state, a plasticity that is probably still lacking in the similar states of most non-human animals.

EROTIC PLEASURE

Another possibility here, one that many people seem to feel is the obvious answer to the question now being considered, is that the object of sexual desire is erotic pleasure. This is because sexual desire is often connected to erotic pleasure. Since erotic pleasure is normally intensely pleasurable, it is not difficult to see how erotic pleasure might be thought of as the true object of sexual desire. That is, that which one desires when one has sexual desire is precisely this erotic pleasure. On this view the other person with whom one engages in sexual activity or the sexual activity that accompanies or leads to the pleasure must be seen as merely a means to achieving that pleasure: as far as sexual desire goes, they are not something desired in themselves.

If, however, one examines how pleasure presents itself to awareness in sexual desire and activity, a rather different picture begins to emerge. For pleasure does not present itself as a detached experience that sexual desire focuses upon and strives to achieve. Rather, it presents itself in awareness as an experiential fabric in which sexual activity resulting from sexual desire takes place. It is thus a phenomenologically supportive structure that provides a constant background for such activity. This background of erotic pleasure, which surrounds and diffuses through the sexual activity, supports the sexual activity by providing a constant affirmation of the desirability of the sexual activity that one is engaged in. It provides affirmation by bathing the sexual activity in a stream of intense satisfaction, much like a display light in a gallery bathes an artwork in a stream of brilliant rays. And just as it is the artwork on display that is typically the focus of our awareness rather than the light that shines upon it, likewise it is the sexual engagement that is the focus of our desire rather than erotic pleasure that accompanies it. One could, of course, try to focus on the erotic pleasure rather than the activity that gives rise to it, but the pleasure remains pleasurable only sofar as it coexists in a supportive relation to an awareness of the activity (actual or fantasized) that it is affirming.

To see how this relation between sexual activity and erotic pleasure works, consider the case of a teenage male who attended parties where the boys and girls would end up pairing off and spending the evening kissing and sexually fondling each other. After several such gatherings this boy came to realize that he never really had a desire to kiss and fondle girls and found no enjoyment or pleasure in it. He was engaging in such activity only because the others were doing so and he did not want to appear different. It then suddenly occurred to him that what he really desired was to kiss and fondle other boys. When he shortly afterward got the opportunity to do so, he then experienced intense erotic pleasure for the first time. This was the beginning of his awareness of his own homosexuality.

Now one could attempt to explain this development in various ways. One might, for example, argue that the reason he turned away from the heterosexual activity was simply that it gave him no erotic pleasure and that, if it had, he might well have no reason to consider engaging in homosexual activity. Perhaps, one might continue, the homosexual thoughts and later behavior were merely a curiosity that grew out of the accidental failure of the heterosexual interactions to generate erotic pleasure. Further, it could well be that the erotic pleasure that ensued from the subsequent homosexual activity was also merely accidental: maybe the male he engaged was simply better at sexual techniques than all the females he had been with.

The problem with this explanation, however, is it does not tell us why heterosexual activity gave him no pleasure in the first place. Although the reason might be that none of the females he was with was good at kissing or fondling, that he happened to be distracted on each occasion, or some other incidental factor, a more likely explanation would seem to be that, as he himself realized, he had no sexual desire toward females. As a result, any sexual activity with females was, from the very start, barred from giving rise to erotic pleasure—unless, perhaps, he could fantasize that the female was a male.

But how is it that lack of sexual desire ensures lack of erotic pleasure? The answer is that if one engages in a sexual activity for which one lacks any sexual desire, then there is no sexual desire present for erotic pleasure to affirm and, as a result, no reason for the appearance of erotic pleasure. As a result, there can be no erotic pleasure in kissing and sexually fondling females if one lacks all sexual desire to do so. Likewise, the probable reason why this individual experienced erotic pleasure in fondling and kissing a male would seem to be that, as he himself realized, he sexually desired such activities with males. Consequently, the erotic pleasure appeared during his homosexual activity as an affirmation of his desire toward males.

This view of erotic pleasure as an affirmation of sexual desire is also supported by a consideration of the relation of erotic pleasure to sexual fantasy. Sexual fantasy, as is well known, is often connected to erotic pleasure through masturbation (Laumann et al., 1994; Reinisch, 1990). In masturbation, however, one does not, it seems, fantasize about erotic pleasure; rather, one typically fantasizes about a sexual engagement that one desires or at least a situation that one finds sexually arousing. The erotic pleasure that accompanies the fantasy and that ought to accompany such an engagement, were the engagement to happen in reality, is then augmented by autoerotic stimulation during the fantasy. That such activity merely augments the pleasure, rather than creating it, is evident from the simple fact that sexual fantazises are erotically pleasurable in themselves. This is why some people are able to have orgasms purely through fantasy alone (Bruijn, 1982a).

The erotic pleasure thus created then provides a backdrop on which the fantasy can unfold, all the while affirming the desirability of the fantasized sexual activity. An example of this can be seen in the following fantasy of a 12-year-old girl. This girl imagined a situation in which a cowboy on a horse rescued her from a runaway stage coach, sweeping her up onto the back of his saddle: "as she imagined how the supple leather of his jacket would feel against her cheek, she suddenly noticed the tingle of a sensation she had never felt before, right where her thighs would grip the saddle" (Maltz and Boss, 1997, pp. 51–52).

The question that arises here is why this tingle of a sensation between her thighs—a common way of describing erotic pleasure—suddenly occurred at this point in her fantasy. There are, of course, various possible explanations. It might have occurred simply by chance—perhaps the way her clothing was rubbing against her—or possibly as she imagined gripping the saddle, she created muscle tensions in her thighs that stimulated her genitals. The fact, however, that the erotic pleasure occurs at the moment in her fantasy in which she is engaged in what looks like a sexually desired activity—holding on to and pressing her cheek against a powerful and daring man who has shown much interest in her—does suggest that the sudden occurrence of the pleasure is a response to and forceful way of underlining the sexual desirability of the activity.

It also seems noteworthy here that she is not, at the moment of the erotic sensation, imagining the feeling of the saddle between her thighs but is rather imagining what his leather jacket would feel like against her cheek. This further suggests that the occurrence of the erotic pleasure is not the object of her sexual desire. The object of sexual desire here is the act of being swept up by a man and pressing against him. The erotic pleasure merely, though nevertheless strongly, affirms that desire.

In fantasies coupled with masturbation there is, of course, the added element of autoerotic stimulation, but the pleasure inherent in this stimulation owes its existence as much to the fantasy as it does to the stimulation. Were the fantasy to disappear or be replaced by sexually repulsive images or thoughts, it seems more than likely that the autoerotic stimulation would quickly be felt to be lacking in erotic pleasure. This would support the view being here presented, namely, that the pleasure that ensues from such stimulation is not the object of sexual desire itself but rather a way of affirming that the fantasized activity is what is sexually desired.

A possible criticism here is that if erotic pleasure is not the object of sexual desire but is rather a way of affirming the desirability of a sexual activity, then it would seem that sexual activity would be desirable even if there were no attendant erotic pleasure. For if erotic pleasure is not the object of sexual desire, then the lack of erotic pleasure during sexual activity should be of no concern. Yet, the criticism would go, the idea of a person desiring a sexual activity that provides him or her with no erotic pleasure seems odd. There are, however, various replies that could be made to this point.

First, if erotic pleasure is, as I have been arguing, an affirmation of the desirability of what one sexually desires, then its failure to appear during an act that one desires might well be experienced as being incongruent or as a form of what Festinger (1957) calls cognitive dissonance. This is why, I would argue, many people tend to be dissatisfied when their sexual activities fail to give them erotic pleasure. It is not that they are so much dissatisfied with the lack of pleasure *per se;* it is rather that they are receiving no affirmation that what they desire (or feel they should desire) is in fact what they really desire.

Or, conversely, a person might be dissatisfied by the fact that a particular sexual experience caused as much pleasure as it did. This can be seen in the case of a man who met and had a sexual interaction with someone whom he thought was a beautiful woman. When he later found out that this person was not a woman at all but a post-operative male transsexual, he became extremely upset (Bork, 2000). What seems to be particularly upsetting for a person in these circumstances, though, is not so much that he was deceived or has engaged in a sexual act that, if he had known the facts, he would have rather not engaged in but rather that he found the act erotically pleasurable. For the erotic pleasure seems to provide a form of affirmation that he in fact desired to engage in a sexual act with a male transsexual. The reason I say "seems to provide" is because erotic pleasure would really provide such affirmation only if the man knew all along that his partner was a transsexual. If the man really believed his partner was a woman, then, of course, there is no affirmation of sexual desire toward a transsexual.

Still, someone in this situation might well begin to wonder why he did not notice that his partner was not a real woman. Men, even surgically and hormonally altered men, have very different bodies from women. Certainly (his thoughts might go) he should have noticed that the hips were not wide enough, that the hands or feet were too big, that the Adam's apple too was prominent, that the vagina was artificial. He might even begin to wonder whether he was not, at some level, really aware that his partner was in fact a male transsexual. Such thoughts could then easily lead him to agonizing doubts about his own heterosexuality.

Secondly, it is evident that some people do desire sexual activity even though it might not be accompanied by erotic pleasure or orgasm. This much is clear from the young girl's fantasy of pressing against the cowboy. For this is something she seemed to desire apart from an awareness of erotic pleasure. This is also supported by the fact that many women who desire and enjoy sexual activity seem uninterested in orgasms and thus the attendant peak-pleasure. And this even seems to hold for women who are quite capable of having orgasms. Discussing the results of a large study on the place of women's orgasms in relation to sexual activity, Bruijn (1982a) says, "three quarters of the women in this sample state flatly that the experience of orgasm contributes little or nothing to their sexual satisfaction" (p. 160). "Orgasmic release," says Bruijn, "is only one of the sources of sexual satisfaction, others being the experience of love, intimacy, sensuality and physical closeness" (p. 159). It might well be that some of the women who enjoy sexual interaction apart from the experience of orgasm are nevertheless enjoying it because of the erotic pleasures associated with the ascending, entering, or floating phases. But judging from the responses of some of Bruijn's subjects, not even this seems important. Here things like warmth and physical closeness are cited as being what is enjoyed.

Evidence is also provided for this view, though in a roundabout way, by the work of Leif and Hubschman (1993) with transsexuals. These researchers found that while there was an increase in orgasm with postoperative female-to-male transsexuals, there was a decrease in orgasm with male-to-female transsexuals, some of whom completely lost their ability to have orgasms. One would suppose that if the object of sexual desire was erotic pleasure, then the male-to-female transsexuals would report lower sexual satisfaction than did the female-to-male transsexuals. Both groups, however, reported increased sexual satisfaction. This suggests—though one must be cautious in interpreting such data—that what each group found sexually satisfying was their new ability to engage in sexual activities that matched their body image and gender identity (the sense of being male or female), not their ability to have or not have erotic pleasure. For even though such persons might still be able to experience the erotic pleasures of the ascending and floating phases, it remains true that they now experience less sorts of erotic pleasure than they did before the operation. It would thus seem odd that, if it were simply the experience of erotic pleasure that was the object of sexual desire, then, upon losing the ability to experience a major type of that pleasure, they would experience more satisfaction.

This view also helps to explain sexual desires and fantasies that involve violence or harm. One of the apparently peculiar facts about persons who have such desires is that they themselves have typically been victims of the abuse that is now the object of their desires. That is, persons whose sexual desires or fantasies involve such things as beatings, for example, tend to have been beaten as children. The connection between such desires and early violence—the erotization of childhood trauma, as Kaplan calls it—is strong enough that Kaplan says, "I can state unequivocally that in more than 7,000 sexual examinations I have conducted over the past twenty years, I have not found a single person who had sadistic or masochistic sexual fantasies, desires, and/or practices who had not been subjected to significant cruelty as a child" (1995, p. 43).

The reason why this connection has an air of peculiarity about it is because being treated cruelly is a terrifying and undesirable experience, especially for a child who is powerless to defend himself or herself against such cruelty. But if such experiences are, when they first occurred, terrifying and undesirable, how is it that they later become the objects of sexual desire? Kaplan's explanation for this is that the erotization of the trauma is a defense against the emotional devastation of the early abuse. Were the memory of abusive events simply left to stand as they are, it would threaten the child's developing psychological integrity. Eroticizing the event, she says, can thus be likened to the development of a protective layer of skin over a wound that enables the wound to heal while being stabilized.

Although such an explanation seems reasonable and fits well with Freud's notion of the defense mechanism of reaction formation, that is, the defending of oneself against anxiety-causing ideas or feelings by an exaggerated expression of their opposites, the explanation nevertheless contains some basic problems.

First, Kaplan's account suggests that such desires or fantasies are merely temporary expedients that will be employed only, to use her metaphor, as the wound is healing. However, as Kaplan herself acknowledges, particular sexual desires and fantasies, including sadistic and masochistic ones, are quite resistant to change—which suggests either that the wound does not heal, that the desire will continue despite the healing of the wound, or that something else is wrong with her explanation.

Secondly, the notion of erotization of a trauma as being a "protective layer" suggests the idea that the resultant sexual desires somehow exist in a passive or stagnant way, standing like a defensive wall between the person and that which the person sexually desires. But as is clear, sexual desire is active and outward directed. Such an erotization is thus not so much a layer that statically encloses the person as it is a dynamic and externally orientated reaching that focuses on the sexually desired activity. And this remains true even for those desires of a sadistic or masochistic nature. Here it could be said that a person's desire for sexual violence defends the person against the pain of the earlier trauma by actively pursuing, either in fantasy or in reality, the sadistic or masochistic activity. Therefore, the metaphor of a protective layer does not seem wholly appropriate. A better metaphor would be that of a frontal assault.

How then does the existence of such desires serve to defend someone against the memory of his or her earlier trauma? One possible explanation here, which follows from the account I am presenting, is that to desire something is usually to see it as being in some sense worthwhile and positive. Consequently, to desire sexually abusive activity, as either the recipient or the perpetrator of the abuse, is to see the abuse as being in some sense positive and therefore as not really being horrendous. In fact, it is to see it as being the totally opposite, namely, as desirable.

But how does one convince oneself that the abusive activity is something to be desired, especially when the original occurrence of the activity was emotionally devastating and not at all desired? This is where the role of erotic pleasure as an affirmation of sexual desire fits in. Here the pleasure that results from the sexual desires, fantasies, or activity serves to affirm the desirability of the desired sexual activity. For if such intense erotic pleasure is the result of violent or abuse sexual activity, then one is at least receiving some affirmation that the activity—and thus the childhood trauma of which it is a reenactment (by taking the role of either victim or perpetrator)—is really desirable and, consequently, that it is not really terrifying after all.

Consider the case of a woman who was as a child badly injured in an attempt of rape and later raped during a date, events that were no doubt emotionally overwhelming for her to suffer. Despite the fact that this woman later had a kind and gentle lover, her most powerful erotic plea-sure came from fantasies of "faceless males who hold my ankles and rape me violently. Eventually, I add all the perpetrators so that they are pene-trating my mouth, my anus, and my vagina. When they start to swear and slap me, I finally come" (Maltz and Boss, 1997, p. 31).

Here we have a case of someone who suffered sexual violence early in life and later takes such violence to be the core of her sexual fantasies. One way of explaining this otherwise peculiar state of affairs is to see that the erotic pleasure generated by the fantasy serves to affirm that her treatment at the hands of her fantasized rapists (and thus by implication her actual rapists), though violent, is nevertheless desirable. For even though the activity that she imagines is clearly horrendous, the intense erotic pleasure that ensues gives the opposite message. It therefore defends her against the painfulness of her memories by giving the message that the sexual assaults she suffered earlier in life were not terrible at all but were, on the contrary, highly desirable. This is even further affirmed for her by the fact that the point at which she "comes," that is, has her most intense pleasure, is pre-cisely the point at which the violence is also at its most intense.

None of this is to say that a person who has thus eroticized a childhood trauma is fully aware of why he or she has done so. Such defense mecha-nisms, as Schad-Somers (1996) points out, typically operate at levels of consciousness where the person is not clearly aware of their existence. Nevertheless, persons engaged in such erotization are sometimes at another level aware that the violent situation that they fantasize about is not one that they are fully pleased with. Thus, in commenting on her recurrent rape fantasy, another woman says, "I don't understand why I replay such a horrible event over and over. I do enjoy the climax, but afterward I cry, probably because I feel so guilty achieving orgasm this way" (Maltz and Boss, 1997, p. 30).

This would explain why these and other sorts of sexual activities are often relegated to the imagery of fantasy and not acted out in reality. It is not that, as some people have argued, the person is devoid of any desire at all to engage in the activity but only that in any particular case there can be numerous overriding considerations and more powerful opposing desires or fears that militate against the activity being carried out. Here one woman says, "But act my fantasies out? Make them come true? No, absolutely not. My real life's not what they are about; I don't want those things to really happen to me, I simply want to imagine what it would be like" (Friday, 1975, p. 274).

This woman is, in one sense, telling the truth. For, in a woman's trying to live out her rape fantasy—say, putting herself in a situation where she was in danger of getting raped—the situation would not, in all likelihood, go according to her plans. She might, for example, get badly hurt or even killed, her reputation and self-esteem would be gravely at risk, she might feel immense guilt afterward, her husband or lover would probably not be accepting of the fact that she purposively put herself in a position to be raped, and so on.

But this does not mean that the person who fantasizes about a sexual activity does not really desire to engage in the activity, only that there might be circumstances surrounding the activity or other considerations either that render the fantasy impossible to carry out in real life (where does one, in real life, find "faceless males," for example?) or that the fantasizer sees as being more undesirable than the activity is desirable.

SEXUAL ACTIVITY

But if erotic pleasure is not the object of sexual desire, what is the object? The foregoing discussion suggests that it might be sexual activity that is the object of sexual desire. For what people sexually desire, I have been arguing, is not erotic pleasure but rather the sexual activity that the pleasure serves to affirm as desirable. There are, however, some difficulties with such a view. First, it is clear that the object of sexual desire cannot be a specific act like, say, sexual intercourse. For this is merely one of numerous sorts of acts that might be related to sexual desire. Someone might, for example, only desire to have her breasts kissed or her legs stroked, and such a desire might still rightly be described as a sexual desire.

To this it seems natural to reply that even though we cannot name a specific sexual act, at least we can say that the object of sexual desire is some form or other of a sexual act, be it sexual intercourse, having one's breasts kissed, legs stroked, and so on. There are, however, two apparent problems with accepting this view. First, it does not tell us how we are to decide which acts are to be considered sexual acts and, secondly, various arguments have been raised against the idea that sexual desire is the desire to engage in an activity. Let us start with the second point.

Shaffer (1978), for example, argues that it is not true that desiring sex implies that one has sexual desire, nor is it true that having sexual desire implies that one desires to have sex. Consequently, he says, sexual desire and the desire to have sex cannot be the same thing.

To show that desiring to have sex does not imply that one has sexual desire, Shaffer points out that a person can desire to have sex for any number of reasons that have nothing to do with sexual desire. Thus, someone can desire to have sex because he or she feels it would be a useful experience, wants to make some money, or wants to get pregnant, none of which implies that the person has any sexual desire.

As for his second point, that having sexual desire does not imply the desire to have sex, Shaffer starts off by referring to the case in which someone sexually desires another person and yet finds it "unthinkable" that he might actually have sex with the desired person. Here he gives the example of an adult who has sexual desire toward a child yet would not want to have sex with the child. Shaffer admits that in such cases there is often a conflict of desires or other factors that might inhibit the person from acting out a real desire to have sex with the child, "but surely," he says, "there are cases in which there may be absolutely no real desire that sex occur, no conceivable circumstances under which the adult would have sex with the other, but, to the contrary, an unambivalent desire that sex not occur and a total horror at the idea of its occurring" (p. 177).

Unfortunately, there are problems with Shaffer's argument. Concerning his first point, that a person can desire to have sex and yet not have sexual desire, this is true enough for the reasons he gives. Nevertheless it does seem false to say that someone could desire to have sex *for its own sake* and yet not have sexual desire. For desiring to have sex for its own sake—one might say for sexual reasons (reasons that we will come to shortly)—looks very much like it implies that one has sexual desire.

Turning to Shaffer's second point, that having sexual desire does not imply the desire to have sex, more serious problems appear. For although Shaffer cites the example of an adult who has sexual desire toward a child but does not desire that sex with the child take place, this looks simply like a case of one type of desire being overridden by a stronger countervailing desire, much like what happens in the case of unacted-upon fantasies. That is, although the adult has sexual desire toward the child, he has stronger countervailing desires—for example, the desire not to damage the child, the desire not to destroy his relationship with the child, the desire not to commit a crime—that stop him from attempting to have sex with the child. Therefore, the reason he does not have sex with the child is simply because various other stronger desires refrain him from carrying out his desire. Consequently, he does desire to have sex with the child.

Shaffer is aware of this objection, but he has no reply to it. All he says is, "but surely there are cases in which there may be absolutely no real desire that sex occur." This, however, is not an argument but merely a plea for us to agree with him (when the word "surely" is used in this sort of way, it is usually shorthand for "although I have no arguments for my position, please believe me anyway"). I, however, do not see why there must be cases of sexual desire with no "real" desire that sex occur. In fact, such a concept sounds contradictory. If John claimed to have sexual desire toward Mary but at the same time honestly asserted that there were no imaginable circumstances in which he would want to have sex with Mary, the only reasonable conclusion would be that he did not understand the meaning of the term "sexual desire" or, alternatively, that he did not understand the concept of having sex.

Moreover, although Shaffer tells us that in some such cases there would even be a "total horror" at the idea of sex occurring, he does not venture to say why someone might have such a powerful feeling. And this is a telling point. For if someone had no inkling of desire to have sex with a particular child, he would probably not have the requisite interest to feel horror at the idea. Such a person would more than likely simply let the idea drift away as he went on to other ideas that were of actual interest to him. However, to feel something as powerful as total horror at the idea of oneself having sex with a child does suggest that one is sufficiently close to carrying out the act—that is, that one has a "real" desire that sex occur—that one is frightened by such desires. And the reason why one is frightened by them is because they bring one into a horrible conflict with other deeply held countervailing desires.

With this it can be concluded that Shaffer has given no reason to believe that sexual desire does not imply the desire to have sex. And this should come as no surprise, for when one examines the experience of sexual desire, it is clear that it intimately involves the idea of having sex or sexual engagement with another's body. For sexual desire is a desire intimately concerned with the body. This does not mean, of course, that sexual desire will operate independently of other desires or factors that are not directly related to the body but only that central to sexual desire itself is the desire to become physically intimate in certain ways with the other person's body.

The problem, however, is that in asserting that sexual desire involves the desire to have sex, we are left with the difficulty that the notion of having sex is one that does not unambiguously point to any specific activity. This is not to say that in having sexual desire one will necessarily have no specific sexual activity in mind, for, clearly, many persons having sexual desire will have very specific activities in mind. Rather, it is to say that there is no specific form of sexual engagement that will necessarily be the object of every instance of sexual desire.

Because of this, it is understandable that someone might be led to believe that sexual desire does not imply the desire for having sex. However, the correct conclusion to draw from the fact that having sex does not refer to any specific activity is not that sexual desire does not imply the desire for having sex but rather that sexual desire does not imply the desire for *any specific form* of having sex, a conclusion that is compatible with the fact that the object of sexual desire is having sex or sexual interaction.

It is thus clear that since sexual desire refers to sexual interaction as its object but not to any specific form of such interaction, it must refer to a more general idea of what is to count as sexual interaction. This is why I prefer here to use the terms "sexual interaction" or "sexual engagement" rather than "having sex." For there is much vagueness surrounding the idea of what is to count as having sex. (For evidence concerning the divergence of opinions here, see Bogart et al., 2000; Pitts and Rahman, 2001; Sanders and Reinisch, 1999.)

Equally ambiguous here are the related terms "having a sexual relationship" or "having sexual relations." These terms present a problem not only for the same reasons that the term "having sex" does but also because it is unclear whether they refer to a one-time event or an ongoing affair in which persons meet regularly to engage in a sexual activity.

Because of this lack of clarity, it is probably best here to avoid using terms like "having sex" or "having sexual relations" (unless they are qualified as in "having oral sex") as ones that are meant to refer to the object of sexual desire. For even if one might not want to allow that sexual interactions that fall short of sexual intercourse are instances of having sex, it seems clear that any of them could, like sexual intercourse, also be the object of sexual desire. That is, genital fondling, cunnilingus, penetrating the vagina with fingers, and so forth could all be interactions that one sexually desires. But if there is doubt concerning whether such encounters are all instances of having sex, there seems less doubt that they are all instances of sexual interaction or sexual engagement.

In saying, however, that the object of sexual desire is sexual interaction, it is essential to see that sexual interaction is something that presents itself as the object of desire in the form of multiple layers of experience and meaning. These phenomenological layers, as they might be called, are here to be understood as moments of awareness that diffuse themselves throughout the sexual interaction and disclose various structures of experience and meaning in the interaction. These structures consist of things like the experience of the other person's body in relation to one's own, one's own body in relation to the other person's, surges of feelings, and the diverse meanings that attend these experiences and seem to spread throughout the interaction. These moments of awareness are best described as layers because numerous such moments of meaning are simultaneously present in the interaction, each with its own force and sort of presence.

The layered quality of this type of awareness in sexual interaction is also evident because some elements of the awareness tend to overlay and obscure others with varying degrees of opacity. Further, although they are layers, they are not wholly distinct layers in the way that layers of cloth might be distinct from each other. For in the sexual interaction it is clear that the different phenomenological layers interpenetrate each other with associations that lead directly into one or more of the different layers.

The phenomenological layers of sexual interaction might thus be compared with a stream, for in gazing into a stream, numerous layers are discernible. On the uppermost layer, for example, the surface of the running water is evident. Gazing deeper, a layer that contains fish might be noticed and below that layer is where plants wave about in the current. Finally, below the plants one might notice waters running over stones and sand on the bed of the stream. Yet none of these layers is wholly distinct, for the waters that constitute them are forever shifting and blending with each other. In a similar way, although sexual interaction is the object of sexual desire, various layers of objects and meaning will nevertheless be discernible in the interaction, objects and meanings that mix with and imply each other. Just how these layers present themselves will be seen shortly.

We can now come back to the other problem with the view that the object of sexual desire is some form or other of sexual interaction. The problem, it will be recalled, has to do with being able to specify what it is that makes an interaction a sexual one. For when one considers the diverse range of sexual interactions, it is not immediately evident what it is that makes them all instances of the same thing. It is tempting to argue here that what makes such interactions sexual is that they involve the genitals. Yet numerous activities that do not make use of the genitals are nevertheless evidently sexual. Few would want to say, for example, that because of lack of genital involvement, a couple engaging in oral-anal, oral-mammary, manual-anal, manual-mammary, or even oral-oral interaction could not be involved in a sexual interaction. For some people such interactions are the most desired form of sexual interaction. As one man says of his favorite sexual practice, "I love it when my face is taken within her cuddling buttocks in a firm grip: Analingus means the culmination of sexual intimacy" (Friday, 1998, p. 139). Indeed, even oral-manual stimulation can well be a sexual interaction, as is evident from the comments of a woman who, discussing her sexual preferences, claims, "I like having my fingers sucked. That can give me an orgasm" (Marrow, 1997, p. 140; see also Zilbergeld [1999], whose sex therapy for men involves suggestions for toe and finger sucking).

The idea of non-genital sexual interactions is also well recognized in Indian treatises on sex. Thus, in the *Ratirahasya*, or *Secrets of Love,* a medieval Indian erotic work by the poet Kokkoka, a love calendar is described in which "on the first day, the lover brings his girl to orgasm by embracing her neck, pressing kisses on her head, pressing both her lips with his tooth-tips, kissing her cheeks, ruffling up her hair, making gentle nail marks on her back and sides, plucking softly at her buttocks with his nailtips, and softly making the sound 'sit'" (Kokkoka, 1964, p. 108).

Still, one could argue that even though analingus, finger sucking, kissing, ruffling up hair, and other non-genital activity can give erotic pleasure and orgasms, this at least is a genital pleasure. Consequently, even though the acts themselves do not directly involve the genitals, the genitals are at least implicated by the fact that genital pleasure is a result, and even an intended result, of such activity.

But why must erotic pleasure or even orgasms involve genital pleasure? One might be tempted to argue here that the very notion of "genital" is contained in the meaning of the term "erotic" and, consequently, that it is simply true by definition that erotic pleasure must involve genital pleasure, if not directly, then at least indirectly. I doubt, however, that our idea of "erotic" or even "sexual" is actually limited to the notion of genital. When we talk about kissing or breast fondling as being sexual activities or erotic pleasures, it does not seem that the idea of an indirect genital pleasure is necessarily implicated.

This view is also supported by an examination of the experience of the pleasure in non-genital sexual activity. The ears and the neck, for example, are sexually sensitive or erotogenic zones for many people. And being kissed or stroked in these places is often experienced as being erotically pleasurable. However, accounts of such an event make it clear that the erotic pleasure resulting from having the neck kissed has little to do with any further pleasure experienced in the genitals. What one experiences as pleasurable is just the soft molding of the lips onto the receptive surface of the neck, the intense intimacy of having someone's face pressed into the vulnerable region of the neck, and the delicate warmth of the person's exhalations rhythmically spreading over the skin. Here a genuine fusion of the kisser and the kissed presents itself to a consciousness that seems to melt into a mixture of indistinct flesh.

The erotic pleasure here displays itself as the tingles of increasing tension on the surface of the neck, tingles that slowly begin to climb up to the ears and up the back of the head. The spreading of the tingles of such a kiss will most likely lead to various tensions and organ tumescence throughout the body, including in the genitals. In this case, however, these genital changes first appear as a result, or one might even say acknowledgment, of the erotic pleasure of the initial contact. And these genital changes, along with other changes occurring throughout the body, might well heighten and intensify the erotic pleasure of the initial touch of the lips on one's neck. But this does not mean that it is these subsequent genital or even bodily changes that are the essence or focus of the erotic pleasure.

One might think, however, that a stronger case for the role of the genital pleasure in erotic pleasure could be made by a consideration of the orgasm. For here it might seem that genital pleasure does play a central role. The problem with this view, however, is that it does not seem that orgasms have to be experienced as a genitally centered phenomenon. Thus, although many women experience their orgasms as involving vaginal contractions, other women and even the same women on different occasions will not show vaginal contractions during orgasm and experience orgasms as being deeply and more diffusely based around the uterus (Beauvoir, 1949; Singer and Singer, 1972). Moreover, genital stimulation is not even necessary to have an orgasm. Some women have orgasms while having their breasts stimulated (Masters and Johnson, 1966), while being penetrated anally (Bergström-Walan, 1981), or while performing fellatio or manually masturbating their partners (Bruijn, 1982b). So if a woman can have a non-genitally-based orgasm and can also have orgasms without any genital stimulation, genital pleasure is obviously not the essence of erotic pleasure.

Still, one might want to argue that with males, at least, the situation is different. In the male's case, because of the external position of the sex organs and the genitally based and orgasm-associated event of ejaculation, it might well seem that the orgasm is experienced as being more genitally centered than the female orgasm. Here, however, it must be noted that for many men, as with women, genital stimulation is likewise unnecessary. Many men have orgasms while dreaming. It is also not uncommon to find cases of men having orgasms by simply touching or looking at a woman (Ellis, for example, gives several such cases).

However, within the complex event or series of events that people indistinctly refer to as orgasm, it is possible to discern at least the phenomena of peak-pleasure and end-pleasure. Now although end-pleasure seems, in the male, closely tied to ejaculation and contractions in the genitals, peak-pleasure has no similar and clearly associated obvious physiological event. Consequently, it becomes difficult to say precisely where peak-pleasure is located, if it is located at any one place. Rather, it is experienced as a sudden rushing upward, a movement that seems to sweep through the entire body, sweeping the awareness of the body away with it. Here it becomes nearly meaningless, even for genitally focused males, to try to say exactly where the event of peak-pleasure is taking place.

It is also important to remember that the physiological aspects of orgasmic contractions and ejaculation are, like other physiological aspects of the sexual process, a physiologically global event and that the release of energy through muscle contractions is something that occurs throughout the body, including in the legs, stomach, arms, back, and face. It would seem implausible to argue that the intense pleasure of this aspect of orgasm is somehow discontinuous with the numerous other events taking place and isolated within those physiological events that occur solely in the genitals.

Further, and more important, the occurrence of orgasms is clearly not necessary for the occurrence of erotic pleasure. There are other sorts of erotic pleasure. Although this is obvious enough, it becomes even more so when it is seen that, for some people, non-orgasmic erotic pleasure can be as or more satisfying than the pleasures of orgasms. Thus, says one woman, "I seem to think I get more out of the friction of intercourse than the orgasm. It's more satisfying to get in there and have the friction, like an itch getting scratched. It's as satisfying as an orgasm. Sometimes its better to have just the friction and not the orgasm with all my nerves firing" (Marrow, 1997, p. 142). And, it should be noted, such preferences are not exclusively a female prerogative. In the words of one man, "Being turned on is the best feeling in the world. It's even better than orgasm because orgasm is an ending while turn-on is a beginning. Makes me feel totally alive and awake" (Zilbergeld, 1999, p. 200).

It therefore seems that although sexual interaction often involves the genitals, it is not limited to such an involvement. But if it is not the participation of the genitals, then what is it that makes an interaction sexual? One possible answer here is that a sexual interaction is an intimate bodily interaction that can involve any part of the body. Although this formulation avoids the problems that come with rendering the notion of a sexual interaction too narrow by focusing on one part of the body, it nevertheless creates other problems. First, it leaves us with the problem of being unable to distinguish between intimate bodily interactions that are sexual and those that do not seem to be sexual. Secondly, it also appears that there are interactions that are in some sense sexual but nevertheless do not involve direct bodily contact or interaction, as is the case with activities like voyeurism, exhibitionism, frotteurism, and fetishism. Let us consider each of these two problems in turn.

When one considers the numerous types of physical interactions that can take place between persons, it seems that some of them are evidently sexual and others not evidently sexual. Thus, for example, two persons who are embracing each other's naked bodies, kissing, and stroking each other would seem to be participating in a sexual interaction, while two fully clothed persons merely briefly touching hands in the exchange of something would not seem to be such an interaction. In between these two extremes there lies a gradation of physical interactions that go from being more evidently sexual to less evidently sexual. The reason I say "would seem to be" or "would not seem to be" sexual and "more evidently" and "less evidently" sexual is because even in cases that appear to have little sexual import, it is clear that, in certain circumstances, such interactions might nevertheless be described as being in some sense sexual.

Therefore, although slightly touching hands in the giving of something might seem to be an obvious instance of a non-sexual interaction, it depends on how the interaction is done. In the brief touching of hands, two people can easily have contact with each other's hands in a way that imparts a sexual meaning to the interaction. In the film *Samsara*, for example, the attractive itinerant worker Sujata visits the monk-turned-farmer Tashi in order to pick up some money that she has left at his house. In receiving the money from him, however, she lightly slides her fingers over the back of his hand in a subtle but unmistakably sexual caress. This action leads immediately to the couple's disrobing and having sexual intercourse.

Further, even the contact of hands is not something that occurs uncon-nected with other behaviors or social contexts: they involve expectations, exchange of glances and words, facial expressions, the presence or absence of other people, and so forth. Thus, in the scene just mentioned, Sujata's touching of Tashi's hand takes place with Sujata's prior awareness that Tashi harbored sexual desire toward her, with an accompanying coquet-tish glance, and with both persons' awareness that Tashi's wife was not home and, consequently, that they were alone.

Plainly, there is a multitude of ways in which the events that make up a simple hand touching can be carried out or interpreted. And some of these ways can easily be sexual. Even the briefest physical contact between two persons walking in the street might, under certain circumstances, be a form of sexual interaction. This is recognized in the *Kama Sutra*, where a particu-lar sort of brief touch is classified as an embrace and thus seen as a form of sexual union. Likewise, in the *Ratirahasya*, different embraces are referred to as "'outer' modes of lovemaking." Here, Kokkoka tells us that "when a man meets a woman on some other errand, and contrives in so doing to touch her body, this is the embrace by touching (sprstakea)." From here, a hierarchy of embraces is given in which each embrace is deeper or more intense than the preceding. Thus, continues Kokkoka, "if they walk together at a procession, or in the dark, and their bodies touch for a considerable time, this is the embrace by rubbing (udghrstaka). If one presses the other against a wall, it becomes the embrace by pressing (pīditaka)" (1964, p. 126) and so on.

With this it appears that it will be impossible to set a limit on what type of bodily interactions might be rightly considered sexual ones. For it is not so much the type of bodily interaction that makes the activity sexual as it is the way in which the interaction is carried out. But this does not seem to put us much further ahead, for now we appear to have the additional diffi-culty of trying to specify what it is about the way in which an interaction is done that makes it sexual. I think, however, that progress can be made here by recalling what was said earlier, namely, that a sexual interaction is not just a bodily interaction but rather an *intimate* bodily interaction.

Now although the idea of intimacy in this context is often taken as referring to the genitals (or perhaps also the breasts or buttocks), I do not think that such a reference need always be the case. That is, we frequently refer to bodily interactions as being intimate even though no genital (or breast or buttock) contact is involved. In this way a man who, for example, takes hold of a woman's ear and strokes it gently can rightly be said to be having an intimate bodily interaction with her. And, indeed, were the woman not sexually attracted to or at least fond of the man, she would more than likely feel that such an action was far too intimate. But what has the man done to the woman's ear that makes us want to call his action an intimate one? The best answer, it seems, is that he has caressed it. And here we arrive at a central point in this inquiry, namely, that sexual activity, which is the object of sexual desire, is an activity that is integrally associated with caressing.

Once it is seen that the object of sexual desire is sexual activity, it becomes evident why it is wrong to say that the object of sexual desire is, strictly speaking, another person. Of course, in the midst of sexual desire, people often say things like "I desire you" or "I want you." But a little reflection shows that such statements are merely shorthand for or polite ways of saying something else. For in saying simply, "I want you," it remains unsaid what I want you for. Such a statement could easily mean I want you to be my financial adviser or interior decorator. But if this is what I really desire you for and is the only thing I desire you for, then my desire toward you is not a sexual one. This problem, however, disappears when I become more specific and instead of saying, "I want you," I say, "I want you sexually." For by adding the modifier "sexually," we now know what the other person is desired for, namely, for something sexual.

This also helps to explain why, contrary to what Scruton (1986) thinks, sexual desire does not essentially aim at an "individual object" (that is, an individual person). For in aiming at sexual activity, rather than at a specific person, it becomes clearer how sexual desire can be desire for sexual activity with multiple partners at the same time. For sexual activity is something that can easily be engaged in and thus desired with more than one person. Although many people do not have desires toward multiple partners, it is clear that many other people do, as is plainly expressed by the depictions of group sex on ancient Greek pottery and by the reliefs of the ancient Gupta temples of India, by Japanese and Chinese woodblock prints, by the discussion of group sex in the *Kama Sutra,* and by the present-day sexual fantasies, of both males and females, of sexual activity with more than one partner (Jones and Barlow, 1990). To try to reject such desires for multiple partners as instances of sexual desire thus has no basis.

Scruton attempts to support his claim by stating that a man should feel cheated if he were deceived by a "cunning device" into thinking he was kissing and having sexual intercourse with one woman when in fact he was kissing one while penetrating another. This, however, is quite beside the point. For if a man did actually feel cheated here (and there is no reason to think he need feel cheated), his feeling would seem to be based more on the fact that he was deceived than on the fact that he was sexually engaging two women at once. This is evident simply because were we to alter the example such that the man knew full well that he was kissing one woman while penetrating another, then the claim that he should feel cheated makes little sense. Indeed, it is just such caressing or being caressed by several partners at once that many people find exciting and sexually desire. Thus, for example, Catherine Millet (2003), in her autobiography, describes her desires for being caressed by several men at once saying,

I took pleasure in this caressing, and in particular when it was a penis that was trailed over the entire surface of my face or a glans that rubbed against my breasts. I liked to catch one in my mouth as it passed by, running my lips up and down it while another came and begged attention on the other side of my outstretched neck, before turning my head to take the newcomer. Or having one in my mouth and one in my hand. (p. 23)

Plainly there is no "individual object" or feeling cheated here.

FROM BARING AND CARESSING TO VULNERABILITY AND CARE

To see the full significance of the idea that sexual activity is integrally associated with caressing, it is important to see that caressing is an activity that, in its very nature, aims at the bare or naked body as its natural object. That is, the act of caressing exists as something that seeks a naked body for its completion. This is why sexual interaction and nakedness so frequently go together and why people tend to enjoy seeing their sexual partner's naked body (Laumann et al., 1994). For the naked body of one's partner is something that invites itself to be caressed. Although one can caress or attempt to caress another person through his or her clothing, a caress is fully or satisfactorily carried out only when one's own body comes into contact with the other person's bare skin. As long as there is clothing or material between one's own body and the body that one is attempting to caress, this will tend to be experienced as a barrier to the completion of the caress (we will discuss apparent exceptions to this shortly). Because of this, it can be said that the desire to caress someone will contain within it a deeper phenomenological layer composed of the desire to have the other person's body, or at least part of her body, in a state of nakedness or bareness.

But this brings us to another point, namely, that in desiring to caress someone, not only do I desire her body to be bare before me, but I also desire, as a further layer of awareness, my body to be bare before her. As Friedman says in *The Hidden Human Image*, "in attitude as well as in physical fact sex means that posture of the ultimate baring of one's self," or as he also says, it is a "mutual baring" (1974, p. 176). But why in this situation do I desire my body to be bare before another person? The answer would seem to be that I desire to engage in mutual caressing with that person. That is, I desire her bare skin to come in contact with my bare skin. Thus, for example, in desiring to caress someone's arm with my hand, not only do I want her arm to be bare for my hand, but I further want my hand to be bare for her arm.

One can, of course, attempt to caress another person's body with an object rather than one's own body—perhaps one might want to stroke another person with a feather or other soft object—but such an action would seem normally to be a preliminary to bringing one's own body into contact with the other person's or perhaps a symbolic substitute for one's own body where the real bodily contact is avoided because of fears, countervailing desires, or some such thing. It is therefore of the essence of the desire to caress that it involves not only the desire to touch another person's body in a certain way, but also to have one's own body touched in a similar way.

From this it can be concluded that to have sexual desire is to have a desire for mutual baring and caressing of bodies with another person. But here we come to a further question: why does someone desire this mutual baring and caressing? A typical response here would be to say, "because it gives erotic pleasure," but as was shown earlier, there are serious problems with such a view. Erotic pleasure will normally tend to be a result of such baring and caressing, but it is only an affirmation, not the object of one's sexual desire. An answer, however, is suggested when one considers a further layer of meaning that is apparent in the phenomenology of baring and caressing and thus in the phenomenology of sexual interaction.

To bare one's body to another person is not only to experience oneself as naked before another person but also, at a further level of awareness, to experience oneself in a vulnerable position before that person. That is, in the experience of nakedness before another person, one can discern the deeper phenomenological layer of vulnerability. This is because an important aspect of clothing is that it allows us to maintain a measure of control over another person's perception of us. With clothing we can draw attention to certain features of our bodies while hiding others, say, something about how we want to be seen, while safely keeping the other person at a distance.

When the nature of clothing is seen in this light—when it is seen as being presented as part of the very body on which it is worn—then the powerful role played by clothing in human interaction, especially sexual interaction, becomes evident. Such is the importance of clothing that

William James (1890) even argues that clothing is part of what constitutes the "material self." When we are clothed, we are disguised and unrevealed in a powerful way. For here we are disguised by something that is at once foreign to us and yet part of us. The disguise thus has an aura of impenetrability to it. This state of affairs, however, is rent asunder in the act of disrobing. For here a person seems to disengage from part of his or her very being (or "material self"), rendering himself or herself vulnerable in a fundamental way. A person in a state of total physical nakedness before another becomes vulnerable simply because there is nothing left to hide. Pretense is no longer possible: his or her body is presented to the other person for all that it is—nothing more, nothing less.

This seems especially true when we consider that in many cultures clothes are also often used for the purpose of sexual enticement (Roach and Eicher, 1979). Such clothing entices by seeming to flow into the very body that it covers and calling one's gaze to penetrate to what lies beneath, thus provoking in the observer the secondary awareness that attempts to separate the naked body from its clothing. Clothing deployed for this purpose can emphasize shapes and curves or be worn in such a way that it barely hides the desired part of the body, thus creating an excited tension in the observer by making him feel at once so close to and yet, because of the sense of impenetrability that clothing carries with it, so far from the desired naked form. As one French fashion designer put it, "a good dress is one which awakens in the man a wish to see the woman wearing it disrobed" (Reik, 1957, p. 474).

That such clothing is not new and has an established place in human history can be seen from the complaint of the Roman stoic Seneca (4 BCE– CE 65) about "raiments of silk—if that can be called raiment, which provides nothing that could possibly afford protection for the body, or indeed modesty, so that, when a woman wears it, she can scarcely, with a clear conscience, swear she is not naked. These are imported at vast expense from nations unknown even to trade, in order that our married women may not be able to show more of their persons, even to their paramours, in a bedroom than they do on the street" (Seneca, 1964, p. 479). Further, it is not just revealing clothing that can act as a sexual enticement but also, and strangely enough, clothing that overtly attempts to hide or desexualize the bodily form that lies beneath. For in the very attempt to hide or desexualize the body, they often draw attention to the fact that there is something sexually desirable that is being hidden and thus in a like manner provoke the attempt to imagine the body freed from the clothing.

Similar things could likewise be said here about perfume, though this works in a slightly different way. This is because perfume is also, or at least is also meant to be, a form of sexual enticement. And just as enticing clothing veils the body and yet draws us past the clothing to the body itself, so too does perfume veil the body and yet draw us past the perfume to the body itself. The difference is that with clothing the covering is a visual one, while with perfume the covering is an olfactory one, presenting itself, as it does, as a halo of scent that lures the observer into the recesses of the body.

Here, it should be noted, women's perfumes frequently imitate the smells of flowers. And the flower, as is well known, is a near universal symbol for the female genitals. Thus, in the 15th-century Indian work *The Ananga Ranga,* or *The Stage of the Love God,* we hear of the beautiful padmini or lotus woman: "Her Yoni [that is, vulva] resembles the open lotus-bud, and her Love-seed (Kama-salia, the water of life) [that is, vaginal fluid] is perfumed like the lily which has newly burst" (Kalyanamalla, 1963, p. 6), while in Japan *Hina Matsuri,* or the festival of girls, is also called the festival of peach blossoms (the peach also being a symbol for the vulva), and in English we speak of the flower of a girl's virginity, of a girl's being deflowered, and so on: the examples are endless. The symbolism here is easy to understand since in the same way that a flower is seen to be a small, scented, and delicate object that opens to display its full beauty, so too can the vulva be seen as such an object.

This further shows that in pulling awareness toward the body itself, perfume operates much like clothing and, indeed, can be seen as a form of olfactory clothing—veiling the real scent of the body in the same way that clothing veils the real shape of the body. For even as clothing directs us to the body by being, as the fashion designer Vivienne Westwood puts it, an expression of the body, so too does the scent of perfume direct us to the body by being an expression of the body. Consequently, the scent of a perfume works to hide and yet remind us of the body's own underlying scent in the same way that clothing works to hide and yet remind us of the body's own underlying contours. This is why perfumes are not meant to reproduce exactly the body's own sexual scents, for if they did, they would not serve the crucial function of subtly hiding those scents.

This interplay between clothing, baring, and sexual enticement is one that reveals the meaning of vulnerability. For once such enticements are removed—the possibility of which is part of their very meaning as enticements—it is always possible that what is left might not be perceived as living up to what the enticements had promised. Even the curvaceous and nearly fully exposed woman in a string bikini still risks that the removal of her bikini may reveal a vulva or nipples that will be seen to be unattractive (much as the removal of her perfume might reveal a body or vulva whose scent is unattractive). And the same is true, with appropriate changes being made, for the man and the revealing of his genitals. Indeed, many individuals and cultures have definite ideas about what constitutes attractive genitals, especially the female genitals. Thus, one man describing his first wife says, "her skin was luscious, she had nice breasts, and an extremely beautiful hairy pussy" (Friday, 1998, p. 210). Further, for the

Nama tribe of southwestern Africa, elongated labia majora are seen to be especially attractive, while for the Siriono of eastern Bolivia, a small and fat vulva is the most beautiful (Ford and Beach, 1952). In the Marquesas Islands of Polynesia excessively red mucous lining of the vulva or course pubic hair are considered unbecoming for a female (Suggs, 1966), while in ancient China a large clitoris was considered repulsive (Gulik, 1961). In the medieval Indian poem the "*Ratimanjari*," or "The Posy of Love," we are told "the queynt [that is, the vulva] of a woman should be like the back of a tortoise, the shoulder of an elephant (or 'cassia blossom'), lotus scented, hairless and well spread: these five are accounted desirable. One which is cold, deep, too high, or rough like a cow's tongue—these four are accounted undesirable by experts in kama-sastra [that is, the study of the sexual arts]" (Jayadeva, 1964, p. 92).

Realizing this, if one thus *desires* to bare one's body before another, then it seems there is an important sense in which one is likewise desiring to be vulnerable before that person. And the same could be said about the desire for the baring of the other person's body. That is, in desiring the bareness of the other person's body, one is at the same time desiring that person's vulnerability.

There are, of course, occasions—such as during a medical examination—when one is naked before another person that do not involve the desire for vulnerability. But this does not go against the claim being made. For here it seems inappropriate to say that we have a genuine desire to be bare before the person who is examining us, let alone that we desire to be bare—and this is the important point—*in order to be caressed*. Becoming naked in such a situation is rather something to which we tend indifferently, and often reluctantly, to submit.

However, as is obvious, such intimate examinations can easily be exploited as an avenue for the expression of sexual desire, both by the physician and by the patient. In a study by Kardener et al., (1973), for example, it was found that of the physicians who reported having erotic contact with their patients, obstetricians/gynecologists—that is, physicians who are routinely exposed to their patients genitals—were in the highest percent. Also, it is not unknown for gynecologists to encounter women who show signs of sexual excitement when being vaginally examined and who request these exams more frequently than necessary (Dr Ronald Cyr, personal communication, 2004). This would suggest that some degree of sexual desire is present in some women's experience of the exam (See also Dickinson and Beam's [1932, 1934] case histories)

Even in those examinations carried out for purely medical reasons, it is noteworthy that the sexual meaning of baring before another person is such that here too the sexual implications of the situation are not always far from awareness. Skrine (1997), for example, describes the case of a man who had much concern over the fact that he might get an erection while having his genitals examined by a female physician and then felt much concern after the examination by the fact that he did not get an erection. Such sexual awareness seems an ever-present possibility. Emerson (1970) here gives an account of how both physicians and patients often struggle to keep sexual meanings from entering such examinations.

Similarly, although there are cultures whose everyday clothing is much more minimal than Western culture, it seems clear that the everyday bareness in these cultures is not something that is desired in order to caress or be caressed. Though, even here, the sexual meaning of baring is often clear enough. Thus, in the Melanesian culture of what Davenport (1965) called East Bay, women normally go about bare breasted. The men of this culture find women's breasts highly erotic and, being free to look where they will, are continually aroused by the sight of the plentiful bare breasts about them. In other minimally clothed cultures the erotic meaning of the naked body can be expressed in the opposite way, namely, through strict taboos against looking at or touching various parts of the body (Marshall, 1971; Merriam, 1971). With the naked-going Kwoma of New Guinea, for example, if a man sees a woman approaching him on a path, he is required to step off the path and look the other way as she passes. Further, there seems to be very few cultures that generally permit women to expose their genitals, at least when Ford and Beach (1952) carried out their classic study. According to Ford and Beach, "the wearing of clothing by women appears to have as one important function the prevention of accidental exposure under conditions that might provoke sexual advances by men" (p. 94).

Moreover, if one considers intimate acts of baring and caressing that involve penetration, one sees how they can forcefully suggest the notion of vulnerability for both sexes. Here the man's penis is submerged into an environment where, despite his nakedness, it is lost from sight, where it loses its boundaries and seems to become swallowed up or absorbed into the woman's body. One can see then how this situation could carry with it the idea that the man might lose possession of part of his body and so suggest the notion of his being vulnerable. This awareness of the male's vulnerability in sexual intercourse is possibly one of the reasons for the existence of the common cross-cultural myth of *vagina dentata,* or the toothed vagina. Although this myth appears in such ancient places as the early Puranic texts of Hinduism (300 BCE–CE 300), versions of the myth still survive in Western culture. Thus, the gynecologist Llewellyn-Jones (1990) refers to the belief that some women can trap a man's penis in their vaginas as being one of the prevalent myths still believed about women.

There are parallels here with Freud's (1908) notion of the castration complex. But in this case, according to Freud, the fear of castration has its genesis in a parental or adult threat of castration designed to stop the male child from masturbating. Consequently, on Freudian theory, the castration complex is acquired prior to and independent of an awareness of acts like sexual intercourse. It is understandable that engaging in these sexual acts may revive castration fears that have been acquired in this way, but prior fears do not seem necessary in order for one to be implicitly aware of the vulnerabilities implied by such acts.

Similarly, for the woman, these acts might also intimate the idea of vulnerability, though probably in a more powerful way. Offit (1995), a sex therapist, claims that a common interpretation of fellatio, for example, is male domination and female submission. Rancour-Laferriere (1985) likewise argues that intercourse and ejaculation into the woman can also be seen in this light. And this is what one might expect, for in being penetrated the woman undergoes the taking in of a foreign object that may hurt or damage her, that might impregnate her, that passes into her and yet remains beyond her control. Another person's body has entered into and opened up hers and so blurred the boundaries of her own body. Penetration, as has been suggested by Bernstein (1990), can thus be seen as a possible threat to the woman's body unity or integrity.

The vulnerability here that comes with a sense of a loss of control over one's body is intensified by the fact that many people experience a further loss of control during the excitement of sexual interaction. This is the view taken in the *Kama Sutra*. Here Vatsyayana says, "the fantasies a man invents under the effect of erotic excitation are not imaginable even in dreams. Like a speed-maddened horse, flying at a gallop and seeing neither holes nor ditches, two lovers blinded by desire and making furious love do not take account of the risks involved in their conduct" (1994, p. 166). Clearly, to place oneself in such a situation is also to place oneself in a state of vulnerability. For here one has a sense of interacting with another person nearly beyond one's control. In such a condition one has less control than normal over how one is presented to or perceived by the other person.

Putting it in psychoanalytic terms, Fried (1960) says that in the intensity of sexual passion, "nearly all acquisitions the ego has made are temporarily given up. These include perceptual organization, thinking capacity of judgment and sense of time. Certain ego defences which have been built up and used since childhood are shed and so the organism is in a rather vulnerable position" (p. 17). This vulnerability through loss of control is closely tied to the vulnerability acquired through the baring of one's body to the other person's gaze and touch. For in carrying out the activities of sexual desire, it is not only one's naked body that is exposed to the other person's view and touch but also the actions of one's naked body—here the spontaneous actions of "making furious love," unprotected by defensive strategies.

To this it could be objected that although such vulnerability is inherent in sexual interaction, this does not mean that it is something that is desired in itself. For perhaps it is just a necessary though undesired consequence of the sexual interaction. That is, although one might well desire to be bare before another person, one might have no desires to be vulnerable before the other person. Or, similarly, although one might desire the other person's bareness, one might not desire the other person's vulnerability. The difficulty, however, is that being bare or experiencing another's bareness, especially in order to be caressed or to caress, is so powerfully tied to our awareness of vulnerability, that it seems unlikely that the one desire does not at some level implicate the other.

Furthermore, it seems that the capacity to enjoy fully sexual interaction depends much on being able to place oneself happily in such a vulnerable state before one's partner while at the same time allowing her to enter a similar state. And here it is not only placing onself in or allowing the other person to enter such a state that is decisive, but, further, that one *desires* to do so. This is what Friedman is referring to, I take it, when he says that "in attitude" sex means the ultimate baring of one's self, or a mutual baring. Consequently, if one desires sexual interaction for sexual reasons, then one also desires a mutual vulnerability of oneself and the other person. To attempt to enter into a sexual interaction while at the same time trying to keep one's bareness hidden or at a distance and also trying to maintain firm control over one's actions is to limit severely the possibility of caressing and being caressed or responding to being caressed. It is to curtail the sense of surrender that is necessary for the occurrence of that spontaneous flow of events that make up the sexual process.

But if the desire for the mutual baring of bodies is a form of desire for mutual vulnerability, what can be said about the desire for mutual caressing? That is, why is it that we desire to caress and be caressed? The answer here is given, I think, by seeing the act of caressing in relation to the desire for baring or vulnerability. For in placing oneself in the vulnerability of bareness before another person, what one desires is to have one's vulnerability responded to with care. One puts oneself in the vulnerable state of bareness before the other person in order that the other person will respond with care. And a physically vulnerable person is cared for by being touched and held. Vulnerability here is thus a state of anticipation that waits upon the care of the caress. Here, in this state of anticipation, vulnerability presents itself to awareness as a diffuse and delicate receptivity that spreads throughout the entire body, a state that looks outward to be fulfilled by the care of the caress. The caress then acts upon the vulnerability both by fulfilling its purpose and by allowing it to continue. It fulfills its purpose by showing care—since vulnerability is desired in order to be cared for—and it allows it to continue by providing assurance that care is being provided.

The caress thus enables one to persist in a state of vulnerability before another person while feeling safe about one's vulnerability. As Marrow (1997) puts it, "women search for a desirable and willing male with whom they feel safe when vulnerable" (p. 149). And the same would seem to be true of male sexual desire. Although many males clearly desire the female's vulnerability when having a sexual encounter, they might nevertheless feel, or want to feel, that they have no desire to be similarly vulnerable before the female. Such feelings, however, founded as they probably are on stereotypic views about masculinity, seem to be at the basis of various male sexual dysfunctions and sexual dissatisfaction (McCarthy and McCarthy, 1998; Zilbergeld, 1999). This is because, according to the account given here, they are feelings that are in conflict with the very essence of sexual desire.

Therefore, the caress is a form of care since it "takes care of" or fulfills the desire to be caressed. Craving to have one's bareness or vulnerability taken care of with a caress seems to be what Reich has in mind when he says that during the sexual process and leading up to sexual intercourse, the male has an urge to "penetrate completely," while the female has an urge to "receive completely." For the penetration of sexual intercourse is also an act of baring and caressing—a baring of the penis to the caress of the vagina and a baring of the vagina to the caress of the penis. Consequently, both sex organs are here in a state of vulnerability and thus in need of care. As one woman puts it, "I finally have an ache deep in my vagina so profound that I have to have the penis inside. With its entrance—it's as if I have to hold my breath till it becomes completely inserted and then I relieve it with a very loud sigh or cry" (Fisher, 1973, p. 206). The same sense of urgency and relief would seem to hold for the male's desire to have his penis in the vagina and the subsequent experience of penetration. Here there is also a deep ache in the genitals that is momentarily subdued or relieved by the penis' entrance into the vagina.

The fact that such penetration is a form of caressing also indicates something further about the phenomenology of caressing. For in being thus penetrated, the woman is caressed to her very depths. That is, here the caress as a physical act does not remain on the exterior of the body but enters within the body. With the male, things are different, for he is not penetrated by the woman's body but rather enveloped by it. Here he is enwrapped in a unified embrace, caressed from all sides at once. Of course, it is not his entire body that is enveloped by the vagina (though, it is worth noting, it once was at the moment of his birth); it is rather just his penis, just as it is not the woman's entire body that is penetrated but just her vagina. In both cases, however, the intensity of the experience of penetration and the vulnerability it involves is such that the boundaries between the sex organs and the rest of the body—boundaries that are in reality obscure—tend to disappear.

This is also true for other forms of sexual penetration. Thus, in accounting her experience of fellatio, Millet (2003) says, "I curl to grab the hardened member so that my lips can feel the soft envelope which slides over its axis. I can mobilise myself into this act so utterly that I feel full up to the brim, my entire body has been put on and filled out like a glove" (p. 173). Further, penetration is typically not an act that occurs independently of other caresses in the course of sexual interaction. Consequently, the precise location and ways of caressing tend to get lost. The experience of penetration melts then into a physically global occurrence, and it is felt to be the entire body that both penetrates and is penetrated.

But if this is the nature of the caress of penetration, it is not altogether different, at least in purpose, from the non-penetrating caress. For in caressing someone's thighs or hips, one is also, in a sense, attempting to penetrate the other person. That is, the caress seeks to go below the surface and engage the body to its depths. This is why caressing often progresses from a light stroking of the skin to an almost kneading of the entire flesh. This seems to be what Sartre (1943) has in mind when he says, "the caress does not want simple *contact*; it seems that man alone can reduce the caress to a contact, and then he loses its unique meaning. This is because the caress is not a simple stroking; it is a *shaping*." This "shaping" is, for Sartre, the process by which one attempts to focus one's awareness on the other person as a body while at the same time trying to have the other person focus on herself as a body. Because of this, in caressing one seeks to bring the entire body to awareness, not just the surface structures. Therefore, says Sartre, "by *clasping* the other's hand and *caressing* it, I discover underneath the act of *clasping*, which this hand is *at first,* and extension of flesh and bone which can be grasped" (1943, p. 390).

Therefore, the caress is an attempt not only to touch the surface of the body but also to reach its inner core. This might well be why the stroking of hair, which Kokkoka recommends, often plays an important part in caressing. Hair is, of course, soft to caress, but its caressing has other features for the person whose hair it is. For although hair is insensitive in itself, its roots nevertheless penetrate the skin and thus come into contact with sensory nerves. Consequently, the stroking of hair is carried further to the roots of the hair, sending waves of sensations below the depths of the skin, almost as if the caress itself had penetrated the body through the hair.

Here it can be seen why although caresses usually involve a gentle touching or stroking, there nevertheless exists a continuum in which caresses can become less and less gentle. For in seeking to caress the depths of the body, the caress can easily become firmer as it seeks to go deeper. Although this may seem initially surprising to some people, a moment's consideration should show that in the intensity of sexual interaction it is sometimes the case that a person no longer strokes the other gently but rather grabs hard at the other person's flesh, biting or digging in with the nails. Alternatively, someone may desire the caressing he or she is receiving to be firmer. This sort of caressing, one that happens in varying degrees in many cultures, was ubiquitous enough in ancient Indian culture that it is discussed in the *Kama Sutra* in independent chapters with such headings as

"The art of scratching," "Biting," and "Blows and sighs." Here Vat-syayana tells us that "sexual relations can be conceived of as a kind of combat," while in the *Jayamangala* commentary on the *Kama Sutra* the 12th century scholar Yashodhara says that sexual intercourse "is in reality a struggle, since in order to assert themselves, both man and woman violently oppose one another, bringing to light a state of mind that could not be achieved by affection" (Yashodhara, 1994, p. 159).

In Ford and Beach's (1952) study, it is pointed out that "among some members of our own society intense sexual arousal may lead a man or woman to pinch, scratch, bite or otherwise bring pain to the partner. And for at least some individuals a mildly painful stimulus can, under certain conditions, result in increased sexual excitement" (p. 55). This is because such a stimulus penetrates the body's inner regions, bringing them into contact with the external caressing. This can be seen in the case of a woman who describes how her husband "pushed both of my breasts together so he could lick both nipples by sticking his tongue out. I asked him to bite my nipples. He did it gently, and I asked him to bite harder. He finally bit hard enough and I got a whole vibration through my body almost to orgasm" (Marrow, 1997, p. 143). Such forms of sexual exchanges are still caresses sofar as they fulfill the person's desire and thus take care of the person's need to be touched in a certain way.

One could, of course, accept that such practices occur in sexual activity but yet still deny that they are properly called caresses. I think, however, that any such attempt to exclude rougher forms of sexual interaction from bearing the appellation of a caress will run into much difficulty. For the firm kissing, pressing of tongues, gripping of shoulders, and pelvic thrusting that are frequently part of sexual interactions are all serving the same purpose and growing out of the same desires as the softer strokes and gentler touches that also occur in such interactions. Moreover, it seems that such diverse actions will, in many sexual exchanges, be blended and mixed to such a degree that any attempt to distinguish them will often fail or at least prove meaningless. At some point, of course, such activities leave the realm of caressing and cross over to become instances of violence and sadism, which also shows how desires for harm or violence can, as referred to earlier in the case of sadomasochistic fantasies, become wedded with sexual desire. A major difference is that here the activity is no longer done *in order to care for* the other person's vulnerability (and here we see the essential connection between the caress and the deeper layer of meaning of care).

In considering the nature of sexual interaction, it also seems significant to note that many of the acts of caressing that are typically involved are, in other contexts, used to comfort and to show concern and care to someone who might be vulnerable. Thus hugging, holding, and stroking, in addition to being forms of sexual activity, are also used to comfort or reassure someone who is sad or frightened or has been hurt. Similarly, kissing, sucking, or nuzzling, which are often part of sexual interaction, are also frequently used to show care and concern. It is a common enough occurrence that a mother, for example, will gently kiss or suck her crying child's finger or other hurt part of its body to show she cares and "to make it better." Or again a child who is afraid of the dark might be kissed and nuzzled while being put to bed in order to be comforted and reassured and to be shown concern. Indeed, many sexologists have explicitly pointed to the close parallels between mother–infant interaction and sexual interaction (see Giles, 1999). Freud (1910), for example, discusses the connections between breast feeding and fellatio, something that has been noted by other researchers. Kernberg (1995) here gives the case of a woman who had "sexual fantasies about performing fellatio, related to the feeling that the orgasm of men represented symbolically the giving of love and milk, protection and nourishment" (p. 79). Ellis (1903), on the other hand, refers to the analogy between breast feeding and sexual intercourse, saying that

the analogy is indeed very close: the erectile nipple corresponds to the erectile penis, the eager watery mouth of the infant to the moist throbbing vagina, the vitally albuminous milk to the vitally albuminous semen. The complete mutual satisfaction, physical and psychic, of mother and child, in the transfer from one to the other of a precious organized fluid, is the one true physiological analogy to the relationship of a man and a woman at the climax of the sexual act. (p. 15)

The relationship between breast feeding and sexual intercourse would seem also to hold for other kinds of feeding and sexually arousing experiences, for it is well known that many people find instances of feeding and being fed to be sexually arousing. In Japanese culture, for example, the connection between feeding and sex is made explicit in the practice of *nayotaimori,* a practice involving geishas—highly trained courtesan-artists traditionally hired by men for sexual and other personal services. Here, the male client eats food off the body of a naked geisha. The obvious implication here is that the sexually attractive body of the naked geisha is at the same time a provider of sustenance (much like the sexually attractive breasts of the mother are similarly a provider of sustenance).

Further, some people—male and female—even incorporate feeding into the caressing of their sexual activity. One woman, for example, describes her ideal sexual experience as being one in which she and her partner smeared food onto each other's genitals and then took turns licking the food from the genitals (Marrow, 1997). Here again the element of caressing as care is also clearly evident. For in licking the food from her partner's genitals, she is caressing his genitals, thus showing him care both by smearing the food onto them and by licking it off—which can also be seen as care in the form of grooming or cleaning—and also, in a sense, by being fed by him. And the same could be said of his behavior toward her.

Feeding in this situation is explicitly connected to caressing because the food is placed on typically erotogenic zones of the body and is done so for the overriding purpose of caressing those zones.

The mouth, however, is also typically an erotogenic zone, and thus feeding can also be done for the purpose of caressing the person who is being fed. There is naturally an indistinct and overlapping boundary between feeding as caring for someone's desire for nutrition and feeding as caring for someone's desire to be caressed. Whether the activity is primarily sexual will therefore depend on whether the desires that motivate the feeding are based primarily on satisfying nutritional urges or on desires surrounding caressing. This shows how the object of sexual desire, existing as it does in multiple layers, can be further complicated by also having relations to elements that, in other contexts, have non-sexual meanings.

THE ATYPICAL SEXUAL VARIATIONS

This brings us to the second problem mentioned earlier, namely, that of activities that are clearly sexual but nevertheless do not involve direct contact between bodies, as is the case, for example, with voyeurism, exhibitionism, frotteurism, and fetishism—practices or desires often referred to as paraphilias or atypical sexual variations. This appears to be a problem for the position I am giving because if the object of sexual desire is mutual vulnerability and care through mutual baring and caressing, then activities like these appear to be counterexamples. They appear to be counterexamples because although they seem sexual, they nevertheless might not appear to involve desires for baring and caressing. I think, however, that such desires, despite their apparently divergent form, still express the basic desire for mutual baring and caressing, albeit in an attenuated way. This fits well with Freud's (1905) observation that the "perversions" are no more than exaggerated or fixated components of the "normal" sexual urge and thus not so perverse after all.

If we examine the case of voyeurism, the relation to the basic desire for mutual baring and caressing is immediately evident. For in many cases of baring before another person in order to be caressed, the naked body is presented not only for the other person's touch but also for his or her view, which is where, no doubt, the expression "caressing with the eyes" comes from. Although the eyes do not actually caress the body, their gaze nevertheless wanders over and enjoys the naked form in much the same way that the hands might. Consequently, the desire to see the bareness of another person, which is central to voyeurism, can also be an aspect of mutual baring and caressing.

An important difference, however, is that while many people's activities here involve mutual baring in order to caress and be caressed, the voyeur (and this term should not be taken to mean anything more than a person regularly practicing voyeurism) stops short of this in at least two ways. First, he does not get involved in *mutual* baring and caressing—that is, he does not seek to have himself bare for or actually caressed by the other person—and, further, he does not even engage in physically caressing the other person's body. That is, the voyeur's interaction here stops at having the other person becoming bare before him. Now although this might seem to render the voyeur's activity radically distinct from mutual baring and caressing, if one looks further it will be seen that the missing pieces are there in disguised form.

First, voyeurs typically masturbate while observing the person they are spying upon or shortly after while mentally replaying or fantasizing about the event (Arndt, 1991). Because of this, although the voyeur is neither caressing the other person nor himself being caressed by the other person, he is nevertheless baring and caressing himself. But in caressing himself he is both bestowing and receiving caresses. Consequently, in addition to the bareness of the person whom he is watching and the baring of himself (in order to masturbate), the elements of caressing and being caressed are also present in the voyeur's sexual act. The difference is that the caresses that the voyeur bestows and receives are performed by himself rather than by the other person and that his baring of himself is for himself alone.

A further difference here is that the person who is undressing or naked before his gaze is not undressing in order to be caressed by the voyeur. Although these are fundamental differences when the voyeur's sexual act is compared with sexual acts involving mutual baring and caressing, they nevertheless seem to be differences that the voyeur is not fully content with sofar as he seeks to overcome them through the use of fantasy. That he seeks to overcome them in this way is suggested by the fact that masturbation, which is employed by the voyeur during his voyeurism, is often accompanied by fantasies of sexual interaction (Westheimer and Lopater, 2002). Thus, although the voyeur may be hiding in a tree while watching a woman disrobe for her bath, it is not this exact situation that is the fulfillment of his desire. For if it were, why would he find it necessary or at least desirable to fantasize about an interaction that is not taking place? Of course, the situation of furtively spying on someone in such an instant creates its own sense of excitement. What if the person sees the voyeur? What if she screams? What if the police come and give chase? All this will have the effect of creating psychological and physical tensions that are not wholly distinct from those of the sexual process. Nevertheless, all this seems little more than a way of supplementing the arousal felt toward the real object of desire, namely, the sexual interaction fantasized during the voyeuristic act.

But then, one wants to ask, why does the voyeur not seek out sexual interaction rather than merely fantasizing about it while secretively watching someone from a distance? Although the answer to this question remains unclear (and there may indeed not be one answer), a possible explanation is suggested by what was said earlier about the reasons for some person's not wanting to act out his or her fantasy. The explanation was that there might be circumstances attending the activity or other considerations that the person sees as being more undesirable than the activity is desirable. This explanation fits well with the fact that, in addition to avoiding real sexual interactions, voyeurs tend to have feelings of inadequacy and low self-esteem and to be lacking in interpersonal skills (Dwyer, 1988). Consequently, secretively observing someone undressing or bathing (or even engaging in sexual activity) enables the voyeur to get as close as possible to a sexual interaction without risking the undesirable event of being seen to be sexually inadequate or being rejected because of poor interpersonal skills. The part of the sexual interaction that is lacking in the voyeur's activity—that is, *mutual* baring and caressing—can then be fantasized to take place. This does not mean, however, that every voyeuristic-like act will necessarily be performed by someone with such sexual anxieties, only that the habitual engagement in these activities, at the expense of actual baring and caressing, will tend to have such anxieties as part of their motivation.

A similar picture would also seem to be true for exhibitionism. For like the voyeur, the exhibitionist is also involved in an act of baring and caressing, though here again the act is not a mutual one. The exhibitionist's participation in actual baring involves only his own body, typically just his erect penis, which he exposes to another person without trying to get reciprocation. Here the caressing and being caressed is once again achieved through masturbation, something most exhibitionists do either when they are exposing themselves or, having fled the scene, shortly after while fantasizing (Freund et al., 1988). Again, there is clearly a heightened excitement that is achieved by the other person's shock or frightened response to the exhibitionist's behavior. It is, however, more likely that this is merely a means of increasing tensions resembling those in the sexual process than it is the real object of the exhibitionist's desire. That the real object of the exhibitionist's desire is still some form of baring and caressing is suggested by the fact that, like the voyeur, the exhibitionist is much dependent on masturbation and fantasy. For this points to the fact that there is something beyond the immediate structure of the exhibitionistic act that is really desired. And again, since sexual fantasies tend to involve some form of imagery surrounding acts of mutual baring and caressing, it seems more than likely that the exhibitionist's fantasy will also include these elements.

The question of why the exhibitionist does not attempt to engage in a mutual sexual interaction rather than merely going part way and then relying on fantasy and masturbation is one that is no doubt complex. It seems, however, that many exhibitionists, like many voyeurs, are also lacking in social and sexual skills, with feelings of inadequacy and inferiority (Dwyer,

1988). Consequently, the act of exposing one's genitals to an unsuspecting person can easily be seen as an attempt to get as close as possible to a sexual interaction while avoiding the social risks of a real sexual interaction—the risks of being rejected or made to feel inferior, for example.

The fact that the person exposed to is "unsuspecting"—something that some people feel is also definitive of exhibitionism proper—and that the act is typically carried out within a few seconds means that the person thus exposed to will have little time to decide how to respond. Under such circumstances, shock will probably be the most usual response. And shock is not, at least, rejection. On the contrary, shock can even be interpreted as intense—if fleeting—interest. And this is no doubt how many exhibitionists seek to interpret the response. Some exhibitionists, for example, feel that the woman will be impressed with the size of their penises (Langevin et al., 1979). This shows just how little the exhibitionist needs to depend on social skills to carry out his trade. Indeed, exhibitionism can be seen as the sexual act that requires the least amount of effort or skill. Even the voyeur still has to find someone who is both undressing *and* has left the curtain open. And, on top of that, he has to be careful enough not to be spotted. But with the exhibitionist, not even this is required. All he need do is simply expose himself to a passerby.

Although it is frequently asserted that voyeurs and exhibitionists are nearly exclusively male, this will depend, of course, on how one wants to define voyeurism and exhibitionism. If one wants to define them, as the American Psychiatric Association (1994) does, as the urge to view or to expose to only "unsuspecting" persons, then it might well be that such practices are engaged in primarily by males—perhaps the coerciveness of these activities is something that society permits more with males than with females, or perhaps such coercion requires a higher amount of aggression than females are interested in showing. But one could always question the role of "unsuspecting" in the definition and argue that either voyeurism or exhibitionism occurs even in cases where the "victim" wants to be seen or wants to be exposed to (as might happen in some cases of performing or watching a strip tease). Here, then, it would seem a little harder to say that either of these two practices was the exclusive realm of males. This is because many women obviously also have sexual desires relating to non-coercively viewing naked bodies and exposing their own bodies.

I mentioned earlier that although the desire for caressing brings with it the desire for a baring of the body and, consequently, that clothing would tend to be experienced as a barrier to caressing, there were apparent exceptions to this. The two main exceptions I had in mind were frotteurism and fetishism, activities that thus seem to present a difficulty for my position. Frotteurism, which is the sexual practice of rubbing one's clothed body up against the clothed body of a stranger (typically done by a male to an unsuspecting female in a crowded place), can quickly be seen to be a "next best" substitute for actual caressing of a naked body. That is, the furtive rubbing of clothed bodies is not the ultimate object of the frotteurist's sexual desires but rather the best he feels he can achieve under the circumstances. This is suggested by the fact that frotteurists often fantasize about having a full sexual interation with the person against whom they are rubbing and also by the fact that many frotteurists are reported to have sexual insecurities, feelings of person inadequacy, and difficulties in forming persisting sexual relationships. (Zgourides, 1996). Consequently, it looks like here too we have a person who desires mutual baring and caressing but, because of various anxieties and lack of ability, finds himself relegated to rubbing his clothed body up against a stranger's clothed body, all the while relying on fantasy to imagine that he is engaged in full acts of baring and caressing.

Here too it is unclear why such a practice is nearly exclusively a male one, though, again, it might well be the coerciveness of frotteurism—inherent in the definition of an act done on unsuspecting persons—that renders it a male activity. Were one to reject this definition and allow that frotteurism could occur with suspecting or even consenting individuals, then it might turn out that there were also females who engaged in frotteurism.

As for fetishism, this seems to present a problem because, at least in its object variety, it appears to involve sexual desires that refer to inanimate objects, such as shoes, gloves, or underwear, rather than to the body. Consequently, if the object of sexual desire is mutual baring and caressing of bodies, then what are we to make of desires that, though evidently sexual, nevertheless make no reference to the other person's body? The first thing to notice is that although object fetishism makes no direct reference to the other person's body, another type of fetishism does. This other type of fetishism, known as partialism, is directed toward some part of the body, say the feet, the breasts, or the hair. The major difference between partialism and other types of mutual baring and caressing is that the partialist's desires center nearly exclusively around baring and caressing or being caressed by the part of the other person's body to which his partialism is directed. Thus, the foot fetishist desires primarily to caress and be caressed by the other person's feet.

These sorts of desires, it should be seen, do not offer a problem for the view being given here. For nothing in this view demands that the object of sexual desire be an interaction with the entire body. And plainly, one does not have to be a partial fetishist to have strong attractions to specific parts of the body. Many males, for example, have clear preferences for the female breasts, buttocks, or legs, while many women seem to have similar attractions to the male shoulders, upper arms, or buttocks. Partial fetishism appears to be little more than an extreme version of these desires.

With object fetishism, however, there is not even part of the body that is the direct object of desire. This does not, however, present a genuine difficulty. For although the direct object of desire is activity involving the fetishistic object, it is obvious that even here sexual desire is still composed of something resembling desires for a baring and caressing of bodies. What the person who has a fetish seems to want is to have the object exposed so that he can fondle or caress it and also to have his body bare to the object so that it can be made to caress him. Bancroft (1989) notes here that it is often the texture of the material of the object against the skin that creates the erotic effect, an experience that might well be described as the object's caressing of the skin.

Further, it is important to see that the non-bodily objects that typically become fetishes are those that are closely related to or symbolize the body, that is, articles of clothing (Chalkley and Powell, 1983). Freud (1905) suggests, for instance, that a fur fetish might ultimately come from the fur's symbolizing the hair of the mons Veneris. Or again, in Friday's (1998) study, a man who had a fetish for rubber aprons claimed that the smell of such aprons was reminiscent of the female genitals. This would seem to indicate that the fetishistic object has, for the fetishist, become an inanimate extension of the body (Bancroft, 1989) or even something of a "fantasized body." This would explain why the fetish is thus often used in masturbation while fantasizing about the part of the body that the fetishistic object comes in contact with. This also makes sense from what was said earlier about the phenomenology of clothing, namely, that clothes present themselves as being merged with the body.

In Freud's (1927) later, controversial view, the fetishistic object symbolizes the fantasized female penis, and attachment to the object is thus motivated by castration anxiety. Although this is a different position from his earlier one, it remains the same sofar as the fetishistic object symbolizes a part of the body. Consequently, we can see that the desires that constitute object fetishism are not altogether at odds with the desires for baring and caressing that we have been describing.

Here too, although fetishism is frequently thought to be exclusively a male behavior, some people argue that it occurs more than occasionally with females (Gamman and Makinen, 1994). With fetishism, however, there is not normally the coercive element that there is with the other variations we have been considering. Nor does it appear to be connected to feelings of inferiority and lack of social skills. Similar things concerning symbolic baring and caressing would also seem to be true of transvestism or cross-dressing, a variation that, at least in some of its forms, seems to be an extension of fetishism. Where transvestism lacks the fetishistic element of sexual arousal, it is usually seen to be an expression of pure transsexualism (Docter, 1988), a condition that is intimately related to the issue of gender. It will be best therefore to postpone discussion of transsexualism until the next chapter.

There are other sexual variations that might also seem to go against the view of the object of sexual desire given in this chapter. I feel, however, that the analyses just presented demonstrate by now a familiar pattern of activities that tend to approximate or symbolize mutual baring and caressing and then deploy masturbation, or a furtive rubbing against someone, and fantasy to fill in the missing parts. In zoophilia direct sexual interaction with an animal will even take place, but here too, fantasy and symbolism seem to play a crucial role (see Chapter 4).

It is also telling that the variations we have been considering are, as Freud (1905) points out, not mutually exclusive activities and that individuals engaging in one of them often engage in others (see also Freund and Seto, 1998). For the more of such activities that a person engages in, the closer he comes to the actual process of mutual baring and caressing, though, albeit, at different times and perhaps with different persons. It thus seems that if an activity is a sexual one, then it will more than likely display a similar structure to those we have just considered (I shall reserve the discussion of necrophilia, masochism, and sadism—variations that have relations to ways of being in love—until Chapter 5).

Were an activity to be totally lacking in any form of baring or caressing, either in reality or in fantasy, then it seems to me there would be little grounds to call it a sexual activity. I do not want to say, however, that the concept of baring and caressing can always be deployed to distinguish beyond doubt between which activities are to be considered sexual and which are not, for baring and caressing are themselves activities with indefinite boundaries. That is, there will always be some activities where it will remain unclear whether they are to be seen as instances of baring and caressing and therefore unclear whether they should be seen as sexual activities. Examples here might include what Stoller (1982) has termed erotic vomiting or perhaps the necrophilious fingering of a decomposing corpse. On the one hand, such activities contain elements that resemble the baring and caressing of sexual activity, but on the other, the elements are attenuated enough that it remains uncertain whether and to what degree they are best seen as instances of baring and caressing. Again, knowing the contents of any fantasies that accompany these activities might prove decisive in enabling us to determine if the activity should be seen as having a relation to baring and caressing.

In addition to the desires that lie behind the atypical sexual variations, there are also, it should be noted, numerous other sorts of desires that are often blended with people's sexual desires. Some individuals, for example, might have desires for a person with a particular type of figure, skin color, or social status, mixed in with their sexual desires. Or again, there are people whose sexual desires might carry with them desires for sexual intercourse in a particular position, setting, or circumstances.

Imagine, for example, the case of a woman whose sexual desires are directed exclusively toward men who are taller than her, who are willing to spend much money on her, and who she feels will let her take control over how their sexual engagement proceeds. Further, imagine that she desires to exchange caresses only in candlelight with romantic music playing. Now although such desires might, for this woman, have always accompanied her sexual desires—that is, her desires for mutual baring and caressing—it should be clear that desires concerning the personal qualities of her partner and the setting in which she satisfies her desires are nevertheless not themselves sexual desires and are only contingently related to her fundamental experience of sexual desire. For were she to suddenly lose these desires, as she might well do (perhaps, for example, she gets bored of men who allow her to dominate them in bed, or she begins to find romantic music distracting), it would not follow that she had thereby lost her sexual desires. What she would have lost in this situation would simply be her preference for a certain type of sexual partner in a certain type of setting. Of course, the woman's desires for a type of partner in a particular setting could be so deeply set in her character that she might feel it impossible to have sexual desires apart from these other desires. But such an impossibility, if it were one, would be only a contingent impossibility, not a conceptual one.

Moreover, even though this woman might have such intransigent desires accompanying her sexual desires, there are other people for whom such factors will play no role at all in their sexual desires. It should therefore be clear that, despite the strength or even exclusiveness of such desires, they are not intrinsic to the nature of sexual desire. They are rather individual preferences surrounding the way in which the object of sexual desire—mutual baring and caressing—is to be achieved.

As I have argued throughout this chapter, the object of sexual desire is not only the desires for baring and caressing but, to be more precise, also the desires for *mutual* baring and caressing between oneself and *at least one other person* (real, fantasized, or symbolized). Consequently, the object of sexual desire also involves the persons who carry out the baring and caressing. Now although persons come with a variety of features, the crucial feature that enables them to become objects of sexual desire—that is, persons with whom one desires mutual baring and caressing—is their gender. That is, in having sexual desire toward someone, the person's gender enters my awareness as that which feeds my desire, that which pulls me toward her in my craving for our mutual baring and caressing. Further, not only does the person of my desires have a gender, but I too, the one who bears the desires, likewise have a gender. Indeed, it is just my having a gender that gives this crucial meaning to her gender and her having a gender that gives a similarly crucial meaning to mine. But what is gender, and how does it work to give these meanings? It is to these questions that I now must turn.

4

The Experience of Gender

Few distinctions within the human condition present themselves as power-fully to us as the distinction between male and female. As each individual enters the world, the first question normally asked about the newly arrived infant is, "Is it a boy or a girl?"—not "Is it big or small?" "Is it healthy or sick?" or even "Is it alive or dead?" From that point on, the treatment the individual receives at the hands of other people, the way he or she responds to them, how the individual thinks of himself or herself, and the directions his or her life will take will all depend fundamentally on the answer to that primal question. And this question is not just primal in the sense that it is the first to be asked about us as we embark upon our lives, it is also primal in the sense that its answer provides the background from which we enter each other's awareness.

When I encounter someone, that person is normally first and foremost presented to my awareness as male or female. Even in the rare event that the maleness or femaleness might be unclear or clearly not even there—as in the case of true hermaphroditism—my awareness nevertheless strives, nearly beyond my notice, to situate the person in terms of this division. In such a case, the maleness or femaleness of a person presents itself like one side of two opposed and competing perceptions of a single Gestalt: each seeking to assert itself at the expense of the other. The bodily form, the facial features, the way of walking, the physical gestures, the type or fit of clothing, the tone of the voice or use of language, and even the style of handwriting, all seem to race forward to me declaring either the maleness or the femaleness of the person.

Of course, this person is other things to my awareness too: he or she is also, say, slender, conservatively dressed, friendly, quick-of-step, and so forth. But all this presents itself upon the background of one or the other side of that primal division. In this way the maleness or femaleness of each person appears as a central feature in which all other features seem to inhere. Thus, what I observe is not simply slenderness, or a way of walking, or even the slenderness or way of walking of a person but is rather, for example, the slenderness of a female or the way of walking of a male. Further, although this distinction might be more emphasized in some cultures rather than others, it is nevertheless one that is of vast significance in all cultures. As Davenport (1987) says in his survey of anthropology and sexuality, "it is not an exaggeration to state that every culture is actually composed of at least two subcultures, one for men and another for women" (p. 207). This does not mean that the distinction between male and female is the only distinction to be made, only that it is a fundamental one.

Despite the apparent immediacy of our awareness of each other's maleness or femaleness, the question of what constitutes such features is one that is surrounded by much confusion. One problem has to do with the fact that in English we have two words here, namely, "sex" or "gender," which are plainly used interchangeably but which some people, notably some feminist thinkers, feel refer to, or at least *should* refer to, different phenomena. Those taking this view sometimes argue that while "sex" refers to biology, gender refers to things like cultural expectations for masculinity or femininity, gender roles, gender identity, sexual orientation, and so on. My feeling is that there is no clear distinction between the normal uses of the words "sex" and "gender," and consequently they are generally accepted as being synonyms. This is supported by the fact that many terms made from these words, such as "sex roles" and "gender roles," are also used interchangeably. But what is it then that the words "sex" and "gender" both refer to? The obvious answer is that they refer to the biological property of maleness and femaleness.

GENDER AND THE GENITALS

This raises the problem of the role of biology in gender. To deal with this, one must first get clear about what constitutes the biological property of maleness or femaleness. The difficulty encountered here is that such a property is one that is constituted of many different levels. Therefore, within the biological property of gender there is at least the chromosomal level, the hormonal level, the level of primary sex characteristics (internal sexual anatomy, reproductive capacity, and basic external anatomy), and the level of secondary sex characteristics (for example, breasts and high voice in the female and beard and low voice in the male).

Now as long as these biological levels are all in agreement with each other, that is, as long as someone who has one gender's characteristics at one biological level also has them at the other biological levels, then any practical difficulty of using biology to decide to which gender a person belongs might never arise. Even in the case of someone whose gender is not immediately apparent, as long as all the biological levels are in agreement with each other, we can always refer to the person's biology in order to get a definite answer.

The complication here, however, is that the biological levels are not always in agreement. For example, in rare cases it is possible to have male sex chromosomes but, because of a genetic disorder known as androgen-insensitivity syndrome, not have a biological sensitivity to male sex hormones. In such a case of pseudo-hermaphroditism, as it is called, the person will, despite the presence of male sex chromosomes and male hormones, develop into what externally appears to be a female (a development that androgen sensitivity would have stopped). That is, the person may have some of both the primary sex characteristics (the external anatomy) and the secondary sex characteristics of a female. This person, however, will not have a uterus or reproductive capacity or be able to menstruate. Nor will such a person have a fully developed vagina. Or, again, a person can have an abnormal number of sex chromosomes and, because of this, show a blending of male and female internal and external sexual anatomy and secondary sexual characteristics. In such a case, which is known as true hermaphroditism, the person will appear to be a biological blending of a male and a female, with the genitals usually appearing to be ambiguous: perhaps a scrotum that resembles the labia majora or an enlarged clitoris that resembles a penis.

Because of such cases, it is not always possible simply to look to a person's biology to get a definitive answer to the question of the person's gender. For when there is a lack of concordance between the different biological levels, the question could always arise as to which level should be considered the definitive one. It is at this point that our *experience* of gender—and thus the role of phenomenological inquiry—begins to assert itself. For even though such a question could be raised, it is evident that not all the biological levels are such that they present themselves immediately to our awareness. The chromosomal, hormonal, and some aspects of the internal anatomical level, for example, consist of entities of which we are usually never immediately aware. This is because entities like these are seen to play a theoretically causal role in the development or workings of those biological levels of gender of which we have immediate awareness, namely, levels like the external sexual anatomy and the secondary sex characteristics. Consequently, these entities do not normally enter our awareness when we perceive a person's gender. What would enter our awareness, however, and accordingly raise an immediate question mark over the person's gender would be the ambiguous or partially developed genitals. In these sorts of cases one might feel inclined to argue that it is the gender identity or gender role that should take precedent and decide the person's gender. Individuals with an ambiguous gender can still develop an unambiguous masculine or feminine gender identity (see, e.g., Hampson and Hampson, 1961). Therefore, a hermaphrodite who has the gender identity of a female should be considered a female.

Although this might well be a convenient way of trying to deal with the problem, it should be evident that it is not really satisfactory. For it does not seem that a male can become a female simply because he has a feminine gender identity. But if this is so, why should a hermaphrodite become a female simply because he or she has a feminine gender identity? One could reply that the male does not become a female because his biological maleness takes priority and thus overrides his sense of gender identity. But if this is true, then it could just as well be argued that the hermaphrodite likewise does not become a female because his or her biological ambiguity (something a female does not have) takes priority and thus overrides the hermaphrodite's sense of gender identity. Further, such a stipulation offers no help in the instance in which the hermaphrodite might have an ambiguous sense of gender identity.

The conclusion to this is that it is not always possible to place a person clearly into the gender categories of male or female. This seems to be the basis of Fausto-Sterling's (1993) suggestion that we should recognize five genders rather than merely two; that is, in addition to recognizing males and females as separate genders, we should also recognize female pseudo-hermaphrodites, male pseudo-hermaphrodites, and true hermaphrodites as separate genders. Fausto-Sterling's argument, however, is based on the premise that hermaphroditic or intersexual conditions are relatively common and thus normal and that the male and female represent merely two ends of a gender continuum.

But as Sax (2002) has shown, Fausto-Sterling has greatly inflated her statistics by including several conditions that most clinicians do not consider intersexual (for example, late-onset congenital adrenal hyperplasia, Klinefelter syndrome, Turner syndrome, and vaginal agenesis). When these categories are removed, Fausto-Sterling's estimation of the incidence of hermaphroditism, which is 1.7 percent of the population, drops to 0.018 percent of the population. This means that rather than there being nearly two hermaphroditic persons born for every 100, as Fausto-Sterling suggests, there is in fact fewer than two such births out of 10,000. This makes the hermaphroditic condition a rare one and takes much of the force out of Fausto-Sterling's argument. (Interestingly enough, in her later work Fausto-Sterling [2000] says that in suggesting there were five genders she was only being provocative and writing tongue in cheek.)

This finding about the ambiguity of hermaphroditism, however, tells us something basic about the ways in which maleness and femaleness present themselves to our awareness. For the ambiguity that leads to this conclusion is not an ambiguity involving gender identity, gender roles, or sexual orientation—a male or female who is ambiguous in any of these areas is, for all that, still seen to be a male or a female. The ambiguity here is rather an ambiguity of biology.

Consequently, it seems that there is something fundamental about the role played by biology in our experience of gender. But the biology of gender, as I have argued, is a biology that is made of several different levels that may not all be in agreement with each other. The question that then arises is whether any of these levels plays a more fundamental role than the others in our idea of gender. One way of replying to this is by looking to the situation in which someone seeks to alter himself or herself in such a way as to alter his or her gender and by noting what exactly it is that he or she is most interested in altering in order to try to become the envied gender. Such a situation can be found in transsexualism.

Transsexualism is a psychological condition that is related to the sense of gender identity. The features that make up transsexualism include an abhorrence of one's own body, especially the genitals (a condition known as gender dysphoria); seeking hormonal and surgical intervention to have one's sex characteristics altered to resemble those of the opposite gender; and the desire to be accepted by everyone as a member of the opposite gender. Its central and definitive feature, however, seems to be the conviction that one is, in some sense, a member of the opposite gender (Wålinder, 1967). But why does the transsexual, who has a conviction that he or she is a member of the opposite sex, place such enormous weight on the appearance of his or her genitals, abhorring especially them and seeking to have them removed or altered? The obvious answer here is that it is because the transsexual is, like anyone else, well aware that it is especially these features of human biology, indeed of the human condition, that are central to our experience of maleness and femaleness.

It is true that there are other sex characteristics—like breasts, bodily figure, and type of reproductive capacity—that also play a role in our idea of gender, but none of these holds the crucial place that the genitals do. Thus, although breasts, for example, are an aspect of female anatomy, females do not acquire them until their teenage years. And the same is true of the female figure and reproductive capacity. As a result, females spend several years of their lives without breasts, the adult female figure, or female reproductive capacity. They are, nevertheless, still females. Further, many adult females have no apparent breasts, have narrow hips, and even lack reproductive capacity. Although this might be seen as making them unattractive as females (and then again it might not), none of it would be enough to call their femaleness into question.

However, were a person to claim to be female while also having a penis and testicles, this would probably be more than enough for most people to reject the person's claims to femaleness and even instead see the person as being a male. And this would seem to hold even in the case where the person had breasts and wide hips (obviously such a person could not have female reproductive capacity). Similarly, were a person to claim to be a male but nevertheless lack the male genitals and instead have a vulva and vagina, most people would also probably reject the claim, pointing out that such sex organs are fundamental to the female gender.

This view receives support from Kessler and McKenna's (1978) findings that the decisive feature in people's perception about another person's gender is genitals. In one study, subjects were asked to guess the gender of the person whom the experimenter was thinking about. In order to do so, the subjects were allowed to ask 10 questions to which the experimenter would answer "yes" or "no." Subjects were informed that they could ask any question they liked as long as the question was not "Is the person male?" or "Is the person female?" Interestingly enough, only 25 percent asked about the genitals in the first three questions, with most subjects asking about gender role and secondary sex characteristics instead. When asked why they did not inquire about the genitals of the person, subjects answered that to do so would be tantamount to asking whether the person was a male or female, a question that had been forbidden. In other words, they saw the having of a vulva and vagina as being definitive qualities of being a female and the having of a penis and testicles as being definitive qualities of being a male.

In a further study, Kessler and McKenna (1978) showed subjects drawings of figures with various gender characteristics and asked subjects, "Is this a picture of a female or a male?" In drawings where the genitals were in conflict with the secondary sex characteristics, the genitals dictated the subject's attribution of gender. Thus, when shown a drawing of a figure with breasts, wide hips, no body hair, long hair, and a penis and testicles, subjects judged the figure to be a male. Similarly, a figure with no breasts, narrow hips, body hair, short hair, and an apparent vulva was usually judged to be female. In other words, the centrality of the genitals for our awareness of gender is such that the presence of the male genitals will lead us to see the owner of the genitals as being male despite the presence of female secondary sex characteristics. Likewise, the presence of female genitals will lead us to see the owner of the genitals as being female even if the person shows male secondary sex characteristics.

Kessler and McKenna, however, claim that there is a discrepancy here between the male and the female case. For although there was nearly a unanimous agreement among subjects that the presence of a penis and testicles is, in and of itself, enough to render the drawing a male, only two thirds of the subjects, say Kessler and McKenna, saw the presence of a vagina as being, in and of itself, conclusive evidence that the figure was a female. They then conclude, "penis equals male but vagina does not equal female" (p. 151).

Unfortunately, however, their study does not warrant this conclusion. First, although they claim that it is the penis alone that dictates whether people will perceive a person as male, their drawing of the figure with female secondary sex characteristics and male genitals has not only a penis but also a clearly drawn scrotum and testicles (see p. 147). This means that subjects viewing this drawing are making their gender attributions on the basis not only of the presence of a penis but also of the presence of a scrotum and testicles. These extra features of the male genitals strongly underline the idea that the figure is a male (It is interesting that in her later book, Kessler [1998] points out how the scrotum is overlooked as part of the male genitals, which is exactly what she does in her discussion here.)

Moreover, although they say that one third of the subjects ignored the vagina in making their gender attributions, the fact is that it is Kessler and McKenna themselves who have ignored the vagina. For in their drawing of a standing figure with male secondary sex characteristics and female genitals, nothing is visible that could be called a vagina. All that is shown in the drawing is a mound that vaguely resembles the mons Veneris, without even two distinct labia majora. For all a viewer of this picture knows, the figure may in fact have no vagina, especially since the secondary sex characteristics are those of a male. Consequently, it is nearly as easy to interpret this figure as a castrated male as it is to interpret it as a female with a vagina. If they had wanted their figure clearly to have a vagina, they should have drawn it in a position that made at least the introitus or the vaginal opening visible, perhaps in a reclining position with the legs open. Thus, because of the clearly distinct penis, scrotum, and testicles in one figure and the absence of a visible vagina or vulva in the other, it is quite understandable that while most of the subjects would see the figure with the male genitals as being male, a lesser amount would see the figure without a visible vagina as being female.

This response to the genitals and their relation to the body also indicates something further about the phenomenology of gender. For although the genitals are fundamental to our awareness of gender, the genitals nevertheless do not exist in isolation from the rest of the body. However, since the genitals are here fundamental, their relation to the body is not an equal one. That is, the genitals are not seen to be merely one more characteristic of gender, on par with other bodily sex characteristics. On the contrary, the genitals are seen to be a center of maleness or femaleness that discloses the meaning of the other sex characteristics. Here the other sex characteristics acquire their meaning as sex characteristics only in the presence of the genitals. Gender can thus best be understood as a bodily Gestalt in which the various peripheral sex characteristics present themselves as male or female characteristics only on the strength of their reference back to the genitals. This is a Gestalt because in themselves none of these sex characteristics carries the meaning of maleness or femaleness. It is only when they are brought into relation to the genitals, which are the core of the Gestalt, that they suddenly transcend themselves, so to speak, and become male or female sex characteristics.

It is as if the genitals were a feudal king and each of the other sex characteristics were lesser lords within the king's realm. For although these lesser lords have power to make themselves heard and in some situations might seem to wield autonomous power, they can do so only through consent of the king. And were any such lesser lord to attempt to rebel and make himself noticed in a way that did not display allegiance to the king, the king's own power would quickly crush such a revolt. In this way, although wide hips and breasts typically have the meaning of femaleness, they do so only by consent of the vulva and vagina. Similarly, although narrow hips and no breasts typically have the meaning of maleness, they do so only by consent of the penis and testicles.

This is why Kessler's (1998, p. 132) obscure remark that there are other ways besides reference to the genitals "to 'do' male or female" makes no sense. For our experience of maleness and femaleness are inescapably tied to our experience of the genitals—and the existence of individuals whose hermaphroditic condition renders them neither male nor female does not change this. In other words, in the realm of gender the genitals reign supreme. Of course, people might one day agree that whether someone is to be designated by the term "male" or "female" is to be decided by, say, the number of friends the person has or by the person's ability to recite the books of the Bible backward. The pitfall here, however, is that these terms would then no longer mean what we mean by them. But even if we could do this, we are still, disappointingly enough, left with the phenomena of the genitals. So to "do" male and female differently, we would then have to either ignore the genitals—and the fact that genitals come in predominantly male and female forms—or use new terms to distinguish between individuals who have male or female genitals. Choosing either of these options might well achieve Kessler's chilling demand that "we must use whatever means we have to give up on gender," but giving up on something by ignoring it or renaming it does not change the fact that it still exists. (For a critique of the view that language creates reality, see Giles, 1994.)

Now, in most cultures the genitals are not something that are on everyday display. Nevertheless, gender awareness is something that imbues all human interaction. Because of this, it might be thought that the genitals are not fundamental to our awareness of gender. That is, the other person's gender is continually presenting itself to our awareness despite the fact that his or her genitals are normally hidden from us. The reason for this, however, is that even though the genitals remain hidden, their presence is something that is always assumed or expected. Not that this assumption would always, to adapt a phrase of Schopenhauer's, appear in our clear consciousness at the sight of another person. Nevertheless, an obscure feeling of this core of maleness or femaleness becomes the fundamental note of our mood toward that person.

What this means is that in ascribing maleness or femaleness to the other person, I am orientating myself to the other person's body in such a way that either female or male genitals are implied. That is, I am orientating myself to the Gestalt of gender. What is implied—the core of the Gestalt—is not situated as a central point or focus of awareness; rather, it is a supportive background that subtly permeates my awareness of the other person and allows me to see the various other characteristics of the person's body as being those of a male or female.

The breasts, for example, are seen to be female sex characteristics only so far as they emerge from a background awareness of the female genitals. This background awareness should not, however, be seen as necessarily taking the form of visual image of the genitals, though such an image remains a possible element of this awareness. Such a background will rather tend to present itself as a web of interconnected meanings that provide the context for an awareness of the genitals as genitals.

Thus, the female genitals may enter our awareness embedded in the idea of a soft, warm, and receiving entrance that nevertheless remains shrouded, gently withholding itself. As Beauvoir (1949) puts it, "the feminine sex organ is mysterious even to the woman herself, concealed, mucous, and humid, as it is; it bleeds each month, it is often sullied with fluids, it has a secret and perilous life of its own." Because of this, the female feels herself to be "absorption, suction, humus, pitch and glue, a passive influx, insinuating and viscous" (p. 386). The male genitals, however, may appear as the idea of transformation from softness to firmness, as an externality that strains outward, searching to fuse itself, both in penetration and in ejaculation, with another body. Here too one finds genitals with a secret and perilous life of their own. For the erection and detumescence of the penis, the elevation of the testicles, and ejaculation all happen—or do not happen—of their own accord, beyond the male's will (hence the Christian philosopher Augustine's concern about his "disobedient members").

But why do we form a background awareness of one gender rather than the other? Plainly, it cannot normally be because of a perception of the other person's genitals, for it is just these that are normally hidden. The answer, of course, is that we form this background awareness on the basis of the other sex characteristics that are not hidden. That is, it is because I observe the other person's breasts, for example, that I form the background awareness of female genitals that permeates my awareness of the other person and calls me to see her as a female. But if this is true, then it seems we have come upon a peculiar problem. For if it is the non-hidden sex characteristics that bring us to assume either male or female genitals, then how could it be that it is the assumption of the genitals that are allowing me to see the breasts as being those of a female? For here it is the breasts seen as female that are leading me to assume the female genitals rather than the other way around.

The answer is that in the same instant that the breasts are seen to be breasts of a female, the assumption of female genitals permeates my background awareness of the person. Or, to put it another way, breasts can be seen as female characteristics only if there diffuses through my awareness at least the obscure feeling that the person who bears them also has female genitals. Indeed, to see the breasts as female characteristics is nothing more than to see them as presenting themselves on the background of the assumed female genitals. Consequently, the priority that the genitals have over the other sex characteristics takes the form of enabling the other characteristics to step forward and present themselves as those of one gender rather than the other. It is a phenomenological priority in which the assumption of the genitals allows a gendered meaning to be given to the other sex characteristics.

Here again the transsexual's case can shed some light on the meaning of the genitals. For according to the available reports (Hunt and Hampson, 1980; Lawrence, 2003; Leif and Hubschman, 1993), transsexuals are quite pleased with the results of their sex reassignment surgery. And this is understandable, for in having his or her genitals surgically altered to resemble those of the opposite gender, the transsexual has altered the fundamental feature of his or her gender to resemble those of the envied gender and thus has brought himself or herself as close as possible to becoming that gender. It will be recalled that one of the main features of transsexualism is a desire to be accepted by everyone as a member of the opposite gender. As I have just argued, this is something that can hardly be achieved as long as one has the genitals of one's own gender. But in having his sex organs removed, the transsexual has removed a major obstacle in the way of achieving his goal.

It is important to note, also, the degree to which the transsexual's operation works in getting other people to accept him or her as actually being a member of the opposite gender. For once the operation has been carried out (and usually not before), people seem at least willing, even in the sexological literature, to refer to a male post-operative transsexual as "she" and a female post-operative transsexual as "he." Non-transsexual female impersonators who retain their male genitals seldom achieve this (unless they are mistakenly thought to be females). Even the sexological terminology used in area of transsexualism reflects the idea of an acceptance that the post-operative transsexual has actually become the other gender. Thus, the terms "sex change operation" or "sex reassignment surgery" imply that the operation somehow changes or reassigns the transsexual's gender. Likewise, the popular terms "male-to-female transsexual" and "female-to-male transsexual" also imply that the operation will transform a person of one gender into the other gender.

At times this scholarly acquiescence to the transsexual's claim to be the opposite gender can even take on a bizarre quality. In one recent medical article, for example, the authors discuss the "gynecological" examination of a post-operative male transsexual, saying, "a 49-year-old female, nulligravid [that is, never given birth] Caucasian female (status after transgender surgery, male to female, in 1991) presented to the ob/gyn clinic for her annual gynecological examination" (Fugate et al., 2001, p. 22). But what purpose is served in telling us that a male transsexual—even if one has decided to call him a female—is "nulligravid"? It is as if the authors believe that the transsexual's operation has made him into a real female who therefore might or might not have given birth. It is thus important clinical information to note during the exam that this particular male transsexual has never given birth. And this sort of acceptance takes place despite the fact that the transsexual's chromosomes, internal sexual anatomy, bone structure, and so on remain that of his pre-operative gender. All this points to fundamentalness of the role of the genitals in our experience of gender.

Yet it seems that the transsexual is, in another way, not fully accepted by others as being a legitimate member of the opposite gender. When, for example, the well-known male transsexual René Richards sought to continue playing professional tennis after his "male-to-female" operation, he naturally wanted to do so in the women's circuit. The official tennis associations, however, protested, claiming that Richards had an unfair advantage over the women because he was stronger than them (Richards and Ames, 1983). But why should Richards' strength be a matter for complaint? There are also many strong women, probably even some who are stronger than Richards. If such a woman were to show up on the tennis circuits, there of course would be no grounds for complaint. One cannot complain against a tennis player simply because she is stronger than other tennis players. But if this is true, then why would the tennis associations feel they had grounds to complain about Richards in this way? The most likely answer to this is that, like many people, they did not fully accept that Richards was a woman. And, not being a woman, he should not be allowed to play in the women's tennis circuits. For the whole point of having a *women's* tennis circuit is that it is a circuit that is reserved exclusively for women.

A similar situation can be seen in the case of male transsexuals who return to their place of work after their operation. One problem that happens here is that often the transsexual's women colleagues do not feel the transsexual should be allowed to use the women's toilets, even though he has undergone a "sex change" operation (see, e.g., Schafer, 2001). Yet a further situation is where someone, usually a heterosexual male, sexually interacts with or is merely attracted to a post-operative male transsexual under the mistaken belief that the person is a female. In the case mentioned in Chapter 3, it will be recalled, the man who had intercourse with the transsexual became extremely upset when he discovered his partner was not a woman but was a post-operative male transsexual. A similar situation is dramatized in Yoshimoto's novel *Kitchen* (1993). Here a man becomes obsessed with the beautiful male transsexual Erico while thinking him to be a woman. When, however, he discovers that Erico is really a post-operative transsexual male, he becomes humiliated to the point that he attacks and murders Erico. In each of these situations it looks like we have a case of people not fully accepting that surgery has managed to change a person's gender. But why would someone feel that a person who went to all the bother to have a sex reassignment operation had nevertheless not been reassigned to the other sex?

A likely answer here is the one given by a male transsexual himself when he says, "I find it hard to relate to having a vagina. I wonder if vaginoplasty [that is, surgical construction of a vagina] is a purely cosmetic reshaping of the penis, which is not in any real way connected to a real vagina. Even when I hear of post-op orgasms I think, 'Is this just a male orgasm coming from a restructured penis?'" (Kessler, 1998, p. 50). Such doubts, thus, have to do with the idea that the transsexual's operation has not given him or her the real genitals of the opposite gender—that is, the fundamental features of the opposite gender—it has merely given him something that cosmetically resembles them. What the post-operative male transsexual acquires is not a vulva and vagina but rather the remnants of penile and scrotal tissue that have been tucked into an incision that has been made in between his legs (Perovic et al., 2000). Likewise, what the post-operative female transsexual typically gets is not a penis and testicles but rather a prosthetic or protrusion of tissue covered with skin grafts taken from other parts of the body along with two testicle-shaped prosthetics placed where the labia majora used to be (Khouri and Casoli, 1997).

Now none of this might be seen as a problem if the genitals were a secondary or inessential sex characteristic like, say, facial hair or tone of voice. For being secondary, their artificiality might be able to be overlooked, as long as the fundamental feature of gender was genuine. But since the genitals *are* the fundamental feature of maleness and femaleness, then artificial genitals carry with them the implication of artificial maleness or femaleness. It is true that males can lose or damage their genitals and thus undergo reconstructive surgery or that females might, typically because of disease, need to have their vulvas or vaginas reconstructed. But in both cases this does not seem to alter drastically the perception of the person as a male or female. The reason for this would seem to be that, having already had the requisite genitals, the maleness or femaleness of the person is already felt to be established despite the incongruence of his or her now lacking those genitals. This feeling is probably strong enough that, as Kessler (1998) suggests, even the male or female who has lost his or her genitals and chooses not to have them reconstructed is still felt to have his or her gender "marked" as essentially male or female. In a way, having previously had the genitals of one gender might work as a default mechanism that is seen to take over and influence our awareness in atypical situations. Something like this, no doubt, also plays a role in the misgivings people have about accepting the post-operative transsexual's claims to be the opposite gender. The suspicion here might be expressed in the question, Since she was once a woman, how can she now be a man?

This, however, cannot be the full story behind such reservations. For if we could imagine a situation in which, rather than undergoing sex reassignment surgery, the transsexual could take a pill or some such thing that magically and faultlessly alters his or her body into that of the opposite gender's body, here it would seem much harder to argue that the person could not be the new gender he or she claims to be. For if the resultant body is in every respect a genuine opposite-sex body with genuine opposite-sex genitals, it would seem pointless to resist the person's claims to now being the opposite sex. The difficulty with the transsexual's operation, however, is that he or she does not get a genuine opposite-sex body with genuine opposite-sex genitals.

This should not, however, be interpreted as saying that there is no point to sex reassignment surgery. Clearly, such an operation enables many people to live their lives with less suffering and more contentment. For this reason alone the operation has immense value. Still, these positive results should not be taken as evidence for the view that the operation somehow lives up to its name of reassigning or changing its recipient into the opposite gender.

This brings us to the question of why the genitals play such a fundamental role in our idea of gender. An answer here is suggested by a discussion given in the *Kama Sutra*, a work whose central concern is the practice of sexual interaction. Here, in the first chapter of the part dealing with sexual union (*samprayoga* in Sanskrit), Vatsyayana seeks to classify types of sexual intercourse in terms of the dimensions of the genitals of the sexual partners. He does this by dividing both males and females into three groups. Males are classified according to whether their penises are small, medium, or large and females according to whether the vaginas are shallow, medium depth, or deep.

But why does Vatsyayana classify males and females according to their genital dimensions? The answer comes when he goes on to discuss the different forms of sexual union. Here he says that there are three equal sexual unions (when a penis and vagina of equal dimensions are brought together) and six unequal sexual unions (when a penis and vagina of unequal dimensions are brought together). From here he argues that the equal unions are the best but also later suggests ways, such as using different positions, in which the unequal type of union can be made better. Thus, Vatsyayana's interest in the genitals is based on the role they play in sexual interaction, an activity, it should be remembered, that is intimately connected to sexual desire. And this seems reasonable enough because the genitals typically play a major role in both sexual interaction and sexual desire.

Could it be, then, that the genitals play a fundamental role in our idea of gender because gender likewise plays a fundamental role in sexual interaction and sexual desire? This also makes sense because sexual desire always takes place within the context of a person of one gender desiring sexual interaction with a person of another (or the same) gender, where the gender of the participants is the basis for the meanings ascribed to the desired activity. That is, the gender of both the person who has the sexual desire and the gender of the person toward whom the sexual desire is aimed are fundamental to the structure of sexual desire. It is this feature of sexual desire that is often referred to as sexual orientation. Therefore, in order to understand the nature of sexual desire, one must first understand the way it is related to sexual orientation.

THE PLACE OF GENDER IN SEXUAL ORIENTATION

A major problem in studying sexual orientation is that different sexologists have different ideas about what the notion refers to or how it ought to be defined or assessed (see, e.g., Sell's [1997] review). Thus, while many sexologists agree that sexual orientation refers to the directions that a person's sexual desires take in relation to the gender of the other person—a view that might be called the desire view—others see sexual orientation as not referring specifically to such desire but rather to the pattern that a person's sexual behavior takes in relation the gender of other persons—a view that might be called the behavior view. A sexologist taking the desire view would thus judge someone's sexual orientation to be, say, heterosexual if the person's sexual desires were directed at persons of the opposite gender. A sexologist taking the behavior view, however, would consider someone's sexual orientation to be heterosexual only if the person's sexual interaction engaged persons of the opposite gender. Yet other sexologists seem to see both the desire and the behavior elements as being equally important components of a person's sexual orientation.

Now since a person's sexual desires and sexual behavior are usually in agreement with regard to the gender of the desired person—for example, heterosexual behavior is usually related to heterosexual desires—then all three views would usually arrive at the same assessment of a person's sexual orientation. A person, for example, who had homosexual desires and engaged in homosexual activity would be seen on all three views to have a homosexual orientation.

Unfortunately, however, a person's sexual behavior toward persons of a certain gender is not always in agreement with his or her sexual desires. For example, a person who engages exclusively in heterosexual behavior might nevertheless have only homosexual desires (a situation I shall discuss shortly). In such circumstances the desire and behavior views of sexual orientation would arrive at opposite assessments of the person's sexual orientation: the desire view determining the person's sexual orientation to be homosexual and the behavior view determining it to be heterosexual.

The combined desire and behavior view, on the other hand, would produce an inconsistent assessment determining the person to be both heterosexual (because of his desires) and homosexual (because of his behavior). It therefore seems that the desire view and the behavior view cannot both be accounts of sexual orientation or at least cannot both be accounts of the same aspects of sexual orientation. For a person cannot be both heterosexual and homosexual in the same way at the same time. This is because being homosexual means being orientated toward persons of the same gender instead of persons of the opposite gender, and being heterosexual means being orientated toward persons of the opposite gender instead of persons of the same gender. A person who is orientated toward persons of both genders is normally referred to as being bisexual. The example just referred to—engaging exclusively in heterosexual behavior while having only homosexual desires—is not what is normally meant by bisexuality.

The question then is whether sexual orientation is to be determined by sexual desire or by sexual behavior or whether both are different aspects of sexual orientation. To answer this, let us ask why someone might in the first place show heterosexual behavior and yet have only homosexual desires. For on the face of it, this is a peculiar situation that stands in need of explanation. Clearly, having homosexual desires is no explanation for why someone engages in heterosexual behavior.

One obvious answer here is that such a person might have guilt, embarrassment, or other negative feelings over his homosexual desires and thus be strongly motivated to appear "normal" and, consequently, engage exclusively in heterosexual behavior. Such a person, as Kaplan (1977) points out, might well be able to learn to become sexually aroused, to engage in sexual interaction, and even to have orgasms within the context of heterosexual behavior. Typically, however, the homosexual desires will remain intransigent. This, according to Kaplan, is because homosexual desires (like heterosexual desires) are not superficial preferences that individuals have, preferences that might easily be switched for other preferences (which is why Gonsiorek and Weinrich [1991] recommend against using the term "sexual preference" to refer to sexual orientation). They are rather a basic part of the individual's psychic constitution.

Some people, however (Baumeister, 2000; Diamond, 1998), have tried to argue that female sexual orientation has more "plasticity" than male sexual orientation and that females who had been, for example, heterosexual early in life can, through "social flexibility," later become homosexual. The trouble with this view is that many women who make such an apparent change describe their early heterosexual behaviors as something they engaged in simply because of social pressures or lack of awareness of other possibilities (Marrow, 1997). When they later discover homosexuality, this is frequently described as a "coming out" or a discovery of their real orientation. Hoeck (2002), for example, gives the case of a 35-year-old woman who did not think of herself as being lesbian but, after being married for eight years with a husband and with three children, suddenly fell in love with another woman. Yet from the time that she was a young girl, she would have romantic feelings for other girls, feelings that she dared not to admit to herself. This woman described her falling in love later in life with the other woman as the moment at which "everything suddenly fell into place." This fits with Kaplan's (1995) observation that although she worked with persons whose sexual desires seemed to change over time, "in all cases, closer scrutiny revealed that it was only the *embellishments* that were altered, while the *basic elements* of the person's fantasy or desire remained fixed" (p. 40).

Therefore, the way that a homosexual who wants to change typically enables himself or herself to engage in heterosexual behavior is not by changing his or her homosexual desires but rather by employing fantasy during the sexual interaction. Thus, while engaging in a heterosexual encounter, the person will most likely attempt to fantasize that he or she is exchanging caresses with a person of the same gender.

Now what can be said of such an individual's sexual orientation? It is true that although he has homosexual desires, he engages in heterosexual behavior. But clearly his heterosexual behavior is a facade. That is, his sexual behavior does not grow out of sexual desires to partake in that behavior; it is rather an attempt to hide or not act out his real sexual desires, desires that, because they are his real desires, he continues to satisfy in fantasy. And just because his heterosexual behavior does not represent his true sexual desires, it seems misleading, if not completely wrong, to say his sexual orientation is in any meaningful sense heterosexual.

One could also imagine the case where a person with only heterosexual desires nevertheless engaged exclusively in homosexual behavior. In this instance the person might be in prison with only same-sex cell mates, lost on a desert island with only same-sex fellow survivors, or an adolescent male from the Sambia culture of Papua New Guinea (a culture that prescribes homosexual behavior for young males). In such a situation the only sort of sexual interaction available to the person would be homosexual interaction. Some people might here choose to (or attempt to) abstain from any sexual interaction, but others might, also with the use of fantasy, engage in homosexual behavior while having only heterosexual desires.

Here too it would seem wrong to assess the person's sexual orientation according to his or her sexual behavior. (See my critique [Giles, 2004] of Herdt's [1999] view that Sambia prescribed homosexual behavior is an indication of sexual orientation or desires.)

All these situations are, of course, unusual with mitigating factors influencing the person's sexual behavior. They nevertheless serve to show the underlying mistake involved in thinking that sexual orientation is a matter of sexual behavior rather than sexual desire or even that sexual behavior is a definitive component of sexual orientation. This conclusion is in agreement with Freud's (1910) view that "what decides whether we call someone an invert [that is, homosexual] is not his actual behaviour, but his emotional attitude" (p. 87).

The conclusion that sexual orientation is essentially a matter of sexual desire does not, however, mean that sexual behavior is irrelevant to the practical study of sexual orientation, for sexual behavior is usually a good indication of a person's sexual desires. Subjects in a study who might be unclear about or unable to verbalize their sexual desires might nevertheless be able to give concrete accounts of their sexual behavior. Also, sexual behavior can be observed in a way that sexual desires cannot. Further, sexual behavior might prove a useful variable for researchers seeking to construct operational definitions of sexual orientation. In doing so, however, it would be important to not be misled into thinking that the operational definition is defining the essential quality of sexual orientation, namely, the disposition of a person to desire sexual interaction with other persons of one rather than the other gender or with persons of either gender.

The idea, however, that sexual orientation refers exclusively to desires toward other persons of one rather than the other gender or with persons of either gender, either in reality or in fantasy—that is, to heterosexuality, homosexuality, and bisexuality—is one that has been criticized. Stayton (1980, 1989), for example, has called this view into question by arguing that "the entire universe is a potential erotic turn on" (1980, p. 5). Stayton's complaint, therefore, is that the three-orientations model of sexual orientation is too narrow. For, he says, in addition to being orientated to other people, sexual desire can orientate toward "me" (one's own self), "it" (animals and inanimate objects), and "Thou" (anything that can be considered ultimate reality). Although Stayton's account is both poorly conceived and poorly argued, the fact that it receives a mention (along with a reproduced diagram) in *The Complete Dictionary of Sexology* (2000) indicates the need for a critical appraisal. This will also help to show the way in which the awareness of gender is fundamental to the idea of sexual orientation.

Why then does Stayton think sexual desire can be orientated in this way, and does his system make an advance on the more common view of sexual orientation? To support his view that a person's sexual orientation can be toward himself, Stayton says, "one of the earliest erotic responses of a child is self-stimulation. If this is not totally inhibited, the person will be capable of having erotic fantasies and experiences with himself or herself throughout the life cycle. There is little question today that autoeroticism is healthy, desirable and probably important to attaining mature adult sexual responsivity. It should be considered not less than, but equal to, erotic response in any other dimension" (Stayton, 1980, p. 5).

But as should be obvious, none of this shows that the categories of heterosexuality, homosexuality, and bisexuality are inadequate or that there exists a separate category of "me sexuality." For nothing in the notions of heterosexuality, homosexuality, or bisexuality rule out the possibility of autoeroticism. That is, heterosexuals, homosexuals, and bisexuals can still engage in masturbation and other forms of autoeroticism without fear of calling their respective sexual orientations into question. Stayton himself seems aware of this when he says that autoeroticism is important in "attaining mature adult sexual responsivity." For this suggests that his notion of autoeroticism is not a separate orientation at all but rather a component of or stage in "mature" heterosexuality, homosexuality, or bisexuality.

The reason why autoeroticism or masturbation need not represent a threat to a person's sexual orientation is because of the role that fantasy plays in autoeroticism, a role that Stayton seems to acknowledge when he says that a person who can have uninhibited erotic self-stimulation will be capable of erotic fantasies. Unfortunately, he does not expand on this. It can easily be seen, however, how fantasy enables a person to maintain her sexual orientation during autoerotic activity. When, for example, the heterosexual person masturbates, she will, as was pointed out earlier, typically fantasize about heterosexual interaction. Since, as was argued in the first part of this section, desire (here expressed in fantasy) is the telling feature of a person's sexual orientation, the heterosexual person who thus fantasizes during masturbation remains clearly heterosexual despite her masturbation. With this it is plain that Stayton is not really giving an account of a separate orientation of "me-sexuality" but merely a defense of masturbation as "healthy" or some such thing.

There are similar problems with Stayton's category of "it-sexuality," where the orientation is toward animals and inanimate objects. To support his view about the existence of an "it" orientation toward animals, Stayton merely says, "it is not unusual for person's to recall erotic experiences with household or farm pets. Many people, both young and old, have had sexual love affairs with pets" (p. 5).

But this is not at all to the point. To "recall" an erotic experience is not the same as having a sexual orientation to the object of that sort of experience. If a woman recalls when she was young having an erotic experience with another girl but since then has desired and engaged in erotic experiences only with men, it would seem strange to say she had a homosexual orientation. For the childhood experience here seems more like a form of sexual experimentation than like an expression of sexual orientation. Likewise, if someone recalls as a child having an erotic experience with a pet but since then has desired and had erotic experiences only with other people, there seems no grounds to say the person has an "it (animate object)" orientation. For someone to have such an orientation, her sexual desires would have to be directed predominantly toward sexual activity with non-human animals with little interest in sexual interaction with people. Here, the sexual activity should be desired in itself and not be accompanied by fantasies of engaging in sexual activity with a person. For if someone were engaging in sexual activity with an animal but all the while fantasizing that the animal was another person, then it would not look like the activity with the animal was desired in itself. In such a case it would seem that the sexual interaction with the animal was merely a substitute for sexual interaction with a person.

Now although it might be possible to find persons whose sexual desires are directed predominantly toward animals instead of people, such persons, I suspect, would be much rarer that those who can "recall erotic experiences with household or farm pets." Further, even in the case of a genuine "it" (animate object)-orientated individual, it is unclear that such an orientation escapes being subsumed within the three-orientations model. For in perusing the literature on sexual activities with and sexual fantasies about animals (see, e.g., Friday, 1998; Kronhausen and Kronhausen, 1969), it becomes clear that the gender of the animal, or the gender that the animal symbolizes, is an important component in the desires and fantasies concerning the animal.

This would fit with Kinsey's remark that if a male becomes erotically aroused at masturbating a male animal, his relationship to animal might indicate a homosexual element. This suggestion is corroborated by Williams and Weinberg's (2003) research on male zoophiles that found that male zoophiles who identify themselves as homosexual are more likely to have strong sexual feelings for male animals. Further, when Williams and Weinberg asked their subjects what made one animal more sexually desirable than another, many subjects referred to the animal's human-like qualities. The researchers felt it was obvious that the men had anthropomorphized their animals in attributing ideal human characteristics to them.

This symbolic relationship of sexual desires toward animals and sexual orientation toward people would seem to be why the animals often used in sexual activity are ones whose genitals are not too distinct from those of human beings or whose bodies at least symbolize the genitals of human beings. Kronhausen and Kronhausen (1969), for example, note that the majority of animal fantasies in erotic literature concern dogs, animals whose genitals bear a resemblance in size and proportion to human genitals.

As for Stayton's inanimate version of the "it-sexuality" orientation, here we are told, "certainly it could be possible to have erotic response to the stimulation of an inanimate object. Bicycles, automobiles, banisters, vibrators, chairs, doorknobs, pillows and rubber artifacts, for example, can be sexually stimulating for some people. These people are not usually hindered in having erotic responses to themselves or others" (p. 5).

But once again, having an erotic response to something—especially if having such responses does not hinder one in having similar responses to other people—is hardly the same as having a sexual orientation to the object. Heterosexuals, homosexuals, and bisexuals can all have erotic responses to banisters, vibrators, doorknobs, and whatever while still maintaining their respective orientations.

The whole point behind the idea of sexual orientation is to be able to describe a person's predominant sexual desires toward one, the other, or both genders. If Stayton wants to expand this notion to include inanimate objects, he cannot do so simply by pointing out that some people can have erotic responses to doorknobs. At the very least he has to show us that there are people who have their sexual desires directed predominantly toward doorknobs. And even if he could find such a person, he would then have to demonstrate that the apparent sexual desires were not in fact based on fantasies about what the doorknob symbolized. For the more likely explanation is not that the person sexually desires doorknobs but rather that the person sexually desires what the doorknob symbolizes. And if a female who appeared to have predominant sexual desires toward doorknobs was in fact fantasizing about penises or if doorknobs had a symbolic relation to penises for her (and such symbolism might well be unconscious), then it would seem that her sexual orientation would best be described as heterosexual rather than "it" (doorknob) orientation, for the focus of her desire is really the male genitals.

Some people do, of course, have sexual desires that focus primarily on inanimate objects. This is known as object fetishism. However, as was pointed out previously, object fetishism usually involves articles of clothing or material (rubber artifacts are the most likely candidate given in Stayton's list). Here, the fetishistic object can best be understood as symbolizing the body. In this way even object fetishism can be subsumed into the three-orientations model of sexual orientation—which is why it is considered an atypical sexual variation rather than an atypical sexual orientation. For here too the fetishist can be seen as heterosexual, homosexual, or bisexual depending on the gender of the body that the fetish is taken to symbolize.

However, the fact that Stayton is not concerned with object fetishism here seems to follow from his remark that "it" (inanimate object)-orientated people "are not usually hindered in having erotic responses to themselves or others." For those with true fetishism can easily suffer such hindrances:

without the fetish, the fetishist is frequently sexually impotent. A similar thing, however, could be said about sexual orientation. For being primarily orientated to people of one gender hinders one from having erotic responses to people of the other gender. This much follows simply from what is meant by sexual orientation. Consequently, it is unclear why Stayton thinks his "it" (inanimate object) category has anything to do with sexual orientation or even what the purpose of the category is.

Stayton's last extra category is "Thou" (anything that can be considered ultimate reality). He presents this "orientation" by giving an example of a Catholic priest who "admitted that there were times in his periods of meditation and communing with God when he felt so close to God that he had an ejaculation without having touched his genitals" (p. 5). We are also told that many clergy have had similar experiences.

But what is this suppposed to show? Do such experiences demonstrate the existence of a "Thou" orientation? The first thing to notice is that it is nothing particular to a so-called "Thou" orientation to have an ejaculation without having one's genitals touched. There are people who, without touching their genitals, can fantasize themselves to orgasms and people who have ejaculations during erotic dreams. In these cases it seems that such persons are merely fantasizing or dreaming about sexual interaction with a sexually desirable person. It is therefore altogether likely that the priest's experiences of meditation and communing with God have much in common with such sexual fantasy or erotic dreams (assuming that the priest's ejaculation is connected with an orgasm). At least Stayton has given us no reason to discount this.

But people who have fantasy-induced orgasms or ejaculations during erotic dreams still have heterosexual, homosexual, or bisexual orientations. And this is true even if they seldom or never engage in sexual interaction. Consequently, there is no reason here to think that the priest does not also have a heterosexual, homosexual, or bisexual orientation—even if he never engages in sexual interaction. If one wants to reject the idea that the priest has such a sexual orientation, claiming instead that he has a "Thou" sexual orientation, then the argument must be based on something other than the fact that he has ejaculations without touching his genitals. And obviously, it must be based upon the content of his experiences of meditation and communing when he has the ejaculation.

In the case of those who can fantasize themselves to orgasm or have ejaculations during dreams, the reason they can still be said to be heterosexual, homosexual, or bisexual is because their sexual fantasies and erotic dreams will typically be about sexual interaction with individuals of one, the other, or both genders or at least with images or ideas that symbolize such individuals. Could it be then that during his meditations and communing, the priest is also fantasizing or dreaming about such sexual interaction with a similarly gendered idea of God? We hear, of course, that

God is supposed to be genderless. But Christianity, and especially Roman Catholicism, has an undisguised view of God as a male. He is typically referred to by the masculine pronoun and as "our Father"; his so-called incarnation, Jesus, was a man; and, for Catholics, his closest representatives on earth—the pope, cardinals, bishops, and priests—are all men. It is therefore not unlikely that a priest who is having ejaculations while meditating and communing with God is in fact sexually fantasizing or dreaming about sexual interaction with an image of a male figure. Here, it is suggestive that Sipe (1995), a psychologist and himself an ex-Catholic priest, estimates that, despite their claims to celibacy, half of American Roman Catholic priests are sexually active (and not with just a "Thou"). Of those involved with children, Sipe estimates that one out of three are involved with boys. In attempting to account for such behavior within the Catholic Church, Sipe refers to what he calls the male matrix and the homosocial structure of the institution.

Roman Catholicism, it should be noted here, also makes much out of the image of a male Jesus hanging, nearly completely naked, on a cross. This is an image that can obviously be arousing to men with homosexual sadomasochistic desires. I have also seen homoerotic variations of this image where Jesus is completely naked with an erection while his disciples engage in homosexual activities at the foot of the cross. Further, the position in which Jesus hangs on the cross is strikingly similar to the ways in which people with sadomasochistic desires or erotic interests in bondage are wont to suspend each other from the wall or ceiling (see Reik's [1940] discussion of sexual masochism and the practice of suspension). All this suggests that the priest's sexual orientation can easily be understood as homosexual. Nothing that Stayton says here justifies the need to introduce the idea of a "Thou" orientation that is somehow distinct from the other sexual orientations.

Stayton's other examples of "Thou" orientations seem to be little more than instances of his equivocating with the term "turn on." Therefore, when he says that math, logic, and astronomy can be objects of erotic response because many people are "turned on" by them, he is relying on the fact that "turn on" can mean both intellectually exciting and sexually exciting. For although it is true that many people are intellectually excited by such academic subjects, it seems false that many people are sexually excited by them. And even if someone is sexually excited by, say, astronomy, it does not follow that she sexually desires astronomy (whatever that could mean). If, for example, I am sexually excited by the scent of a woman's perfume, it does not follow that I sexually desire the scent of her perfume (whatever that could mean). Consequently, if Stayton expects us to believe that many people sexually desire astronomy, he has to do much more than simply tell us that many people are "turned on" by it.

Another view that might be thought to question the fundamental role of gender in sexual desire is the view that one of the sexual orientations itself, namely bisexuality, is an example of sexual desire that does not seem directed to any gender in particular. Here, it might be argued, a person has sexual desires toward other people regardless of their gender. Consequently, with bisexuality, it might be continued, we have an example of sexual desire in which, far from playing a fundamental role, gender plays little or no role. But if the gender of the other person is inconsequential in one type of sexual desire, then clearly it is not an essential element in sexual desire. This might suggest, then, that the importance that heterosexuals and homosexuals place on the gender of the person is something peculiar to heterosexual and homosexual desires, not to sexual desire itself.

This, however, is only one interpretation of the phenomenon of bisexuality. On another interpretation the bisexual is just as sexually interested in the gender of his or her partners as the heterosexual and homosexual are, the difference being that the bisexual is interested in both genders. According to this view, some of the bisexual's desires are exactly similar to the heterosexual in that the bisexual also desires sexual interaction with the opposite gender. His or her other sexual desires, however, are exactly similar to the homosexual in that the bisexual likewise desires sexual interaction with a person of the same gender. In both cases the bisexual's desire focuses, as do the heterosexual's and homosexual's desire, on sexual interaction with a person with a certain type of genitals. Where the bisexual parts company from the other two orientations is in his or her not lacking sexual desire for people of both genders.

This view is supported by Tripp's (1988) observation that there is a near universal tendency for bisexuals to say that although they enjoy sexual interactions with both genders, the two experiences are entirely different. As one bisexual man put it, "I have sex with my wife as often as possible and . . . I enjoy it tremendously (so does she!). Sex with men is just different and so exciting that I have to have it also" (Klein and Schwartz, 2001, p. 244). This is so, says Tripp, because the bisexual employs a double value system that enables him to "shift gears" from one gender to the other and enables him to respond sexually to each gender's particular male or female qualities. This suggests that the bisexual's desire is not indifferent to the gender of his partner but is showing the same sort of desire as the heterosexual when engaged with the opposite gender and the same sort as the homosexual when engaged with the same gender.

A similar view is also found in Shively and De Cecco's (1977) two-dimensional model of sexual orientation, a model that was expanded upon by Storms (1978, 1980). On this view heterosexuality and homosexuality are separate and independent factors in which a person can be either high or low. As a result, a person can be either high or low in heterosexuality while at the same time being either high or low in homosexuality. A bisexual, according to Storms, is someone who is high in both heterosexuality and homosexuality (someone low in both is, he says, asexual). There is, however, a terminological problem in putting things this way. For the idea of heterosexuality is normally meant to refer to a sexual orientation that is primarily toward persons of the opposite sex *rather than* toward persons of one's own sex. Similarly, homosexuality is normally meant to refer to a sexual orientation primarily toward persons of one's own sex *rather than* towards persons of the opposite sex. Thus, it is in fact contradictory to say that a person could be both, at the same time and in the same way, high in heterosexuality and high in homosexuality, for to be high in heterosexuality is to be low in homosexuality and vice versa.

One way around this difficulty is to employ instead the idea of heteroeroticism or heterosexual desire and homoeroticism or homosexual desire. These could then refer to the content of a person's sexual fantasies and desires rather than to a person's sexual orientation. Although Storms sometimes speaks this way, at other times he refers to "homoerotic and heteroerotic orientations" and "homosexual and heterosexual eroticism" without ever clearly distinguishing between what he means by these different terms. If, however, one were to make such a distinction, then it could be said that a homosexual is someone who is high in homoeroticism and low in heteroeroticism, while the converse is true of a heterosexual. A bisexual would then be someone who is high in both homoeroticism and heteroeroticism.

It should also be noted, however, that although Storms offers his theory as an advance on the Kinsey scale (1948, 1953), there is nothing in his account that is essentially at odds with Kinsey's scale. The Kinsey scale is a seven-point scale for rating a person's degree of sexual orientation. It ranges from the category of exclusively homosexual to that of exclusively heterosexual, with bisexuality in the middle and varying degrees of heterosexuality and homosexuality on either side. Storms criticizes this scale saying it implies that bisexually orientated persons will have only a moderate amount of heteroeroticism and only a moderate amount of homoeroticism.

But nothing in Kinsey's scale forces us to interpret it this way. Being situated in the middle of the scale need not mean that bisexual persons have less heterosexual desires than do exclusively heterosexual persons or less homosexual desires than do exclusively homosexual persons but only that in addition to their heterosexual desires they also have an approximately equal amount of homosexual desires. This is because nothing in Kinsey's scale implies anything about the amount of heterosexual or homosexual desire. For example, in the category of "exclusively homosexual" there is nothing to imply that a person fitting this category must have high amounts of homosexual desire, only that the desires that he does have—be they few or many, weak or strong—are exclusively homosexual.

This is also why it is problematic that Storms labels people with low amounts of sexual desire as having an asexual orientation, as if asexual were a separate category of sexual orientation. By most indications, people with low amounts of sexual desire are not asexual in the sense that they lack any orientation to the same, the opposite, or both genders. Rather, they seem to be heterosexuals, homosexuals, or bisexuals who because of various problems have lost desire for certain sexual interactions (Basson 2001; Kaplan, 1995). Such persons will typically show receptivity to sexual stimulation in the right circumstances (see, e.g., Cawood and Bancroft, 1996) where this receptivity takes place within an established sexual orientation. (It also seems relevant to note that sexual inactivity within a marriage is usually a signal of other problems within the marriage [Donnelly, 1993]). In cases like these it seems wrong to label the person as having an "asexual" orientation. The usefulness of Storm's account, however, is that by extracting one interpretation of Kinsey's scale, it avoids the ambiguity that Kinsey's presentation contains. It further enables us to differentiate between those who have higher and lower amounts of the various desires.

The reason, then, why a bisexual is not indifferent to his or her sexual partner's gender is because when a bisexual has sexual desire toward another person, his or her desire is, depending on the gender of the desired person, of the same sort desire as that of either a heterosexual or a homosexual. That is, the bisexual is here, like the homosexual or heterosexual, a person of one gender desiring sexual interaction with a person of another (or the same) gender, where the gender of the other person works to give various meanings to the desired sexual interaction. The fact that the bisexual is capable of having sexual desires toward both genders does not mean she is indifferent to the gender of the person's whom she desires; it simply means she finds more genders to be sexually desirable than do the heterosexual or homosexual.

Thus, if we could imagine a case where a male bisexual, for example, has sexual desire toward another male, it would not be a matter of indifference to him that the person with whom he desires sexual interaction is a male. Indeed, his sexual desire toward the other man would be focused, like the male homosexual's desire, on the maleness of the desired person. And this maleness, as I argued, is something that emerges in awareness from a background of awareness of the male genitals. Here, consequently, the awareness of the desired person as someone with male genitals would be an integral element of the sexual desire. And the fact that on another occasion the same male bisexual might desire sexual interaction with a female, similarly focusing on the femaleness of the desired female, does not change this.

With this, the relation of sexual desire to sexual orientation becomes evident. For sexual desire is such that its structure includes the orientation toward a gender. That is, sexual desire is the desire for sexual interaction with a person with male or female genitals where the person, and therefore the genitals too, can be actual, fantasized, or symbolized. But this seems to raise another problem, for genital activity is not a necessary component of sexual activity. That is, kissing, stroking of the legs or hair, and other forms of non-genital bodily caressing can all be sexual activities even if no genital activity is involved. But if this is true, then in what sense can gender, whose essence is the genitals, be fundamental to sexual desire? The answer is provided by noting what was said earlier about the Gestalt relation of the genitals to gender. For here it was seen that although my awareness of another person's gender immediately implicates an awareness of either male or female genitals, such an implication is not a focal point in my awareness. Rather, my awareness of the genitals presents itself as an all-encompassing background that dispenses meanings onto other sex characteristics. It consequently both supports and permeates my awareness of the other person as male or female.

Therefore, although sexual desire aims at sexual activity with another body with male or female genitals, it does not necessarily aim at activity involving the genitals of the other person's body. The important thing is simply that the desired body has the desired genitals, that is, that the person is male or female. Although this might initially seem strange—why desire a body with specific genitals if the genitals are not to be engaged?—a brief reflection on the relation of sexual desire to sexual activity will easily demonstrate this. Consider the case of a heterosexual male who, because of his sexual desire, is engaged in the activity of having a female perform fellatio on him. Now, as far as the simple physical technique of fellatio may go, it seems neither here nor there that the person performing fellatio is a female or male. For it seems a male should be able to perform fellatio as a female. And were the man not able to see or touch the person who was performing fellatio on him, it is altogether unlikely that he would be able to tell the gender of his fellator. Yet, because of his heterosexuality, it would be of paramount importance to him that the person with whom he is having oral sex be a female; that is, it would be crucial to his sexual desire and satisfaction that his partner has a vulva and vagina.

Of course, other things might be important too. It might be important, for example, that his partner have a particular body shape, that she is attractive, or that she has particular feelings toward him. But all such features would enter into consideration only once the person was assumed or perceived to have a vulva and vagina. And this desire that his partner has the requisite female genitals would persist even though he may never desire to engage them in his sexual activities. Why is this? It is because the gender of the desired person is fundamental to sexual desire even though the genitals of the person—that is, the basis of her gender—are not fundamental to sexual interaction.

THE TWONESS OF GENDER IN SEXUAL DESIRE

The gender of the desired person is not, however, the only instance of gender involved in sexual desire. There is also the gender of the person doing the desiring. For, as mentioned earlier, sexual desire always takes place within the context of a person of one gender desiring sexual interaction with a person of another or the same gender. Because of this, in every instance of sexual desire, the element of gender will make its appearance at least twice, namely, once as the awareness of one's own gender and, second, as an awareness of the other person's gender. It is important here not to confuse this idea of the twoness of gender in sexual desire with the idea of opposite genders, for the idea of opposite genders is the idea of maleness and femaleness. But in sexual desire it is not necessary that the two genders be that of male and female, for in homosexual desire the two genders are the same. Twoness here refers simply to the fact that sexual desire involves a person with a gender desiring sexual interaction with another person with a gender regardless of which combination of genders are involved. This twoness of gender is the minimum requisite in which sexual desire can take place (in sexual desires directed to more than one person, then twoness would need to be replaced by threeness, fourness, or some such combination).

The notion of twoness itself is one that holds a distinguished place in the history of ideas. For example, one of the earliest Greek philosophers, Anaximander (600–546 BCE), accounts for the origin of the world in terms of the continual struggling and balancing of pairs of opposites. Thus, the physical features of wet and dry, hot and cold, rare and dense were all seen to be instances of twoness in which one of the elements attempts to overwhelm the other, only later to have to pay recompense for its injustice and itself be similarly overwhelmed. Likewise, Empedocles (492–432 BCE), another early Greek philosopher, saw the origin of all change as being based on the two cosmic principles he called Love and Strife, the former being the principle of unification, the latter that of dissolution. He also personified these principles as the goddess of love and the god of war.

In ancient Hawaiian thought there is also the notion twoness expressed in the idea of the ancestral god Ku and his consort the goddess Hina. Ku, which means "rising upright," presides over the rising sun and hence over the morning. Hina, which means "leaning down," presides over the setting sun and hence over the afternoon. The principle of Ku is expressed in standing stones and upright plants, whereas that of Hina is expressed in flat or rounded stones and trees whose branches lean downward.

Similarly, in ancient China we find the "Appendices" of *The Book of Changes* setting forth the principles of yin and yang, two opposing cosmic forces whose interactions accounted for the flux of the universe. Here yin refers to what is earth, female, passive, soft, wet, and absorbing, while yang refers to what is heaven, male, active, hard, dry, and penetrating. This doctrine of yin and yang and the harmony of opposites later spread into much of Chinese thought. It lies, for example, at the basis of Chuang Tzu's (369–286 BCE) Taoist notion of the equality of all things and opinions. For, according to Chuang Tzu, apparent opposites, such as here and there, beauty and ugliness, and even existence and non-existence, are all relative to the place or situation of the observer. To see this is to see the equality of all things.

In Taoist thinking after Chuang Tzu, the doctrine of yin and yang becomes explicitly related to sexual practices and the idea of a male and female exchange of yin and yang elements through sexual interaction. Thus, in a Taoist work known as *Joining of Yin and Yang,* the author recommends that, to initiate sexual intercourse, the man should "stroke around the neck, then down to the hollow of the collarbone, over the nipples, across the belly, and up to the ribs. Reaching the vulva, massage the clitoris. Suck in energy to vitalize the spirit, and you can see forever and survive as long as the universe" (Cleary, 1999, p. 27). Here we see how the male draws in the female's yin through the touching of her genitals. Although the origin of these early ideas of twoness is obscure, it seems altogether likely that they come from the idea of the sexual interplay of two genders.

Because, however, the object of sexual desire (and thus sexual desire itself) involves not just the awareness of two genders but also a desire for the bringing together (in sexual engagement) of two genders, then it will also involve an extra awareness of two genders in a state of sexual fusion. This awareness might take the form of an image, but its salient feature will be the numerous meanings that surround such awareness. Fisher (1989), from whom I get the term "twoness," refers to this fusion, "whether the action is hetero- or homosexual," as the creation of "an interpenetrating two-body gestalt" (p. 266). Here is why the term "twoness" is perhaps preferable to the similar term "duality." For although the idea of duality carries with it a clear implication of opposition, this does not seem to be an essential aspect of the meaning of idea of twoness. Twoness can refer to opposition, but it also seems to encompass the idea of the interconnectedness of two things, such as an interpenetrating two-body Gestalt.

Although Fisher does not expand here on what he means by a Gestalt, it is easy to see that in the moment of sexual interaction my own body and consequently my own gender—which is also a Gestalt—is organized in relation to another body and thus to another body's gender—which is likewise a Gestalt—in such a way that my gender becomes fused with that of another gender. Through the caress of bare skin by bare skin, the boundaries of my gender in relation to the other person's gender become obscured. Here the meaning of my gender as something that separates me from the desired gender changes as I now see my gender being that which enables me to fuse with the desired gender. This is especially true in those forms of sexual activities that involve the penetration of one body by another. Here my body, which is the bearer of my gender, seems to be both extended by and mixed together with another body, which is the bearer of the other person's gender. Consequently, a Gestalt-like structure emerges that is more than the sum of simply two genders considered individually.

Yet to desire the bringing together of two genders, I must first be aware of the two genders as existing individually and separated from each other. Indeed, it is just this separation that sexual desire seeks to overcome. Consequently, the phenomenology of gender in sexual desire is such that it contains a tripartite structure, namely, an awareness of my own gender, an awareness of the other person's gender, and an awareness of our genders brought together. Let us now look at how each of these elements presents itself in the structure of sexual desire.

When I have sexual desire toward another person, a central feature of that desire is an awareness of the place of my own gender in relation to that of the other person's. A prominent element in this is the awareness of the incompleteness of my own gender. That is, my gender presents itself as only half of an interlocking twoness. The element that appears in my awareness as that which offers completion of my gender is the gender of another person, a gender that, in sexual desire, manifests itself as existing at a distance from mine. In this way my gender appears to me as being cut off from the other person's gender. It is as if my gender, whose incompleteness puts me in search of another gender, brings me to the edge of a precipice from which I can go no farther. Here, in the midst of sexual desire, there looms before me an emptiness that continually reflects back to me a sense of the incompleteness of my own gender.

This emptiness, which permeates my awareness, is a general structure of my gender that can take many specific forms. It can appear, for example, as the particular urgency that characterizes the awareness of the distance of my gender from that of the other person or as the sense of a promise of the completion of my gender that might or might not be fulfilled. Or it can appear as the vacuum that pulls me forward through the ascending phase of the sexual process and as the unknown destination of the subsequent rushing upward. Here the movement is driven by a sense that the gender I lack is somehow waiting for my gender at the end of an uncharted journey. Despite the apparent differences between these forms, each form reveals behind itself the same emptiness at the core of my gender.

It is this aspect of the awareness of my gender in sexual desire that discloses a further feature of my gender. This feature is the dynamic quality of the incompleteness of my gender. For not only does my gender present itself as an emptiness, but it further presents itself as an emptiness that moves toward being filled. This is evident from the fact that I do not experience the incompleteness of my gender in a static way. It does not sit before me as an indifferent feature disconnected from all other structures of my awareness. For in the instant that this incompleteness appears before me, there is already a striving toward completion, that is, toward a solution to my incompleteness. This searching is a movement toward fulfillment, which is the dynamic structure of the emptiness at the heart of my gender. It is a structure that works like a suction, continually pulling toward a filling of the emptiness and thus toward a completion of my gender. Here is the sense in which one can rightly speak of sexual attraction, for even though I am actively searching for that which would fill my emptiness, this carries within it a sense of being passively swept along.

The movement, however, is not one that is unilateral. It is not an instant in which the other person's gender is felt to be stationary and only mine is felt to be pulled in that direction. It is rather a case of bilateral movement. Here I feel my gender being pulled toward the other person's gender while at the same time feeling her gender being pulled toward mine. In the first movement I experience her gender as calling to my gender and as wresting me loose from any apparent sense of completeness. She does this by displaying her gender before me and thus disclosing the incompleteness of my own gender. In doing so she sets in motion the dynamic structure of my emptiness. I am then drawn toward her gender in a search for the filling of the emptiness of my gender. In the second movement I experience my gender as being that which draws her gender toward mine. In this case my gender is not only being swept toward hers but is also sweeping hers toward mine. As she appears before me, I thus feel my gender acting like an undercurrent that slowly draws her gender down into mine. What her gender is being drawn into is the empty space within my gender.

In all this, it is as if she moves toward the empty core of my gender bearing promises of fulfillment and completion. This imminent sense of completion seems to gather force as her gender rushes in on me, positioning itself to overwhelm me much like each of Anaximander's elements overwhelms its opposite. These movements of gender are movements that take place in sexual desire and are thus always movements in relation to the other or desired gender. This shows the interconnectedness of the twoness of gender in sexual desire. In considering the place of my gender in sexual desire, it has been, in the same stroke, necessary also to consider the place of the other gender. For in sexual desire the awareness of my own gender and how it presents itself is necessarily tied to my awareness of the other person's gender and how it presents itself. Although this is similarly true for my awareness of the other gender—since this must also be tied to the awareness of my gender—it is here also possible to focus on the way in which the other gender enters my awareness. In doing so it becomes apparent that my awareness of the desired gender also involves the awareness of the desired gender's incompleteness. Here the other gender likewise appears as only half of a twoness, an incompleteness that also reveals an emptiness.

This emptiness, however, is not something different from the other gender but instead reveals itself in sexual desire as an integral part of the other gender. It is experienced as the place into which the other gender pours as it rushes outward toward me. It is thus something that works to give the feeling that the desired gender is, by its very nature, situated at a distance. And here the dynamic feature of the other gender's emptiness can be seen. For in situating the desired gender at a distance, her emptiness acts to move herself away from my gender.

This moving away, however, is only one feature of the dynamics of the desired gender's emptiness. Another is a sense of an opening outward. In this case it is as if the emptiness is offering a secret path through which the desired gender can be reached. It is much like an escape tunnel through which the desired gender is calling for my gender to help her break free. And as she calls, it is as if I hear her voice echoing through a vault, assuring me that the way toward her is open and free. But this openness is still a distance that I must traverse to reach her: it is an emptiness that her gender has of necessity laid between us.

Although such an experience has clear allusions to the filling of the vagina with the penis, this is only one instance of the filling of an emptiness of gender. For there is also an emptiness that surrounds the penis, especially the erect penis, before it enters the vagina. Here there is a sense of incompleteness that is experienced as the need to have the space around the penis filled, that is, to have the penis contained or held. Here it is the woman's body that moves to penetrate and fill the space into which the penis extends. This is a fact that is captured in Salvador Dali's painting *Young Virgin Autosodomized by Her Own Chastity*. Here a penis is moving to penetrate a woman from behind whose buttocks are surrealistically depicted as though they were also penises. In this way the painting is implying that penetration of the woman will at the same time involve a phallic-like penetration by her buttocks of the spaces around the penis that is moving toward her.

To this it could be objected that the space around the penis is not part of the penis, and so there is no sense of penetration here that is analogous to vaginal penetration. But what is vaginal penetration? In one sense it is simply the filling up of the actual or possible space that lies between the anterior and posterior walls of the vagina. When the vagina is penetrated, it is not the walls of the vagina that are penetrated but simply this space. However, what is essential to this penetration in order that it be experienced as penetration is that the surface of the penis and the walls of the vagina come into contact during the forward movement of the penis against the walls of the vagina or vice versa. Were the penis somehow able to enter the vagina without coming into contact with the vaginal walls, then the act would be lost upon both the male and the female, and neither would undergo it as an experience of penetration.

But the space between the penis and the testicles is also a space, as is the space between the penis and the stomach. These are also spaces that are penetrated in sexual intercourse, and here it is the vagina (or, rather, walls of the vagina together with the labia, the mons Veneris, and the perineum) that penetrates them. And here too the surface of the penis comes into contact with the vaginal walls during the forward movement of the vagina or vice versa. The spaces around the penis are not, of course, internal spaces in the way that the vaginal space is an internal space, and herein lays a fundamental difference for the genders in the phenomenology of sexual intercourse. Still, this should not blind us to the fact that in sexual intercourse there remains a primary similarity between the experiences of the male and the female. This similarity is the infiltration by one body of the spaces intimately associated with those of another body. And this is not just true for sexual intercourse but also holds for the experience of any sexual interaction between the opposite or same genders. Consider the following description by a woman of her sexual interactions with another woman:

There is a yin and yang to sex. When I am yin, I feel open, and I allow my lover to touch me and go with the changes in my body. I feel that I draw her energy into me and when I do, I experience a charge, a rush, a shaking, a flow, a deep sucking in of who she is into my gut. I want her to take a turn at being yin. That means I can be yang. I touch her and push my energy into her. It's not just my touch of her. I visualize that something of my substance goes into her and changes her in a way that she feels exquisite pleasure. (Marrow, 1997, p. 165)

This woman's description is revealing not just because of her relating the idea of the twoness of yin and yang to a sexual exchange (along with their lack of relation to specific genders) but also because of her account of the sensation of the mutual infiltration of body spaces during sex—even though there is no sexual intercourse or vaginal penetration taking place. Here she explains how she feels "open" to her lover's touches and how she draws the other woman's energy in, experiencing a "deep sucking in of who she is into my gut." She also feels she penetrates her lover experiencing that something of her own "substance" enters the other woman.

The description becomes more concrete when she also tells us that "I can run my tongue along her teeth and gums and then penetrate her mouth forcefully with my tongue . . . then go to the ears and lick around and penetrate her ear with my tongue. While I'm doing that I might pull her hair lightly with my hand and gently push my index finger of my other hand into her other ear" (pp. 165–66). (Here it is relevant to remind ourselves what was said earlier about hair stroking and its ability to penetrate the body through the roots of the hair and send sensations rippling under the skin.) In all this it is clear that a central element in the sexual interaction is the interpenetration and mutual filling of two bodies.

Even in sexual interactions that do not involve overt bodily penetration, the basic element of filling an emptiness is still discernible. In the sexual desire for kissing, for example, there is an emptiness that presents itself about the desired gender's lips and mouth. Here too the desired gender places a dynamic emptiness before itself by simultaneously moving away and beckoning after. In this case the offer for the filling of her emptiness is expressed by the beckoning of her lips and mouth. The lips and mouth here present themselves as existing in a space that calls to be filled. The fullness of the desired gender's lips attracts me just because they reveal a space that is being filled. This fullness suggests the possibility of these lips filling my own emptiness. To experience this awareness as a call for kissing those lips, that is, as one directed at my own mouth and lips, I then, at this point, have to experience the emptiness of my own gender as emanating from my own mouth and lips. Of course, in the actual occurrence of sexual desire it is never just the lips and the mouth or just the penis or vagina that present themselves as existing in an emptiness that calls to be filled. It is rather the entire bodily Gestalt whose gender emerges on a background of awareness of the genitals. The focusing on this or that activity is merely the focusing on one particular way of engaging the incompleteness of gender.

The gender of the desired person thus presents itself as an emptiness with at least two dynamic functions. One is the creation of a sense of moving away and being situated at a distance, and the other is the creation of a sense of calling and of offering a way forward. Although these two functions appear opposed to each other, they are nevertheless complementary and supportive to each other. For one of the things that makes me experience a calling to move forward is the fact that the desired gender is situated at a distance and is moving away. None of this means, however, that the person whom I sexually desire is intentionally generating a sense of moving away or calling me forward (though, of course, this intention lies behind much of courtship behavior as, for example, when a woman walks away from a man while glancing back at him over her shoulder). For this is merely the way that her gender presents itself to my awareness whether she intends it or not. Someone whom I sexually desire might have no awareness of me in the moment I have sexual desire toward her. Nevertheless, these two functions will in the same instant make their appearance.

This simultaneous moving away and calling forward lies at the heart of what can be called the exoticism of the desired gender. The desired gender is something exotic because it presents itself as something mysteriously different (and thus moving away) from my gender. This difference fascinates me and thus lures me toward the desired gender, much like an explorer is lured to an unknown land. This feature of exoticism is clearly evident in the nature of heterosexual desire. For here the desired gender is the opposite gender. Consequently, the desired gender is situated on the other side of the primal division between maleness and femaleness.

Thus, the heterosexual male sees the female genitals, the core of the female gender, as being the antithesis of his own. Whereas his genitals extend from the body and carry on their biological sexual process—erection, ejaculation, and loss of erection—in full view, the female's are self-enclosed and for the most part hidden within the body. Here the major changes of the sexual process—lubrication, vaginal contractions, lowering of the uterus, and so forth—take place hidden away in the recesses of the body. Even the exposed parts of her genitals—the labia of the vulva—seem to fold and point inward.

Similarly, for the heterosexual female, the male genitals present themselves as the antithesis of hers. Whereas hers rest within her body, his seem to be, in stark contrast to hers, appendages precariously attached to the surface of his body. (Here, no doubt, is where the expression "opposite gender" is felt to get its legitimacy.) In erection the penis appears to move beyond the body in an attempt to dissociate itself from the body. This attempt even seems carried to fruition in ejaculation from the erection. For here the ejaculate actually does dissociate itself from the male's body. This is quite foreign to the structure and sexual actions of the woman's own genitals. Of course, vaginal fluids can also dissociate themselves from the female body, but such dissociations tend to be more in the form of gradual secretions. In this way, the genitals of each gender will tend to present themselves to the opposite gender as having an exotic quality about them.

Because it is these exotically different genitals that present themselves as the core of the desired gender and because it is the opposite gender that is desired in heterosexual desire, it is quite understandable that in heterosexual desire the desired gender takes on an exotic quality. But how does this view fit with homosexual desire? For what the homosexual desires is a person of the same gender as himself or herself. But if the desired gender is the same as the person who has the desire, then it clearly cannot present itself as having an exoticism based on the structure and actions of a different type of genitals.

The answer here, I think, is that having opposite gender genitals is only one way in which the desired gender can present its exoticism. Another way is that the desired gender can have the same genitals that, though the same in some ways, nevertheless present themselves as being crucially different in other ways. For the homosexual this difference seems to be based on what Tripp (1988) calls a "felt-shortage" of one's own gender. On Tripp's view the homosexual is someone who intensely admires the attributes of same-gender persons. The homosexual does this because he feels himself to be lacking in these attributes. This intense admiration is engaged in to the point that the person begins to eroticize the same-gender attributes and seeks to absorb them into himself by sexually engaging same-gender persons. "It is," says Tripp, "the contrast implicit in this distance which determines a person's appetite for same-sex attributes and, consequently, his readiness to admire them, to eroticize them, and to import still more of them" (1988, p. 76).

Tripp is careful here to point out that it is not the actual difference between the homosexual and the admired same-gender person that is important; rather, it is the perceived distance between them that counts. Thus, "even the confident and utterly secure male who has eroticized male attributes is ready to improve what he has by sexually importing refinements and additions from an admired partner" (1988, p. 78). This is true, says Tripp, for both male and female homosexuals, with the difference that, in contrast to male homosexuals who can easily eroticize an admired male stranger, female homosexuals will usually have an emotional tie to the admired person before the erotization sets in.

This should not be taken to imply, however, that there is anything "pathological" or "abnormal" in the homosexual's felt-shortage. For, as I have argued, the same sort of experience takes place in the purportedly "normal" heterosexual's case. The difference is that while the homosexual has a felt-shortage for his own gender, the heterosexual has it for the opposite gender. One might still try to argue, I suppose, that there is something delusional and hence pathological in thinking one can acquire some of another person's gender through sexually engaging him or her. But if this is how the argument would go, then it is evident that the same argument could be raised in the heterosexual's case. But just as one should reject the idea that, on this ground, heterosexual desire is pathological, so should one reject the similar idea that, on this ground, homosexual desire is pathological.

Here, then, it can be seen how the homosexual finds exoticism in the genitals of persons of his own gender. For in both his felt-shortage of his own gender and his intense admiration of same-gender persons, the homosexual sees the sex characteristics and related qualities of his own gender as something mysteriously just beyond his grasp. Even though he has these characteristics himself, they nevertheless seem to escape him in some inexplicable way. In this way, for the homosexual too, the desired gender presents itself as a simultaneous moving away and calling forward. For the moving away is the distance between himself and the admired same-gender person, while the calling forward is the perceived admirableness of the other person's gender. But it is just this moving away and calling forward that lends an exotic flavor to the desired gender. Consequently, the characteristics of the same-gender person deliver themselves to the homosexual as being exotic. These characteristics, of course, can be numerous, but what lies behind them, what defines them as gender characteristics, is, as I have argued, the genitals. Thus, to find same-gender persons to be exotic is to find same-gender genitals to be exotic. Consequently, the homosexual finds the genitals of persons of his own gender to be exotic.

This general account of the exoticism of the desired gender is supported to some extent by Daryl J. Bem's (1996, 1998) "exotic becomes erotic" developmental theory of sexual orientation. On this theory a person develops his or her sexual orientation by originally seeing the desired gender as different from himself or herself and thus as exotic. What determines whether a child will see the opposite or the same gender as exotic and thus later as erotic is the extent to which the child feels himself or herself to be most similar in gender-role behavior to girls or boys. If, for example, a boy feels himself to be most similar in gender-role behavior to boys, girls will be seen as exotic, and the boy will later tend to eroticize females. On the other hand, if a boy feels himself to be most similar to girls, boys will be seen as exotic, and the boy will later eroticize males. This similarity or dissimilarity will be determined, says Bem, by biological factors like temperament (it is here, and only here, feels Bem, that genetic factors might play a role in sexual orientation).

The trouble with this theory, however, is that it focuses on gender-role behavior as being the exotic and thus erotic element. But gender-role behavior, as argued earlier, has little to do with gender itself, for the decisive feature of gender is the genitals. This would suggest that what the child originally sees as exotic and thus later as erotic—or, better, what stays exotic but also becomes erotic—is the genitals of the dissimilar child (on this version, the reason why a child would see the genitals and thus the gender of another child as being exotic would then be explained by the dynamics of the Oedipal triangle and the process of identification with one of the parents. See Beiber et al., [1962] and Fisher [1989]).

To this it might be replied that the genitals are something that would not be as apparent to a child as would gender-role behavior. But as is evident to anyone who has observed young children, the genitals play a major role in their awareness of themselves and others. Galenson and Roiphe (1974) have shown that by six to seven months of age, boys begin to play with their genitals; that by 10 to 11 months, the same is true for girls; and that for both genders, masturbation is established by 15 to 16 months. This early interest in their own genitals naturally leads children to an interest in the genitals of others. This interest takes a striking turn when they discover, as they quickly do, that not all people have the same sort of genitals. For example, upon seeing his mother's genitals, one two-year-old boy threw his hands up in the air and said, with a laugh, "Peepee gone!" Here was his authoritative statement that her genitals were different from his: he had a penis (peepee), but hers was gone.

Moreover, as Freud (1908, 1910) points out, children as young as three years old already have a notion of sexual intercourse, involving themselves in much speculation and research in an attempt to understand the differences between the genitals of the two genders and the origin of babies (I have seen infants as young as 10 months old engage in interactions resembling the motions of sexual intercourse). This does not mean that such young children have the cognitive abilities to conceptualize fully the definitive role that the genitals play in determining gender, only that even by this early age there is an intense awareness that the genitals play some special role in something.

However, as one study showed, 40 percent of three-year-olds, four-year-olds, and early five-year-olds are able to make the clear connection between a person being a specific gender and the person having that gender's genitals (Bem, 1989). I suspect that this percentage, which is based on an American sample, would even be higher in cultures that, unlike American culture, do not routinely cover up children's genitals, hide adult genitals from the view of children, or avoid discussions of sex with children or avoid sexual behavior in front of children. In Marquesan culture, for example, young children have ample opportunity to observe adults having sexual intercourse, frequently partake in group masturbation, and, by about the age of seven, will play "mother and father." This game involves the boy and girl lying or standing in the face-to-face position for sexual intercourse while their naked genitals come into contact (Suggs, 1966). It seems unlikely that such children are unaware of the genital basis of gender. (See also Goldman and Goldman's [1982] study, which shows North American children to be far behind Australian, Swedish, and British children in their ability to describe the genital differences between the genders.) Consequently, even though it might be gender-role behavior that originally alerts a child to the fact of her similarity or dissimilarity to one or the other gender, it seems that the genitals of the dissimilar gender would quickly become the exotic element of that gender.

This brings us to the third appearance of gender in sexual desire, namely, my gender and the desired gender brought together in an interpenetrating Gestalt of sexual interaction. This third appearance of gender differs from the individual appearances because here the two genders are brought together in such a way that their interpenetration gives rise to a new awareness. It must be seen, however, that this is often a projected awareness that the various movements of our genders present themselves as moving toward. That is, it does not mean that this interpenetration need be taking place as an actual sexual interaction for it to be an element of sexual desire. For sexual desire usually makes its first appearance well before sexual interaction (though, of course, it also continues throughout the sexual process and sexual interaction). It is rather perceived as an element in the desired goal toward which I am both moving and being called. It appears as an image or a complex of meanings surrounding the idea of sexual union of two genders.

This new awareness involves the idea of the process of fusion of my gender with the gender of the other person. Here the fusion appears as a simultaneous filling of the emptiness of each of our genders by each other's genders, an instant that Watts (1958) describes as "a melting warmth between the partners so that they seem veritably to flow into each other" (p. 179). And this is what one would expect from the foregoing analysis of the separate appearances of the individual genders. For in seeing that there is both an incompleteness to each individual gender and a striving toward completeness, the mutual filling of each other's emptiness is the obvious goal of these movements.

But how exactly does this mutual filling appear to awareness? The answer is provided by simply looking to what happens in the actual intimacy of sexual interaction. For what happens here is the basis for the third appearance of gender as an interpenetrating twoness. It might be felt that this means that only someone who has experienced sexual interaction can thus entertain such an awareness; otherwise, how could someone know what it would mean to bring two genders together in an interpenetrating Gestalt? And this might well be true. But since sexual interaction involves not only sexual intercourse but also other warm and physically intimate interactions, including those experienced in infancy, most if not all people will have something upon which to base their awareness of an interpenetrating twoness.

It is noteworthy here that even in early infancy one frequently comes across the bodily interpenetration of mother and infant. For in breast feeding it is common enough that the infant reaches up and puts part of itself (its fingers) in the mother's mouth, perhaps in an attempt to imitate the mother's putting part of herself (her nipple) in the infant's mouth. Here the mother's nipple penetrates the infant's mouth—which, as Ellis points out, is a striking analogy of sexual intercourse—while the infant's fingers penetrate the mother's mouth (the beginnings, no doubt, of some people's sexual practice of having their fingers sucked). Such an event might well be the primal occurrence of bodily interpenetration.

It also cannot escape our notice that in the very process of birth, something that even precedes infancy, another type of bodily penetration occurs. This is the penetration of the fetus into the birth canal from the cervix. Here the fetus penetrates one part of the woman's body by entering it from another. And, significantly enough, that part of the woman's body that is penetrated in this backward fashion by the fetus is just that part (the vagina) that was originally penetrated in a forward fashion by the penis.

Thus, in the moment of sexual fusion, I feel the gender of my partner, her warmth, her scent, her entire femaleness—all of which takes its meaning as femaleness on the background of her female genitals—streaming into my body. (And here is another basic function of smell in sexual desire, for not only does the scent of the desired person direct me toward her body and specifically towards her genitals, but it is also that aspect of her gender Gestalt that streams into my lungs, filling me in a further way with her femaleness.) Through her caress of my bare skin, I feel myself filling with her femaleness in such a way that it merges with my maleness. This is a process of melting in which her femaleness, her gender, seems to dissolve and diffuse itself deep into my core. It is much like the gradual immersion into a warm bath. As the water envelops the body, there is an eruption of tingling that races under the skin. As this subsides, waves of warmth are sent in pulsations deep into the body's core. This warmth, originally felt as the warmth of the water, then loses its sensation of separateness as it diffuses throughout and becomes one with the body.

At the same time I feel my body melting into hers. That is, not only do I feel her femaleness penetrating into me, but I also feel my maleness penetrating into her. The movement here is one of spreading outward and into her body. As I embrace and caress her, my own body seems to disperse over top of hers, spreading out over her like mist on the surface of a pond. In the same moment, however, my body presents itself as seeping into hers, working its way into the emptiness at the core of her femaleness. My maleness seems thus to sink into and commingle with her femaleness, precisely the inverse of what her femaleness is simultaneously doing to my maleness.

This mutual spreading outward and into each other's body—something that Millet (2003) nicely describes as an "unfurling" of bodies joined together—is a process that is bathed in a sense of softness where I feel my gender dissolving within the emptiness of her gender while having her gender similarly dissolve softly within the emptiness of mine. The softness is the sense of receptiveness with which her gender accepts and absorbs mine while mine accepts and absorbs hers. Yet because of the elements of the physical elements of the sexual process—the vasocongestion, myotonia, increased breathing rate, and so on—this softness appears as riding on a wave of mounting tension.

When seen from the phenomenology of gender in sexual desire, this mounting tension is experienced as the mutual filling of the emptiness at the core of each other's gender. It is not, however, that the increasing tension destroys the softness. That is, the sense of the mutual filling of genders does not remove the sense of receptiveness of each gender to the other. Rather, the tension and the softness are mutually supportive, the increase of one giving rise to that of the other. Thus, the more the tension escalates, the softer our merging becomes, while the softer our merging becomes, the more the tension escalates. Or, in other words, the more our genders fill the emptiness of each other's gender, the more receptive to such filling our genders become, and, conversely, the more receptive our genders become to such filling, the more they are filled by each other. It is in this intense receptivity to the other's gender that my own sense of gender is finally brought to a state of fusion with the other gender. Because of this two-way movement of mutual filling, the emptiness of my and the other person's gender here become fused in the form of an interpenetrating Gestalt.

The rising of tension and softness, however, is not the only mechanism that serves to blend one's sense of gender with that of the other person's gender.

Another such mechanism is that of the bursting phase, namely, the experienced pinnacle of orgasm. As was seen in Chapter 2, one of the possible outcomes of the early elements in the sexual process is the arrival at the point in which the rushing-upward phase at last crosses over into the bursting phase. There I referred to this point as involving a bursting of the barrier against which all tensions were straining. With the investigation into the phenomenology of gender in sexual desire, the central meaning of this bursting now becomes evident. For what bursts here is the sense of barrier between genders interlocked in sexual contact. In the buildup to this bursting, the barrier against which I am straining is the barrier that separates her femaleness from my maleness. It is as if in absorbing her femaleness into my maleness, I at last reach a point where that which contained my gender, that which kept her femaleness distinct from my maleness, suddenly bursts at the seams.

As just mentioned, an immediate precursor of this bursting is the experience of a rushing upward. Here, then, the meaning of this rushing upward becomes apparent, for this is the point where I sense the other person's gender suddenly swelling up inside me. No longer being merely absorbed, her gender races in to fill the last corners of the emptiness within me and, with no place left to go, shatters the obstruction between us. Although this shattering and that which precipitates it is experienced primarily as bursting of my gender by that of the other person, the fact that my own gender is likewise felt to be filling hers means that this outward flowing of my gender will also tend to play a role. For in sensing that my gender is being absorbed into hers, I likewise sense what might be called the increasing vulnerability of my gender. That is, the barrier that keeps my gender distinct from hers seems to lose its strength to resist hers.

Therefore, the more I feel my gender penetrating into hers, the less my gender seems to be distinct from hers. Consequently, what her gender rushes into is another gender whose boundaries are becoming more and more vulnerable to rupture. But this vulnerability is just what I desire (here, then, the desire for vulnerability, already present in the phenomenological layer of baring and caressing, makes a further appearance at the layer of gender). In this sense it is both the outward flowing of my gender and the inward pouring of hers that are felt to give rise to the final bursting of orgasm.

Throughout this discussion of the twoness of gender in sexual desire, it has proved necessary to take account of the element of emptiness in gender. As stated earlier in this section, the concept of emptiness is also one that plays a fundamental role in Taoist philosophy and thinking about sexuality. Thus, in the fourth chapter of the *Tao Te Ching* (Lao Tzu, 1927; my translation) Lao Tzu (about 604 BCE–?) tells us that

The Way is emptiness, but forever inexhaustible:
It is an abyss, as if it were the ancestor of all things.
Blunting sharpness, resolving tangles, and softening lights

It subdues all turmoil.
How deep and endless it is.
Whose offspring it is I do not know:
It exists even before the notion of god.

Although scholars disagree about what exactly Lao Tzu means by the Way (Tao in Chinese) or how it could be inexhaustible or blunt sharpness, reading Lao Tzu with a view to understanding sexual desire—which is just what the later authors of the Taoist sex manuals did—allows many of his ideas to fall into place. Lao Tzu himself suggests this reading when he tells us in Chapter 6, "The valley spirit [that is, emptiness] never dies, it is the gateway of the mysterious female." Here we find an explicit connection between never-dying emptiness and the female genitals or "gateway" and thus gender (See also Chapters 10 and 61). And as I have tried to show, the Way to the desired gender is indeed paved with emptiness. That is, the reason I move toward the other gender in sexual desire is because of the emptiness I sense at the core of my own gender, and the reason I feel her thus moving toward me is because of her emptiness, which situates her at a distance and presents her as an opening outward.

This emptiness is, as Lao Tzu puts it, forever inexhaustible, deep, and endless because, as pointed out in an earlier discussion, although my desire is fulfilled in the moment of sexual union, it nevertheless can continue unabated; that is, fulfillment does not mean cessation. It is like an ancestor not only because of the role of sexual desire, and thus emptiness, in human generation but also because it underlies our gender, that primal distinction that cuts its way throughout human existence. This emptiness blunts the sharpness of the urgency of desire, subduing all turmoil, by giving rise to softness. This takes place in the interlocking twoness of the third appearance of gender in sexual desire. Here, in the instant of penetration, the urges of fore-pleasure are momentarily subdued and the turmoil is lost. I do not know whose offspring it is—that is, where it comes from—simply because it is a primitive element in my awareness of gender. It's existing even before the notion of god shows the primordialness of our experience of gender.

With this we have arrived at the place where the account of sexual desire can be filled out by adding the element of gender to its overall structure. As was concluded in the Chapter 3, the object of sexual desire is the mutual baring and caressing as a bodily expression of mutual vulnerability and care. Further, as argued in this chapter, sexual desire is intimately connected with the awareness of one's own gender, the awareness of the other person's gender, and the awareness of these two instances of gender brought together in an interpenetrating Gestalt.

However, neither the desire for mutual baring and caressing nor the desire for the bringing together of two genders is an independent event. They are each fundamental elements woven together in the fabric of sexual desire. For the body I want bare before me in order that I may caress it is not just any body; rather it is at least the body of someone with the desired gender. And what I want to bare before the other person in order that she might return my caresses is not a genderless body; it is rather my body with its specific gender. Thus, to have sexual desire for someone is to desire mutual baring and caressing of someone of a particular gender where both one's own gender and the gender of the other person are seen to be brought together in an interpenetrating Gestalt, an interpenetration that is achieved precisely through the acts of mutual baring and caressing.

As has been mentioned various times throughout this study, the inherent complexity of sexual desire is further complicated by the fact that in many such instances of desire, the person for whom one has sexual desire is also a person for whom one feels romantic love. The time, therefore, has come to focus on the nature of romantic love and its special relation to sexual desire.

5

The Structure of Being in Love

BEING IN LOVE

A central feature of the relation between love and sexual desire is that being in love seems to imply having sexual desire. This is suggested not only by everyday experience but also by the fact that the sort of love that implies sexual desire, namely, romantic love, is also referred to as erotic or sexual love. Although the relation between such love and sexual desire might seem an obvious and natural one, it is difficult to say precisely what the nature of the relation is and why there is such a relation. However, the fact that such a relation appears to exist suggests that to understand fully the nature of sexual desire, its connection to love must also be understood. Yet to do this we must first start with exploring the nature of love itself. For only by understanding the nature of love will we be able to see the way in which its structure relates to that of sexual desire.

The interest in romantic love, like the interest in the sexual process, has an ancient history. Thus, in Plato's (1973) celebrated dialogue the *Symposium,* various persons at a drinking party are called upon to say something about such love. One of the speakers cites a story in which it is said that there were originally three sexes: man, woman, and hermaphrodites, here meaning beings consisting of a man and woman joined together. As a punishment for the hermaphrodites' self-satisfaction, the gods split them in two. Now, consequently, they are always in a state of desperate longing for their other half. It is just this longing for union with the beloved, the dialogue tells us, that is the essence of erotic love.

Despite the striking relevance of this ancient Greek account, various scholars have tried to argue that the notion of romantic love is a construction of modern Western culture (see Averill, 1985; Rougement, 1983; Walsh, 1991). Others, however, have argued against this view pointing to the biological or evolutionary roots of love (Buss, 2003; Fisher, 1995; Mellen, 1981). As I have shown elsewhere (Giles, forthcoming, a; forthcoming, b), there are serious flaws with both the social constructionist and the biological accounts of sexual desire. Since sexual desire is an integral part of romantic love, it seems that there will also be similar flaws with both accounts of love.

Here, however, it is worth noting that a perusal of what has been written about love in diverse epochs and cultures does seem to suggest that the experience of love is one that is common to humankind, an observation that in turn suggests that something is amiss with the social constructionist account (but does not mean that love must be explained biologically). Thus, in the Old Testament we find the poem known as The Song of Songs. Although this poem has been given religious interpretations, most scholars now see the literal historical meaning to be one dealing with human sexual love (Murphy, 1990). It is possibly written by Solomon to a peasant girl and is a dialogue full of expressions of desires and longing for the loved person. The same sort of desperate cravings for union with the loved person can also be found in the 17th-century Sinhalese poem "*Kuveni Asnaya*," or "The Legend of Kuveni" (Holt, 2002). Likewise, in a collection of love songs written in southern China in the early 19th century, we find the poet Jiu Ji-yung declaring,

Now he hates; now he loves. Now he loves, now he hates;
Love and hate, inconstant both. I feel in a daze.
I am like a ship on the high seas, driven to the centre of the ocean,
Unable to reach land on either side. How can I unite with him? (Morris, 1992, p. 128)

Or again, as Jiu Ji-yung beautifully puts it, "You made my heart a flag in the wind; and I could not haul it down" (p. 78). Such romantic outpourings of longing, pain, and fluttering of the heart do appear to fit remarkably well with the Western idea of love.

This idea of love being a state of longing for oneness with the loved person is something that modern thinkers have also laid stress upon. Freud (1930, p. 66), for example, claims that "at the height of being in love the boundary between the ego and object threaten to melt away" and that "against all evidence of his senses, a man who is in love declares that 'I' and 'you' are one, and is prepared to behave as if it were a fact." More recently, social psychologists have offered similar definitions. Thus, Hatfield and Walster (1981, p. 9) have defined this sort of love as "a state of intense longing for union with another" that, if achieved, leads to "ful-fillment and ecstasy" and, if unrequited, to "emptiness, anxiety, or despair." This sort of craving for union with another person seems strangely reminiscent of the sexual desire for merging of genders discussed earlier. The similarity of these sorts of desires, along with the fact that they often make their appearance together, might well be why many people see romantic love and sexual desire to have some sort of essential relation.

Here, however, it is important to keep in mind the distinction between sexual activity and sexual desire. For it can easily be the case that someone who is in love with another person never engages in sexual activity with that person. But this does not mean that he or she does not have sexual desire for his or her beloved. For there are numerous reasons why someone might choose not to act on his or her sexual desires. He or she might, for example, have much guilt surrounding sexual activity, have a fear of preg-nancy or disease, be single and feel that sex outside marriage is wrong, and so forth. But having such ideas or feelings is quite compatible with having sexual desire. So it cannot be concluded that love and sexual desire have no basic connection simply because some people have no sexual activity within their love relationships.

Yet the relation between being in love and having sexual desire does not seem to be such that if a person has one of these desires, he or she must also have the other. For everyday experience suggests that a person can have sexual desire without being in love (I will explore this point later). In what follows I shall examine some of the better-known theories of love before presenting a phenomenological analysis of being in love and the diverse paths it can take. This will then help to reveal its relation to sexual desire. But before I set out on this project, it will be useful to clarify some of the peculiarities surrounding the use of the word "love."

It is a cause for some wonder that in English the word that we use to denote one of our deepest and most meaningful experiences can also be used to describe our relation to various activities or objects to which we are merely positively disposed. I may say, for example, both that I love someone and that I love playing cards or love a certain vase. Despite the use of the same word in each of these instances, there is, however, an important difference that separates the first use of the word "love" from the other two. For although in each example "love" functions as a transi-tive verb, only in the first example can it also function as an intransitive verb. Only when I love someone can I, strictly speaking, be said to be *in* love. It is true we can take the intransitive expression "in love" and, mak-ing it transitive, say such things as "I am in love with this vase," but in these cases—when what we claim to be in love with is not a person—it is evident that "in love" is being used metaphorically as a convenient hyper-bole. This is suggested by the fact that when it is left in the intransitive form, as when I declare simply, "I am in love," it is normally understood that what I am in love with is a person. Of course, someone could always claim to be non-metaphorically in love with a vase or some other physical object, but then it would seem that the person has used fantasy to endow the object with human-like qualities and that it is the fantasized projection of the object that the person believes herself to be in love with.

Why, then, must it be a person with whom I am in love? Why cannot I be, strictly speaking, in love with a vase? The most obvious answer to this question is because only a person is capable of loving me back. But why should it matter to me if that with which I am in love is capable of loving me back? Plainly because in being in love with another, I want that person to love me back. This is a point that is well made by Sartre (1943, p. 375) when he says, "love is the demand to be loved." Sartre's point is based on a phenomenological analysis, but it is also a point that would be predicted on the basis of equity and social exchange theories of interpersonal attraction. For according to these views, what persons in a social relationship want is that the ratio of their own inputs to outcomes is equal to the ratio of the other person's inputs to outcomes (Byers et al., 1998; Hatfield and Rapson, 1993; Sprecher, 1998). This is because the lack of equity here could be seen to create a cognitive dissonance that the person would then be motivated to eliminate. Consequently, to be in love with someone would be to invest a high amount of input into a relationship that, if the other person did not reciprocate to an equal level, that is, show love back, would naturally lead to an uncomfortable dissonance. It is therefore understandable that love wants love in return.

Some psychologists, however (e.g., Mills and Clark, 1982), have questioned the equity theory of love claiming that what they call "communal love" guides romantic relationships more that does considerations of equity. In communal love, persons are more concerned about the welfare of each other and benefiting each other than they are about ratios of inputs to outcomes. And this, of course, might be true in many cases, especially when it comes down to mundane concerns about the give-and-take of everyday goods and services (though in many other cases it might not be true). But when it comes to the exchange of love itself, then it seems wrong to say that people in love are unconcerned about equity and any lack of reciprocation. For the very essence of romantic love seems to be that it longs for just this reciprocation.

However, one must be careful here. For being in love is not just the demand to be loved: I may demand to be loved and yet not love the person on whom I place this demand. I may, for example, want to be loved merely because I am narcissistic and being loved feeds my narcissism. But in such an instance I am clearly not in love with *the person* whom I want to love me. Further, although being in love may be to want the one I love to love me back, this still does not explain what it is that I want to do to the other person or what is it I want the other person to do back to me.

(And herein lies the lacuna in Sartre's account, for although he gives subtle descriptions of the diverse ways in which a person in love will attempt to control the other person's love while at the same time wanting the beloved to give freely of her love, the question of what love itself is—that is, what it is that is being controlled and wanted to be given freely—is never fully addressed.) To understand what being in love is, we must therefore go straight to the question of what it is that I want reciprocated in this way.

Although there is a wide range of literature on interpersonal attraction that has some relevance to the notion of love, various findings (e.g., Rubin, 1974) seem to suggest that romantic love operates in a way that diverges fundamentally from other forms of liking or interpersonal attraction. This distinction is borne out when we consider the ways in which love is known to differ from liking. There is, as has been mentioned, the special relation that love has to sexual desire. Liking does not seem to have such a close connection to overt sexual desire. One can begin to desire sexually a person whom one used merely to like, or one can begin to like a person toward whom one originally only had sexual desire. But in neither case does the development seem to be an integral part of the liking process. The liking of friendship does not, as a matter of course, imply overt sexual desire, and sexual desire seems, if anything, to lead more to love than to merely the liking of friendship.

Secondly, while the gender of the other person does not seem, for most people, to play a crucial role in determining which persons one can like, it does seem to play such a role in determining which persons one can fall in love with. While it is true that some persons can fall in love with persons of both genders, here I would argue that, for essentially the same reasons given earlier in the discussion of bisexuality, the gender of the loved person is never a matter of indifference and is in fact crucial to the nature of the love. Of course, in the feelings that make up liking, the gender of the other person is also never a matter of indifference, if for no other reason than the meaning of gender points beyond mere liking to the prospect (or lack of prospect) of sexual desire. However, there seems to be nothing in the nature of liking itself that implies that people will tend to like persons of only one gender.

Thirdly, in contrast to liking, which develops gradually, love seems to make its appearance swiftly. This is one of the meanings, no doubt, of the expression "to fall in love." For falling is not something one does slowly. In an instant, one slips and plummets over the cliff, racing through the air at unbearable speeds. This falling can have its origin in the most diverse of backgrounds. In one case, perhaps I meet someone on different occasions but do not take much notice of her. However, during one of our meetings, I seem to see her more deeply than I had previously. Suddenly I sense her attractiveness: the way she tilts her head, her smile, and the way her gaze seems to penetrate me. In an instant, I feel myself drawn to her, to want to be near her, to want to know her. All of a sudden, I find myself filling with romantic desire for her.

In another case, perhaps the person is someone I have known well for a long time. She is a good friend and someone whose company I enjoy. Perhaps there are even sexual undertones between us. Even so, it would be wrong to say I am in love with her. But then on one occasion, things abruptly change. Something she says, the way her hand accidentally brushes mine, or perhaps her altered way of looking at me unexpectedly sets my love in motion. Now I look at her in a new light, now I cannot stop thinking about her.

In a further situation, it might well be love at first sight. A new person suddenly appears in my world, her attractiveness shaking me loose from all other projects and plans. Here the appearance of my love is simultaneous with the appearance of the loved person. In each of these cases the appearance of love seems to be anything but gradual.

Fourthly, although liking seems to be a reasonably stable relation, love often appears to be more fragile and volatile. As is well known, persons in love can see their feelings swept away in a moment. Here, for innumerable reasons, intense feelings of love can suddenly evaporate, explode into hate, or find themselves looking elsewhere. An awareness of this fragility is often manifested in the sense of insecurity that can attend being in love. Moreover, this sense of insecurity is something that can grow with the intensity of the love. For the more intense the experience of love, the more catastrophic the lover feels its end would be. In such cases the lover seems aware that the structure he or she has entered shares something in common with a house of cards: here too things could suddenly come tumbling down. In this way romantic love also differs from other forms of love relationships. In familial or parental love, for example (something I will come to in the next section), the experience of love tends to persist through various difficulties. It is not a regular occurrence for parents and their children to "break up" and end their relationships in the way that it is for lovers.

Although some evidence suggests that not everyone experiences love in this fragile and volatile way (Dion and Dion, 1973), this might well have to do with differences in the experience of love at its various stages of development. In the early stages of love, people are often overwhelmed with the newness of the situation, with learning about the other person, and with adjusting their lives to the presence of the loved person. Clearly, this a more fragile and volatile state of affairs than later in the relationship when both persons have come to know each other well and have built lives around each other.

The fact that a love relationship might develop in this way should not, however, lead us into accepting the apparently common view that the intensity of the experience of love necessarily diminishes over time. While this plainly does happen for many people, any observer of human relations can easily discern that there are also people who remain as intensely in love with their partners as they did when they first met. What changes here are simply the newness of the situation and the rapidity of the adjustments in one's life.

A fifth way in which liking differs from love is that, while liking is often thought to be based on actual rewards that persons give each other in an interaction, the intensity of love seems to be more connected with the persons' anticipation or even fantasizing of the future rewards that the relationship has to offer. It is well known, for instance, that the person in love is continually contemplating the next meeting with the loved person: when they will see each other again, where they will go, and what they will do. A person in love will spend much time imagining what it will be like to see the beloved again, what it will be like to kiss her lips, smell her hair, and hear her laughter again. Even once the lover is in the arms of the beloved, there is still frequently a sense of expectancy and excitement about what is to come. This projection to the future directs the gaze of love forever forward, tying it precariously to imagined possibilities.

Finally, while experiences that are normally thought to be noxious or punishing—for example, suffering, frustration, rejection, and fear—tend to reduce liking, they appear not only not to reduce love but even to intensify it (see Berscheid and Walster, 1974). Thus, it is common enough to see relationships in which one of the partners responds to rejection by the other by clinging all the more intensely to the rejecting partner. Here the rejected partner suddenly experiences an intensification of the love he has to the person who is about to leave him. Even though such treatment at the hands of the beloved might increase feelings of love, it will probably decrease feelings of liking. The practice of relentlessly pursuing an ex-lover—even to the point of stalking her—often seems driven, at least in part, by such intensified and desperate feelings of love. Or again, someone who is continually frustrated in her attempts to have her lover show his feelings or respond to her in a desired way can react to such frustrations with deeper feelings of love and the determination to change him.

Nothing here, however, should be taken to imply that there will never exist instances of interpersonal attraction that appear ambiguous and seem to lie somewhere between the liking of friendship and the love of romantic desire. The intense feeling for or thoughts about a same-sex best friend held by an apparently heterosexual person might be a case in point. A person with such feelings might, for example, display no overt sexual desire for the best friend and not be aware of having swiftly or abruptly developed his feelings for the other person but nevertheless experience his feelings and desires in the friendship in a volatile and fragile way, fantasize about seeing the person again, and even cling to the other person in the face of rejection.

I think, however, that any ambiguity between liking and romantic love here is only an appearance of ambiguity and not a real ambiguity. For were such feelings to manifest themselves in a relationship, most people, I feel, would suspect that there was more to the attraction than mere friendship (even more than "best friendship"). The fact that the person is experiencing his feelings for the other person in a volatile way, fantasizing about seeing the other person, and clinging to the other person, even when being rejected, would strongly suggest that at some time there was in fact an abrupt onset of feelings and, further, that somewhere below the person's immediate awareness there are sexual desires for the other person. This in turn would suggest that the person's desires are in fact ones of romantic (homosexual) desire and not those of mere friendship.

These various ways in which love differs fundamentally from liking has encouraged investigators to develop distinct empirical techniques and theoretical accounts for both assessing and explaining romantic love. The result of this work has been the appearance of a variety of theories, many of which approach the notion of love from quite different perspectives. Walster and Berscheid (1971), for example, give an account where they argue that love is an emotion and therefore will be explicable in terms of Schachter's (1964) two-component theory of emotion. Using this theory Walster and Berscheid suggest that a person will experience love when (1) he or she is intensely aroused physiologically and (2) situational cues indicate that it is appropriate to label the arousal as "love."

Although there is evidence to support the two-component view (for example, Dutton and Aron, 1974), it does not seem that all persons recognize emotional arousal as being a part of love (Dion and Dion, 1973). One way of explaining these findings would be to see that the two-component theory is not so much an account of what is involved in love as it is a causal explanation of one of the ways someone might develop a romantic interest in another. The fact that persons might fall in love under emotionally arousing conditions would help to explain why love, in opposition to liking, tends to be swift in its onset. A good example here comes from D. H. Lawrence's (1922) "The Horse Dealer's Daughter," where the characters Jack Ferguson and Mabel Pervin fall suddenly in love during the intensely emotional circumstances in which Ferguson saves the Pervin from an attempt of suicide by drowning. Here the situational cues—the man's display of intense care in the act of saving, the intimate acts of drying, undressing, and changing of the woman—all work to suggest that it might be appropriate to label the arousal as love. Indeed, the meaning that all this takes on for the woman becomes plain when, upon asking "Who undressed me?," and receiving the reply "I did" from the man, she then asks "Do you love me, then?"

However, after someone has fallen in love in such emotional circumstances—which is not to say this is the only way of falling in love—then the arousal or feeling component of love, as opposed to certain nonemotive components, need not be experienced as an essential element of love. This is why it is wrong to say, as many people do, that love is essentially an emotion. For although emotive elements frequently accompany and blend themselves with the other elements of love, the degree to which the emotive elements make their appearance is something that is highly variable, even to the point of not appearing at all. There are, however, other components of love that do not have such a liberty, for with their disappearance, love itself disappears. Just what these components are is something I will come to shortly.

Sternberg (1986) offers a different theory in which romantic love is presented as being one sort of love that, like other sorts, is explicable in terms of a "triangle" of the basic components of intimacy, passion, and decision/commitment. According to Sternberg, these three components are all important though varying parts of loving relationships. The different types of love can therefore be explained by the way in which the strength of each of these components varies relative to the others. "Companionate love," for example, is said to be high in intimacy and decision/commitment but low in passion, while "empty love" is supposed to be low in intimacy and passion but high in decision/commitment.

Unfortunately, Sternberg does not explain why a relationship that has little intimacy or passion deserves the title of love, even that of "empty love." Indeed, saying that a relationship of "empty love" is a type of love sounds very much on par with saying that a decoy duck is a type of duck. And just as most people would reject the idea that a decoy duck is a type of duck, so, I feel, most people would reject the idea that empty love is a type of love.

In contrast with the other types of "love," Sternberg presents romantic love as being high in intimacy and passion but low in decision/commitment. But again, claiming that romantic love is low in decision and commitment seems more like stipulation than analysis. For nothing in the experience of romantic love suggests that the individual in love need be low in her decision or commitment to the person she loves. On the contrary, a person in the throes of romantic love normally seems to feel she has found the perfect partner and begins to imagine a future with the beloved. Such ideas hardly seem to be instances of "low decision/commitment."

As for the passion component of romantic love, Sternberg sees this as being "highly and reciprocally interactive with intimacy" (p. 122) and also as being sometimes predominated by sexual needs, though, strangely enough, he does not attempt to explain why either of these might be the case. It is also peculiar that Sternberg seems to think it is only passion that is related to "sexual needs," for intimacy itself is something that also is strongly connected to sexual desire. Indeed, a couple's having intimacy without the intimacy leading to sexual desire is an unlikely situation. This is because as such intimacy deepens, it naturally leads to desires for the intimacy of sex. For only in such an exchange does intimacy find itself fulfilled.

Yet another theoretical approach to love is Hazan and Shaver's (1987) attachment theory of love. Hazan and Shaver argue that love is best conceptualized as an attachment process. They refer to the work of Bowlby (1969, 1973, 1980), who studied the processes whereby infants forged attachment bonds to their primary caregivers and argue that adult romantic love can be "translated" into or understood in terms of these early attachment bonds—a view that is basically Freud's Oedipal theory of the ontogeny of love. In their study Hazan and Shaver found that Bowlby's three attachment styles (secure, avoidant, and anxious/ambivalent) are about as prevalent in adulthood as other researchers found them to be in infancy. These results were interpreted as giving some support for the view that childhood attachment styles might provide the basis for different forms of adult romantic relationships (see also Morrison et al., 1997).

Although this view is useful in pointing to the developmental origins of love, it does not explain the differences between attachment and love, how it is that the same thing (that is, love) can be expressed in three such distinct ways, or what exactly it is that the secure, avoidant, and anxious/ambivalent styles have in common, that is, why they all deserve to be listed under the title of love. In other words, it does not explain the nature of love itself.

And similar things could be said about Lee's (1977) well-known typology of the styles of loving. Lee's view is that there are six styles of loving, namely, what he calls *eros, storge, agape, ludus, mania,* and *pragma*. The *eros* style of loving, for example, focuses on the sexual aspect of love, while *storge* aims more at quiet affection. *Agape* refers to a style of loving that is other-focused and *ludus* to a playful style of loving in which love is a pleasant pastime with little commitment. *Mania* is then said to be a combination of *eros* and *ludus* and *pragma* a combination of *ludus* and *storge*. This theory has received much attention and development, especially by Hendricks and Hendricks (1986, 1993). The problem, remains, however, that, like the other accounts just mentioned, it is one that also stops short of telling us what love itself is. That is, although we are told of the different ways in which people display their love, we are left none the wiser as to what it is that people are displaying in different ways.

Part of the difficulty, I feel, is that many theories of love have neglected to deal with love from the place where its inner structures can most easily be discerned, namely, from the place in which love presents itself to the awareness of someone in the throes of love. Such an attempt to see love from the inside, as it were—that is, to give a phenomenological account—makes it much more difficult to overlook the way in which the constitutive elements of love structure our awareness of our relation to the loved person. Yet only in disclosing this structure of awareness can we hope to have an adequate understanding of love itself.

An important step in this direction, however, is given by May (1969), who says, "the paradox of love is that it is the highest degree of awareness of the individual self and the highest degree of absorption in the other" (p. 308). This gives us a good starting point because it suggests that love as an experience must be understood as a complex of simpler constituents, namely, an intense, simultaneous awareness of the self and the other (or, as I would prefer to put it, constructed image of the self [see Giles, 1997]).

Although May feels it is a paradox to be immersed in such an awareness, the "paradox" disappears, it seems, once we see *how* it is that we are aware of self and other. For if the earlier definitions are taken into account, it appears that this awareness must involve the elements of longing, craving, or desire. And desire must be desire for something. Therefore, if I love someone, my absorption in that person will be in the form of intense desires toward that person while at the same time intensely desiring that the person I love bears similar desires toward me. Consequently, the awareness in love is an awareness of myself and the person I love tied by the relation of desire. This would help to explain why love seems to be based on anticipation and fantasizing of future rewards, for in desiring something, especially in powerfully desiring it, we often anticipate and fantasize about what it would mean or what it would feel like to fulfill the desire. It also suggests one of the connections between love and sexual desire.

LOVE AS THE DESIRE FOR VULNERABILITY AND CARE

The question then arises: What are the contents or objects of these desires? That is, what is it someone desires when he or she experiences love? Again, an answer is suggested by noting what was said previously, namely, that an integral feature of romantic love seems to be sexual desire. For if love is related in this way to sexual desire, it might well be because love shares a common structure with sexual desire. Looking back to what has already been discovered about sexual desire, it will be recalled that the object of sexual desire was found to be mutual baring and caressing. This baring and caressing was in turn seen to be a physical expression of the desire for vulnerability and care.

Turning now to the experience of love, what presents itself to awareness is a similar structure. For here what is disclosed are also the desires for vulnerability and care. In this case, however, the characteristic structure of these desires—a structure that distinguishes them from mere sexual desires—is that the desires here reach beyond physical vulnerability and care (that is, beyond baring and caressing) to grasp also at psychological vulnerability and care. (Here the idea of psychological vulnerability and care is meant to refer to all aspects of our mental constitution that might be vulnerable and thus in need of care. This will typically, though not necessarily, include the aspect of emotional vulnerability.) That is, at the very core of the experience of love lies a complex of intense desires involving the desire to be vulnerable before another person in order that one may be nurtured or cared for by that person and, at the same time, the desire to have the other person vulnerable before oneself in order that one may nurture or care for that person.

Here too it must be seen that the object of desire is one that is permeated with diverse meanings. In this way the element of vulnerability carries with it both the meanings of "psychologically in need" and "susceptible to injury or harm." That is, gazing at the path of one meaning immediately leads us—like watching the shooting star within the meteor shower—to notice the path of the other. Here we see that to be psychologically in need is also to be susceptible to a form of injury. Consequently, although vulnerability as a component of love typically bears the meaning of being in psychological need, the fact that it also bears the meaning of injury or harm shows that both these meanings will often play a fundamental role in various instances of love. Indeed, as I shall try to show, the very fact that the two meanings are so closely related suggests that the feature of injury or harm will be intimately woven into the fabric of any love relationship, at least in the form of an ever-present possibility on the horizon of awareness.

For now it should be noted that the notion of care is also one that has various meanings. Heidegger (1927), for example, sees care (*Sorge* in German) as one of the fundamental ways in which human existence is related to the world. This is because, to be human is already to care in some way about the world: human existence is such that it is never purely neutral toward the world. Further, according to Heidegger's phenomenological analysis, other relations that resemble care, such as will, wish, dependence, and urge, are all derivable from the more basic relation of care.

On this view, then, care is a primordial relation we have to things and thus means "take notice of or have concern for." Here there is no particular object of or way in which we show care. In this instance care refers simply to the general and non-neutral engagement we have with the things about us. Such an engagement encompasses, of course, the person we love. But our engagement with the loved person is different from our engagement with other objects in the world. The care shown here is of a different order than merely taking notice of or having concern for something. To arrive at the place where care becomes a specialized element of desire within the context of love, its most appropriate meaning should be described as "to look after or show concern for fulfilling the psychological needs of someone." Here, the object of care—the needs of someone—and the way in which we show concern—desiring to fulfill the needs—are much more specific. Still, these two meanings are clearly related. For the only way I can look after or show concern for fulfilling the needs of someone is if I have the ability to take notice of or have concern for the world about me, part of which is the needs of the person I love.

With these definitions of vulnerability and care in place, the relation between the element of vulnerability and the element of care in love becomes evident. For the desire to be psychologically in need before someone already suggests the desire to have someone look after or show concern for one's needs. And the same could be said about the reciprocal desire for the other person to be psychologically in need.

The notion that care is an element of love is one that seems obvious. For a fundamental feature of the experience of love is the desire to minister to the needs of the person one loves while at the same time desiring to have one's own needs ministered to by that person. This sort of tending to and showing concern for the needs of another person while having the other person respond similarly to one's own needs is something that can best be described as mutual care. This is supported by the work of various researchers (e.g., Fromm, 1956; Kelly, 1983; May, 1969) who identify a similar notion of care as being an integral part of love.

The element of care as a part of love is likewise evident in non-Western cultures. The Mangaians from the Cook Islands, for example, also see care as being essential to love. As one Mangaian man explains, "What is being in love? It is caring about someone, taking care of someone, showing care" (Harris, 1995, p. 120). Further, the Japanese psychiatrist Doi (1981) argues that the Japanese notion of *amae*—a word that cannot be directly translated into English but that involves the idea of "the desire to be cared for"—is, in Japanese culture, an inseparable concomitant of love. Despite the lack of an equivalent word in English for *amae,* Doi nevertheless feels that the phenomenon that *amae* refers to is a universal aspect of love (he suggests that Balint's concept of "passive object love" and, to some extent, Freud's concept of identification capture the idea of *amae*).

When care is understood as the element in love that encompasses the feature of looking after or showing concern for someone's needs, then the notion of identification with the loved person, an element that some theorists see as playing a role in love, can easily be recognized as a relative of care. Thus, Balint (1948) argues that an essential element of love is identification with the loved person in which his or her interests, wishes, and so forth are seen to be about as important as one's own. Such identification, however, seems essentially related to the notion of care just given. For inasmuch as I see the loved person's interests and so forth as being about as important as my own, I care about her interests to the same sort of degree that I care about my own. Therefore, given that I care about my own interests, my identification with the person I love has embedded within it my care for the person I love. It is worth noting that May (1969) even goes as far as to refer to this sort of identification as care itself. For

May, care is "a state composed of the recognition of another, a fellow human being like oneself; of identification of one's self with the pain or joy of the other; of guilt, pity, and the awareness that we all stand on the base of a common humanity from which we all stem" (p. 285).

Here too, I feel, is where the notion of idealization might have some relation to the experience of love. Various people (for example, Averill, 1985; Balint, 1948; Jankowiak and Fisher, 1992) have tried to argue that the process of idealizing one's partner is a basic feature of romantic love. Here the person in love overestimates certain qualities of the beloved and sees them in an unrealistically positive light.

While such idealization plainly occurs in some love relationships, I see nothing in the nature of love itself that implies idealization is a fundamental aspect of love. Idealization can occur in contexts other than love—as when someone idealizes an admired role model—and many people in love have only fully realistic perceptions of their beloved. Where the notion of idealization perhaps gets its foothold in some theories of love is in its relation to the notion of care. For to care strongly about another person—an essential feature of the experience of love—is something that can also be an expression of the mere idealization of the other person. That is, because someone sees another person in an unrealistically positive way, he might want to demonstrate his admiration by bestowing much care on that person. Because of this, it might seem that the desire to care—which is fundamental to love—must be motivated by idealization. But it should be obvious that the desire to care can also be motivated by non-idealized romantic attraction to the person. Here there need be nothing unrealistic or delusional about my perception of the loved person; here I simply see her and am attracted to her for what she is.

Unlike care, however, the idea of vulnerability as an element of love is one that has received little notice. This is odd because in perusing the literature on love one regularly comes across references to the importance of vulnerability, of being able to be vulnerable to the other person, of being attracted to the vulnerability of the other person, and so forth. Despite this, different accounts of love either ignore the element of vulnerability completely or devote little attention to it, treating it as merely a peripheral aspect of love. Yet when we examine other elements that are said to play a central role in love—for example, intimacy (Harvey, 1995; Jankowiak, 1995; Sternberg, 1986), trust (Driscoll et al., 1972; Holmes and Rempel, 1989; Milsten and Slowinski, 1999), and self-disclosure (Altman and Taylor, 1973; Byers and Demmons, 1999; Rubin et al., 1980)—what we discover is that they all cluster around the more basic experience of vulnerability.

Thus, if one considers the experience of intimacy, one can easily see its relation to vulnerability. To achieve the deep sort of intimacy required in love, we must be willing to put ourselves at risk and place our private and innermost workings in each other's hands. That is, we must divulge ourselves to each other and, through such a sharing of personal feelings and information, enter into a state of mutual psychological vulnerability. And here we see the central role that vulnerability plays within the experience of intimacy.

This also brings us to an understanding of the relation of vulnerability to self-disclosure. For the sharing of personal feelings and information, which establishes the mutual vulnerability of intimacy, is just what is involved in self-disclosure. It is the lowering of defensiveness and an exposure of the vulnerable aspects of ourselves. Giffin and Patton (1976) give the example of a girl who nervously self-discloses to a male classmate that she had experienced an attempt of rape on the previous night. This is personal information by which, in disclosing, she renders herself quite vulnerable to her conversational partner. In doing so, say Giffin and Patton, she has shown not only positive feelings toward her male classmate but also that she trusts him.

It is in a similar manner that we can explain the importance of trust. When seen from the context of a love relationship, trust is best understood as the expectation not to be betrayed on a personal level, that is, not to have one's needs disregarded or certain confidences broken. But I can be thus betrayed only if I have placed myself in a vulnerable position before the other person, that is, if I am psychologically in need before that person or have shared confidences. It is apparent, therefore, that the importance we place on trust in love can, like the importance of intimacy and self-disclosure, similarly be traced back to the more basic experience of vulnerability.

A possible objection here—one that echoes a previous objection about vulnerability and sexual desire—is that although vulnerability may be present in love, this does not mean that it is something we desire. Perhaps vulnerability is merely a necessary but undesired consequence of the interpersonal closeness involved in love. However, once we allow that the desire for care is basic to the experience of love, then it seems we must also allow that the desire for vulnerability is likewise basic to the experience of love. This follows from the fact that the desire for care can be understood as an element of love only if it is seen in its relation to a corresponding desire for vulnerability. For if we remove the desires for vulnerability from their corresponding desires for care, what we are left with will fall short of what we normally understand by romantic love, for I can easily want to care and be cared for without experiencing love. I might, for example, merely want to set up a mutually supportive relationship with someone that is built on reciprocal care, none of which implies the existence of romantic love.

Although such a relationship might well be described as one that involved love, such love would be the love of friendship and not the love of romance. This is because although I here desire to care for the other person, I do not likewise desire that she be in need of my care (that is, that she is vulnerable before me). Similarly, although in this instance I desire that the other person might care for me, I do not also desire that I am vulnerable before that person (that is, that I am in need of her care). In such a relationship, even though I desire to care for the other person, I might well be indifferent to or even dismayed by the fact that the other person is in need of my care and vulnerable before me. Consider the case of a devoted physician or nurse who cares for her patients. Here is an instance where someone might desire to care and yet not desire the other person's vulnerability. Likewise, I might also be unhappy with the fact that I am vulnerable before the other person. I might, for instance, be a patient who, despite my desire to be well, is nevertheless in need of care. Here the element of vulnerability is indeed an undesired aspect of the relationship, and, consequently, the desire to be cared for here would not be an element of love (my desires here also fall short of love because I do not desire reciprocity; that is, I as a patient do not likewise desire to care for the physician or nurse or desire that she be vulnerable before me).

However, once we introduce the desires for reciprocal vulnerability, then the relationship changes in a dramatic way. Here I not only desire to be cared for by the other person, but I now also desire to be in need of care before the other person. Further, I not only deeply want to care for the other person, but I also yearn to have the other person to be in need of my care. With these desires, my relation to the other person has acquired the essential elements of love.

Another reason for seeing the element of vulnerability as a basic constituent of love is that it enables us to account for some of the central features of love that distinguish it from liking. Thus, it seems that the experience of vulnerability underpins much of the fragility and volatility of love. For the experience of vulnerability is, as I have just argued, an unstable state. That is, it is a state that cries out to us as demanding a solution. This is why although, in love, I desire to be vulnerable before the loved person, I do so only in order to be cared for. Here care is experienced as the longed-for response to vulnerability. Nevertheless, the other person's response of care does not remove my desire for and sense of vulnerability. For these continue by the very fact that I am in love with the other person. It is these that drive my continued desire to be cared for, that is, my continued experience of love. It is therefore clear how love, which is filled with the experience of vulnerability, is something that remains highly volatile and fragile.

In addition, the element of vulnerability also enables us to account for the fact that normally noxious experiences seem to intensify love. One explanation of this could be that such experiences confirm the fact that one is vulnerable before the other person, that is, that one of the basic elements of love is present in the relationship. Of course, what is desired in love is to be vulnerable before the other in order to be *cared for*. But as I have tried to show, the experience of vulnerability is one that bears not only the meaning of "in need of care" but also the meaning of "susceptible to injury or harm." It is therefore no mystery that someone who loves another and yet fails to have the other person respond to his or her vulnerability with care might nevertheless accept that suffering, frustration, rejection, and fear are at least an acknowledgment of his or her vulnerability (an essential element in love) before the loved person.

We are now in a position to see what is involved in the phenomenological structure of being in love. When I am in love with someone, I experience myself as being enmeshed in a network of desires, and what I desire is that (1) (a) the person I love be vulnerable before me in order that I may care for her and also that (b) I may be vulnerable before her in order that she may similarly care for me. Further, since to love is to want to be loved, then another component of my being in love is my desire that (2) (a) the person I love desires to be vulnerable before me in order that I may care for her and also that (b) she desires me to be vulnerable before her in order that she may care for me. In both (2) (a) and (2) (b), the object of my desires is the desires of the other person. Thus, (2) is merely my wanting the person I love to have the same desires toward me that I bear toward her.

It is essential to see here that the elements of vulnerability and care present themselves in each of their appearances as already implying or pointing toward one another. That is, the desire to have the other person vulnerable before me already contains the desire to care for the other person, while my own desire to be vulnerable before the other person contains, in the same stroke, my desire to be cared for by the loved person. Likewise, the desire to care for the other person already encompasses the desire to have her vulnerable before me, in the same way that my desire to be cared for by her also carries with it the desire to be vulnerable before her.

The same is true for the elements of the desires I want the other person to have toward me. Therefore, although the structure of being in love is such that it contains numerous distinct elements, these elements are nevertheless fused together in a mutually supporting network of meanings and implications. This does not mean that various of the elements cannot come to stronger expression than the others or even be completely replaced by other elements, only that in doing so the resulting structure diverges further and further from what we normally experience as being in love.

It is telling that this structure of desires for mutual vulnerability and care, which lies at the core of being in love, has remarkable similarities to the structure of the relationship between mother and infant. Since there is a close connection between sexual interaction and mother–infant interaction, it seems likely that, given the ties between love and sexual desire, there will also be similarities between the structure of romantic love and the mother–infant relationship.

This is borne out by the observation that one of the most salient features of an infant is its complete vulnerability. Arriving helpless in the world, the infant presents itself as being in immediate need of care, both physically and psychologically. Indeed, the first cries of the infant can easily be seen as primitive expressions of the desire to be cared for, expressions that become more and more conscious within the first few months of life. Fortunately for the infant, most mothers have a strong desire to provide the required care. Indeed, not only does the mother typically have a desire to care for the infant, but, further, she also typically desires the infant to be vulnerable before her. That is, she wants the infant to be in need of her care. Significantly, it seems it is just this vulnerability that gives the infant its attractiveness to the mother.

Therefore, already at the moment of its birth the infant finds itself in a relationship that bears some essential aspects of a relationship of romantic love, namely, a relationship in which someone desires its vulnerability in order to show it care. Where the mother's feelings toward the infant normally differ from romantic love is that although the mother has these desires toward the infant, she does not typically desire that the infant have similar desires toward her. That is, she does not desire that the infant likewise desire her vulnerability in order that the infant might show care to her.

Moreover, if we consider the relationship from the infant's side, here too some basic elements of romantic love can be discerned. For as just mentioned, the infant quickly begins to express something resembling the desire to be cared for by the mother. This is also suggested by Doi's (1981) arguments that love's constitutive element of *amae*, or the desire to be cared for, is first expressed by the infant at the mother's breast. Where the infant's desires toward the mother fall short of being romantic love is that although the infant expresses something like the desires to be cared for by the mother, it does not seem, at least in the very early stages of life, to desire to be vulnerable before the mother. This seems true if for no other reason than the young infant simply lacks the cognitive ability to entertain such a desire. (Here, then, it seems that the desire to be cared for is more primitive than the desire to be vulnerable, which is understandable since the idea of care is a component of the idea of being in need of care, that is, of being vulnerable.)

Nevertheless, it is noteworthy that within the first year of life most infants begin to show something like a desire to be vulnerable and in need of the mother's care. It is a common enough occurrence, for example, that an infant who has just started to crawl will get itself apparently trapped in a certain position and then call to its mother for help. Yet closer observation will show that the infant is not really trapped but merely wants to appear as though it were trapped in order to have its mother come to help and show care. This looks like an expression of the desire to be vulnerable and in need of care before the mother.

Infants also, of course, as Mahler et al., (1975) have demonstrated, express the desire to separate and free themselves from the mother. But this is a desire that exists side by side with the desire to be in need of care and in no way cancels it. Indeed, the *rapprochement* phase described by Mahler and her colleagues—the phase in which the infant oscillates between physically moving away from the mother and briefly returning to her—shows the coexistence of these two desires. Put in terms of the account being here presented, the fact that one has a desire for love does not mean that one lacks a desire for independence.

Another way in which the infant's desires toward the mother differ from the desires that make up the experience of being in love is that the infant does not desire the mother's vulnerability in order to care for the mother. Again, the reason for this probably has much to do with the infant's lack of cognitive abilities. But here too it is significant to note that the developing infant quickly learns to copy the maternal caregiving behavior. Thus, as mentioned earlier, a nursing infant will often put its fingers in the mother's mouth, perhaps in an attempt to imitate its mother's breast-feeding and thus caregiving behavior. Or, again, also imitating its mother, the infant might attempt to share its food with or show other caregiving behaviors toward its mother.

Such behaviors probably make their first appearances as simple instances of imitation driven by little more than the desire to imitate. However, the developing cognitive abilities of the infant are quickly bound to give rise to the related awareness that the desire to imitate encompasses the desire to be like the person being imitated. And if the person being imitated is desiring vulnerability and giving care, then the desire to imitate that person will likewise come to encompass the desires for vulnerability and giving care.

What all this shows is that the rudimentary expressions of the complex of desires that constitute the structure of being in love are already present in the primary mother–infant relationship. This also shows that a mother's love for her child and the child's love for its mother can, like romantic love, also be understood within a structure of desires for vulnerability and care.

THE NON-EXCLUSIVENESS OF LOVE

One purported feature of love that needs to be examined here is that of exclusiveness. It is often asserted that what distinguishes romantic love from other kinds of interpersonal attraction is the fact that it is exclusively directed toward one person. Thus, although I can like several people, I cannot have romantic love for more than one person, or, again, although a woman can have motherly love for all her children, she cannot have romantic love for more than one man. In other words, although there is nothing in the structure of other forms of interpersonal attraction that prevents one from being able to have these feelings for more than one person, there is something in the structure of romantic love that prevents one from being able to love romantically more than one person.

The peculiar thing about this view is that although it seems to be widely held in Western culture, it is also one that is plainly false. Although it is true that there are people who have ever romantically loved only one person, it is also true that there are people who have romantically loved more than one person. Many people go through more than one love relationship, falling in love with one person, only later to terminate the relationship before (or after) falling in love with someone new. In such a case, the feelings of love are clearly not exclusive to only one other person. Here, of course, the feelings of love for different persons are occurring at different times; that is, first I am in love with one person and then later, when that is finished, I am in love with another. And this, it might be felt, does not really offer a challenge to the view that love is exclusive. For the view that love is exclusive is not the view that I can never have love for more than one person but rather that I can never do so at the same time.

But is it true that I must be completely finished with my desires of love for one person before I can embark on having such desires for another? Everyday experience clearly speaks against such a view. One need only observe the relationships occurring about oneself to see that people can easily be in love with one person, only to develop suddenly, at the same time, similar desires for another person. Such a multiple occurrence of desires would seem to lie behind many instances of extramarital relations, having affairs, keeping a mistress, or "two-timing," as it is often pejoratively called. Of course, such occurrences are also often based purely on sexual or other motives (for example, to bolster one's self-esteem, to assert independence, to get revenge, and so forth), but it is evident that at other times they are frequently based on a genuine love for the second person.

Many people, however, might feel that to fall in love with a second person while still claiming to be in love with a present lover only serves to show that the first relationship is not really one of love, is in a stage of dissolution, or some such thing. And this, in some cases, might well be true. But to assert that it is necessarily true in all cases simply goes against the evidence and thus seems little more than prejudice. (See, e.g., Rubenstein's [1983] study where various persons claimed to be in love with several individuals at the same time. See also Bell [2002].)

One way of resisting this conclusion might be to claim that although it is possible to be in love with more than one person at a time, such a multiple appearance of the desires of love is inherently unstable. As a result, such a state of affairs never lasts for long. Therefore, if love is going to endure, it must, in the end, be held exclusively for only one other person.

Two things could be said to this. First, whether or not being in love with more than one person is unstable does not change the fact that it is possible to be in love with more than one person. Love itself is a fragile and volatile state of affairs. But the fact that love is fragile and volatile does not mean that it does not exist. And, likewise, the fact that being in love with more than one person might be unstable does not mean that being thus in love does not exist (that is, that love must be exclusive). Indeed, because the desires of love for one person are in themselves fragile, it is to be expected that two or more instances of such desires, when considered as a whole, would be doubly or multiply more fragile. For here there are at least two possible places, as opposed to merely one, where the desires could break down. Still, the fact that something is fragile does not mean that it will necessarily break, which is why love, be it directed to one person or to more, can also endure.

Secondly, if being in love with more than one person is unstable, it would seem that much of this instability is the result of cultural strictures rather than something inherent in the relation itself. In Western culture, being in love with more than one person at a time (and even, to some extent, at different times) is highly censured. Not only do institutions of Western culture refuse to acknowledge the validity of loving more than one person by refusing legally to acknowledge marriages between more than two persons, but, further, people displaying such feelings are socially rejected, attacked as being selfish, dishonest, or, because of love's relation to sexual desire, as being "oversexed." And this social criticism seems to redouble when the person displaying the love is a female.

Further, persons who accept their lover's being in love with another person are chastised, pitied, told they should feel jealous, laughed at, and humiliated. Consequently, each of the beloveds of the same lover are under much pressure to change the situation, either by terminating her own relationship with the lover, by pressuring the lover to terminate his relationship with his other beloved, or by directly confronting the other beloved. As a result, the person in love with more than one person is typically under much censure not only from the wider culture in which he lives but also from within his relationships with the persons he loves.

Here, of course, is where deception comes in. If someone is genuinely in love with two persons, then he no more wants to terminate either of the relationships than he would want to terminate his one relationship if he were only in love with one person. Yet he is typically under much pressure to do so. One desperate solution to this dilemma is for the person to try to keep the fact that he is doubly in love hidden as much as possible, both from general view and from that of each of the loved persons. But such a solution, or rather temporary expedient, carries with it the seeds of its own destruction. For, as I have tried to show, at the heart of love lie the desires to be vulnerable and thus open before the other person. It is a desire that implies self-disclosure, intimacy, and trust. But with the practice of deception, these elements of love are immediately damaged. For in deceiving the other person one is drastically limiting the possibility of self-disclosure and intimacy while also destroying one's trustworthiness. One is withholding one's vulnerability rather than offering it. And this flies in the face of love.

It is thus little wonder that instances of being in love with more than one person might be unstable, for when they take place under such circumstances their demise seems all but certain. It is vital to remember, however, that the destructive elements that serve to distinguish love for more than one person from love for just one person (as opposed to the destructive elements of fragility and volatility, which both types of love share in common), have nothing to do with the nature of love itself but rather have to do with the cultural traditions in which the love takes place.

Even the common idea that the presence of a third person spoils the magic of the lovers' world does not go against this. For the third person that most people have in mind here is someone to whom neither of the lovers have any romantic relations. Here the third person's ability to see the relationship from the outside works to remove the lovers' awarenesses from the internal view of the relationship. When the third person is also someone in love with one of the two lovers, then this point no longer seems to hold. For here, the third person is no longer fully an outsider but someone who is intimately connected to the love relation so far as she is in love with one of the lovers who is also in love with her. This pulls her deeper into the interior of the other two persons' love relation because she herself is receiving the same sort of desires (her beloved's way of loving) that her beloved is also directing to his other beloved. The third person's position as an outsider would even become less clear in that not-unheard-of situation where the third person is in love not only with the lover but also with his beloved. For here she is now intimately tied to both persons in the relation and is thus an essential element in both their love lives.

What this means, then, is that as far as the desires for reciprocal vulnerability and care are concerned, there is nothing in their nature that implies that they can be directed at only one person. Of course, in each of their expressions these desires are directed to a definite individual, but there is no reason why there need be only one definite individual to whom all such desires are directed.

It might be argued, however, that there is a further feature inherent in being in love—and thus not essentially the result of cultural strictures—that threatens the state of being in love with more than one person in a way that it does not necessarily threaten being in love with only one person. This is the feature of jealousy. Although not a *structural* feature of being in love itself—that is, there is nothing in the complex of desires for reciprocal vulnerability and care that could be described as jealousy—such jealousy, some people feel, is a *dispositional* feature of being in love (e.g. Buss, 2000). In other words, being in love is a state that, under certain circumstances, has the disposition to give rise to jealousy. This would be much like arguing that brittleness is a dispositional feature of glass. For although nothing could be found within the structure of glass itself that could be called brittleness, glass nevertheless has the disposition to break easily under certain circumstances. This is just what is meant by saying that glass has brittleness. And just as this disposition of glass to break is a basic feature of glass, so is the disposition for jealousy a basic feature of being in love. Such jealousy, it could then be argued, is destructive to love because it puts a pressure upon the person to terminate one (or more) of his love relations while at the same time breeding resentment toward the loved person who is applying the pressure.

To this it must be agreed that jealousy, like love itself, seems to be a phenomenon that is experienced across various cultures: references to feelings of jealousy can be found in the literature of different ages and different cultures. Yet, as Hupka (1981) has pointed out, jealousy is most prevalent and threatening in cultures that emphasize personal property, require marriage as the only legitimate way to engage in sexual activity, highly value the idea of personal progeny, and use marriage as a basis for economic security and social recognition. However, in cultures that do not emphasize such things, where sexual satisfaction is readily available and where the group is more important to one's welfare than are offspring or a spouse, jealousy is mild and infrequent. Such a state of affairs flourished in the polyandrous culture of the Todas of the Nilgiri Hills in southern India. Here, upon marrying, a woman was automatically considered to be married to all her husband's brothers. Also, before or even after marriage there were few restrictions of any kind on who may have sexual intercourse with whom. As a result, sexual gratification was easily obtainable. Consistent with this approach to sexual intercourse, children were accepted in Toda culture for their own sake, and the Toda male showed little interest in knowing whether a child was his. Consequently, in Toda culture jealousy was virtually non-existent (Rivers, 1906).

Also, in some cultures jealousy is seen not so much as a reaction to the fact that one's lover is in love with another person but rather that one's lover is, or might be, more in love with another person than he or she is with oneself; that is, it is a reaction to seeing the third person as a rival who threatens one's own relationship. In such cultures the important thing then is not that one does not engage in multiple love relationships but rather that one does not do so in a way that makes one's lovers feel threatened by each other.

This is why Vatsyayana—who wrote within and addressed his work to a polygamous culture—suggests ways of avoiding rivalry among one's lovers or spouses. This is because for the culture in which Vatsyayana wrote, jealousy was not an inherent aspect of a relationship involving multiple lovers. It was rather more of an aspect of those multiple relationships in which favoritism or unfairness worked to generate rivalry. Consequently, the way to avoid such jealousy was to avoid displaying favoritism and unfairness. Thus, Vatsyayana says of the man who will avoid jealousy among his wives, "he gives pleasure to one by strolling in the garden, to another by making love, to a third by gifts, by praising those who are cultured, by giving secret appointments. Thus he keeps them all satisfied" (1994, p. 302).

Therefore, although jealousy exists across cultures, there is a wide variation in the degree and extent to which it thus exists. This variation in jealousy is also something that occurs within a specific culture. If we consider modern Western culture, for example, it seems that, for the most part, it contains those of Hupka's features that favor jealousy. Yet here too it is obvious that there are immense individual differences in how jealousy is experienced. Consequently, it seems that other factors—like gender, the nature of the particular relationship, or a person's character structure—also play a large role in the disposition to jealousy. For example, here females tend to show more jealousy when their partners are romantically involved with another person than when they are merely sexually involved. The reverse, however, seems to be true for males. In addition, jealousy-provoking behavior tends to be less threatening for people who know their beloved is already involved with a third person than it is for people who believe their relationship to be monogamous (Bringle and Boebinger, 1990). Also, for some people in Western culture, jealousy is simply a basic way in which they undergo their love relationships. For such people, even the idea of being treated equally with the beloved's other lovers or knowing beforehand about the extrarelationship affairs of the beloved would hardly be enough to assuage feelings of jealousy and make the situation acceptable.

The fact remains, however, that not everyone in love experiences jealousy and, consequently, that jealousy cannot be a fundamental feature, or even a fundamental dispositional feature, of being in love. This can also be seen from the fact that jealousy, in contrast to love, has little do with one's desires toward the other person. Rather, in such circumstances it has its deepest roots in the jealous person's character as low self-esteem or fear of a loss of self-worth. This would especially seem to be true of persons displaying what has been called "suspicious jealousy," that is, jealousy that occurs in the absence of any clear evidence of a partner's romantic or sexual activity with a third person (Bringle and Buunk, 1991).

Why jealousy might appear to have its basis in a relation to the other person is because jealousy seems to be a fear about the loss of the loved person. But this is only on its surface. If one looks a bit further, it becomes evident that jealousy is not so much a fear of a loss of the beloved as it is a fear of the loss of the beloved *to another person*. But if someone's concern is with losing the beloved, why should it matter whether the beloved was lost to another person? The answer is that what makes this essentially different from a simple fear of a loss of the beloved—as when the lover fears abandonment by or disappearance of the beloved—is that loss of the beloved to another person carries with it the stark and unavoidable implication that the beloved sees the new person as more attractive, valuable, and worthwhile than the lover and, consequently, that the new person might well be more attractive, valuable, and worthwhile than the lover. With abandonment for other reasons, the person might also get the message that she was not worthwhile enough for the beloved. But here, the harsh comparison between the lover's own attractiveness and that of another person is not an essential element of the abandonment.

Therefore, the quintessence of jealousy as a character trait is not so much the fear of the loss of the loved person as it is the fear of the loss of one's own self-worth. This is supported by White and Mullen's (1989) review that suggests that jealousy is connected to feelings of inadequacy, feelings that are directly related to feelings of low self-worth. Consequently, the jealous person forsakes the love relation, a relation that should tie the lover to the beloved in a complex of reciprocal desires, and instead focuses his awareness on the tenuousness of his own feelings of self-worth and his overwhelming fears of losing them. Thus, the jealous person looks into the eyes of his beloved much like other people look into a mirror. And what the jealous person is here straining to see is a reflection of his own self-worth.

But these features have their roots in the character of the jealous person, not in the structure of being in love. Consequently, there are people who are genuinely in love with someone who is himself or herself also in love with a third person but, having no fears of a loss of self-worth, do not experience the triangle—or polygon, as it may be—in a jealous way. As one woman from a Mormon polygamous (and legally unrecognized) marriage put it, although she was deeply in love with her husband, she did not mind sharing him with his other wives, women whose friendships she also enjoyed. Sharing him with his other wives gave her time to pursue some of her own interests and also relieved the pressure for her to have sexual intercourse more than she liked.

Someone might want to object here that if this woman does not mind sharing with other women the person she claims to love deeply, then she cannot really be in love. Such an objection, however, seems like little more than begging the question. It is an attempt to define love from the start as something that can be had for only one person at one time rather than looking to see how romantic love, in its different varieties, is in fact experienced.

WAYS OF BEING IN LOVE

The analysis of being in love into a complex of simpler desires for mutual care and vulnerability not only discloses the immediate structure of the experience of being in love—that is, how being in love presents itself to awareness—but, further, enables us to chart the diverse paths that instances of being in love can take. Moreover, it enables us to say why such diverse paths can still be seen as instances, or at least attenuated instances, of being in love. Here it can be seen how the experience of being in love—what might be termed a reciprocal orientation in love—can also appear in other orientations that are related to being in love in various ways. These orientations, to which I will now turn, are those of dependency, paternalism, masochism, sadism, and necrophilia. Let us examine each of these in turn.

One common way of being in love is to desire to be in a state of dependency before the other person, that is, to have what may be called a dependent orientation in love. In such a case the person undergoes his or her experience of love in a non-reciprocal way. Here the person desires to be dependent on the loved person while not wanting that the loved person be similarly dependent on him or her. This way of being in love can take numerous forms. It can present itself as submissive, passive, indecisive, or helpless behavior before the beloved, all of which are meant to provoke the beloved to respond with concern and care. Examples of this sort of orientation are given by Nir and Maslin (1982) in their case studies of various women's "lovestyles" (which is not to say that it is only women who display such an orientation). In their discussion of one such case they say, "It is not a mature mutually reciprocal relationship that she wants. Rather, Dianne is desperately, frantically searching for someone to care for her in a total all-encompassing way. . . . What she really wants is a man who will take care of her and care about her in the same way that a parent acts as a protector to a helpless child" (p. 197).

In addition, this orientation seems closely connected to feelings of possessiveness toward the other person and desires for exclusiveness in relationships (Pinto and Hollandsworth, 1984). It also seems tied to jealousy (Bringle and Buunk, 1986). It is important to see, however, that such connections are merely contingent and therefore extrinsic; that is, they are not intrinsic to the phenomenological structure of the dependent orientation. This is evident from the fact that nothing in the phenomenology of the dependent orientation discloses the features that lie at the basis of possessiveness, exclusiveness, or, as has just been shown, jealousy.

What is it, then, about such a state that enables it to be seen as a way of being in love? On the view given here it can be said that such a form of dependency has an essential relation to love because it is constituted by at least part of the complex of desires that make up love (which does not mean that all aspects of the dependent orientation will surface in a reciprocal love relationship). What the dependent lover wants is to be vulnerable before someone who will care. The person with such an approach to love has little desire to have the other person vulnerable before him or her, and, further, the dependent person does not want to care for the one who will care for him or her.

This is not to say that dependency will only be expressed in love by someone with a dependent orientation. On the analysis just given an aspect of such dependency, namely, the desire to be vulnerable before the other person in order that the other person may show care, is also a definitive aspect of love. This is because, as stated previously, part of the experience of being in love is to have the desire to be vulnerable before the loved person in order that one may be cared for, that is, to desire to be dependent on the other person. The difference here is that the person with a reciprocal orientation, unlike the person with the dependent orientation, also desires the other person's dependency. As a result, instances of such dependency will tend to make their appearance within a love relationship simply because it is a love relationship. This fits with Reiss' (1960) account, which refers to mutual dependency as being an integral process in the love relationship. Here, then, we can see the structural connection that the dependent orientation has to being in love and thus why the dependent orientation delivers itself to us as a way, or at least an attenuated way, of being in love.

This lack of desire for a reciprocal relationship also makes its appearance in what may be called a paternalistic orientation or paternalism in love. A person showing such an orientation in love is someone who, like the dependent lover, also experiences being in love in a non-reciprocal way. What the paternalistic lover wants, however, is to have a one-sided relationship in which it is the other person who is dependent on her and in which it is she who ministers to the other person. The paternalistic orientation can thus be seen as the complement of dependency, for the paternalistic lover's desires fulfill what it is that the dependent lover wants from the other person, while the dependent lover's desires fulfill what it is that the paternalistic lover wants.

This orientation seems related to what Berne (1977) calls the "parent ego state." According to Berne, "an 'ego state' may be described phenomenologically as a coherent system of feelings, and operationally as a set of coherent behavior patterns; or pragmatically as a system of feelings which motivates a related set of behavior patterns" (p. 123). One such system is that of the feelings and behavior typical of a parent. When this system of feelings and behavior manifests itself as a person's primary mode of showing romantic love, then we have paternalistic orientation in love.

But why might such a paternalistic orientation be seen as a way of being in love? The answer is because despite the lack of desire for reciprocity, the paternalistic orientation is still made up of at least part of the desires that constitute being in love. On this account, the paternalistic lover is explained as being someone who desires to have the other person vulnerable before herself in order that she may care for that person. She does not, however, similarly desire herself to be vulnerable before or cared for by the other person. Thus, the paternalistic orientation is not something completely foreign to love, for here, as with the reciprocal instance of being in love, there is the desire to have loved person's vulnerability in order to show care.

Because of the constitutional role that this aspect of paternalism plays in the complex of desires that make up love, instances of paternalism will, like instances of dependency, also tend to manifest themselves within the reciprocal orientation. The reason for this is that desiring the other person's vulnerability in order to show care (part of paternalism), like desiring to be vulnerable in order to be cared for (part of dependency), is also an integral part of being in love.

When being in love is based on a reciprocal orientation, then the person in love will desire to respond to the loved person's desire for dependency by showing its complement, namely, paternalism. That is, she will want to respond to the loved person's vulnerability (which is something she desires in order to show care) by showing care. This also follows from Reiss' view of the integral role of dependency in love. For to desire the loved person's dependency (which is part of the desire for mutual dependency) is simply to desire the vulnerability of the loved person in order to show care. But this is, at the same time, to desire to show paternalism. The paternalism here, however, is like the dependency of being in love, a reciprocal paternalism. Lacking this reciprocity is where the paternalistic orientation parts ways from the reciprocal orientation.

Care, however, is only one response that is related to vulnerability; another response is hostility. And such a response should not strike us as totally inexplicable: we need only note that when we experience someone's vulnerability, one of the things we sense is the person's defenselessness, that is, the person's exposure to possible harm. This is why, no doubt, the element of vulnerability brings with it not only the meaning of "in need of care" but also that of "susceptible to injury or harm." So already woven into the experience of vulnerability is the meaning of harm. Because of this dual meaning it is easy to see how the expression of vulnerability might be used by someone who desires to be harmed or controlled rather than to be cared for. Such a person might desire to be vulnerable before another person in order to be harmed or controlled by that person. When this occurs, together with a lack of desire for reciprocal relations, then we have what can best be described as masochism.

As pointed out by Rathbone (2001), "masochism, if not only a blanket term, at least refers to an extremely heterogeneous phenomenon which transmutes everytime one attempts to grasp it" (pp. 83–84). Maleson (1984) and Grossman (1986) also complain that the idea of masochism is something that has been used with little precision and thus has acquired a confusing array of meanings. However, several writers (e.g., Bowlby, 1969; Coen, 1992; Leary, 1957) seem at least in agreement that masochism is best understood within the context of interpersonal relations. Other writers, like

Berliner (1947) and Schad-Somers (1996), also see it as intimately tied to the attempt to find love. Rathbone herself starts off her book on masochism by claiming that "when a 'love'-relationship is not loving, it is usually sado-masochistic" (2001, p. v), thus pointing to the close connection between love and masochism. Schad-Somers makes this connection more explicit stating that "the quest for love (or the illusion of it) is the central mecha-nism operating in the psychic economy of masochism" (p. 46).

Although Schad-Somers does not fully explain why she qualifies "the quest for love" with the parenthetical remark "or illusion of it," this can easily be explained on the present view. This is because being in love con-sists of the desires for mutual vulnerability and care. The person with a masochistic orientation in love, however, is one who has little interest in the other person's vulnerability or in showing or receiving care. His or her interests revolve primarily around his or her own desire to be vulnerable in order to be harmed. Consequently, the masochistic lover has dispensed with much of the complex of desires that constitute being in love: not only is the element of reciprocity now gone (as it is with dependency and pater-nalism), but, in addition, the element of care is also gone. And, to remove his or her desires even farther from those that make up love, the masochist has replaced the element of care with that of something quite adversative to care, namely, harm.

Therefore, if dependency and paternalism are attenuated ways of being in love, then masochism is an even more attenuated way. Yet for all that, a pivotal element of being in love—namely, the desire to submit oneself in an intimate way and to place oneself in a vulnerable position before the other person—remains. It is probably this peculiar blend of elements apparently antithetical to loving (the desire for harm instead of care) with those crucial to loving (the desire to be vulnerable) that leads Berliner to describe masochism as a "pathologic way of loving," with the term "pathologic" referring to the apparently foreign elements and the term "loving" referring to the central elements.

The problem, however, in using such a description is that it can easily lead one to think that there exists a "normal" way of loving that lacks the "pathologic" masochistic elements. But one of the peculiar features of romantic love is that experiences that are normally thought to be noxious or harmful—such as suffering and rejection—appear to intensify love.

Consequently, at the very heart of love lies a mechanism that responds to being harmed by strengthening the feelings of love. Although this is not fully masochism, it is nevertheless well on the road to masochism. For if suffering, rejection, and harm intensify feelings of love and intensified feel-ings of love are what one desires (as many people in love do), then it is a small step from being in love to desiring suffering, rejection, and harm. If these desires remain non-reciprocal and begin to override the desires for care (which is easy enough considering they would not comfortably coexist with the desire for care), then masochism has made its appearance. It is this ease of transition from love to masochism that no doubt accounts for the various instances of masochism that are wont to appear in otherwise reciprocal ways of being in love.

But how could it be that a complex of desires like love, which has the element of care as such a basic element, can suddenly slip into a complex of desires whose essence is to seek out harm? The answer lies in the pivotal element of vulnerability. For in having the desire to be vulnerable at its core, that is, the element that enables the desire for care to be part of love, love has, in the same stroke, taken the basis for masochism into its core. For the basis of masochism is also the desire to be vulnerable. This is because, as I have argued, the idea of vulnerability is intimately connected to the ideas of both care and harm.

Masochism, however, is not the only way in which harm can make its appearance in the context of a love relationship; another way is in a sadistic orientation. As with masochism, the sadistic orientation is also a non-reciprocal one. Here, however, rather than desiring to be vulnerable before the other person in order to receive harm, the sadistic lover desires the other person's vulnerability in order to bestow harm. The person with a sadistic orientation in love desires neither himself to be vulnerable nor to give or receive care. The sadistic orientation, being the mirror image of masochism, is consequently the fulfillment of the desires of the masochistic orientation. As a result, in the same sort of way that the paternalistic orientation in love is the complement of the dependent orientation, so is the sadistic orientation the complement of the masochistic orientation.

There is, of course, something odd about the idea of sadism as being a way of loving, for the idea of desiring to harm the loved person seems, on the face of it, anathema to the idea of love. Yet one need only open one's eyes to see that numerous love relations are fully infiltrated with, and even based upon, the desire to harm the other person: wife beating and murder, violent jealousy, humiliation, coercion, emotional cruelty, and rape seem to abound in what might otherwise be described as love relations.

The question that one wants to ask then is how it is that such desires can be related to being in love. And here again the answer is to be found in the pivotal element of vulnerability, for the desire for the other person's vulnerability, which is fundamental to love, is also fundamental to sadism. The difference is that whereas the person with a reciprocal orientation desires the other person's vulnerability in order to show care, the sadistic lover desires it in order to show harm. Here again it is vulnerability's Janus-faced quality of meaning both "in need of care" and "susceptible to injury" that enables it to exist happily at the basis of otherwise quite opposed orientations.

Because, however, sadism is often thought to be essentially the desire to inflict pain or harm on another person, it might appear that the desire for the other person's vulnerability is not basic to sadism. But it should be evident that with sadism the desire to inflict pain is closely wedded with the desire for the other person to be vulnerable. This would explain the importance the person with a sadist orientation places on controlling the other person—something that is well expressed in the typical sadistic practice of binding and gagging another person—for to control a person is to have that person vulnerable before the one who is in control. Indeed, the very practice of inflicting pain on or torturing another person can also easily be seen as a powerful form of control. For in causing the other person to undergo pain, the sadist is at the same time in vital control of the other person's consciousness. Here the sadist fills the other person's consciousness with the dreadfulness of pain, thus controlling the person's awareness by driving it in a direction chosen by the sadist. Because of the horrific nature of inflicted pain, few victims are able to escape such control.

However, the fact that it is the sadistic rather than the love orientation that focuses on the other person's vulnerability in order to cause harm does not mean that sadism will never appear in reciprocal orientations. For, with the desire for the other person's vulnerability as a fundamental element, love already has the germ of sadism planted in its soil. Again, this is because the meaning of vulnerability points equally in the directions of both care and harm. Therefore, in experiencing the loved person's vulnerability, that is, in truly knowing that the loved person is now vulnerable before him, the lover sees the beloved's defenselessness and susceptibility to harm or injury as an integral part of her need for care. Consequently, the idea of harm is in the lover's awareness, if only but an obscure inkling, just so far as he desires the other person's vulnerability.

This does not mean he will therefore desire her vulnerability *in order* to harm her rather than *in order* to care for her, only that the conditions are fertile for such a development and that, like masochism, instances of sadism can easily find their way into a love relation. Whether and the degree to which this happens will depend on things like the nature of the love relation, the culture in which the relation takes place, personality factors, and so on. However, as Schad-Somers (1996) says, "if one accepts the fact— and I believe one must—that childhood is never without trauma, that men raised in the nuclear family never completely lose their awe, fear and envy of women, then it would follow that a certain and minute element of perversion—as well as perversity—and sadomasochism are present in the relationships between all men and women" (pp. 87–88).

There are, however, those cases in which the non-reciprocal desire to cause harm appears unaccompanied by the corresponding desire for the vulnerability of the other person. But this brings us to a new level of interpersonal orientation, for here the fundamental link to love—the desire for vulnerability—has at last been severed. When the desire for harming the other person occurs by itself as an orientation (and here, because of the absence of the desire for vulnerability, we can no longer say "an orientation *in love*"), we then have a case of necrophilia rather than of sadism. As has been argued by Fromm (1973), the distinction between sadism and necrophilia is the distinction between the desire to dominate or control and the desire to destroy. Although Fromm allows that there will always be some amount of destructiveness linked with sadism, this he feels is merely a result of the more basic desire for domination and control over others (on my account, these desires would be analyzed further in terms of non-reciprocal desires for the vulnerability of the other in order to impart harm). The sadist, says Fromm, desperately needs the other whom he controls in order to remain in control.

Sadism, therefore, despite its desire for harm, does not essentially include the desire for the elimination of the other person. Necrophilia, however, aims precisely at the destruction of the other person and thus has little to do with the maintenance of control. Consequently, the necrophile's interests skirt around the issue of vulnerability. The necrophile's desires lie rather with death and destruction. Thus, in forsaking the issue of vulnerability, the necrophile has turned his back on the last remaining element in the complex of desires that constitute love. With masochism and sadism, even though the apparently foreign element of harm has made its way into the complex, there still remains the desire for vulnerability, that is, a residual but nevertheless central element in love. But with necrophilia even this vestige of love is gone. What is left is simply the desire to destroy, a desire that is often expressed in murder or the mutilation of a corpse.

The idea of necrophilia is usually associated with the idea of necrophilious sexual practices, just as masochism and sadism are often associated with masochistic and sadistic sexual practices. Although such practices exist, this does not mean that masochism, sadism, and necrophilia refer only to sexual practices, for they are also, as just shown, orientations. When they occur as sexual activities, then we have behaviors that also fall under the heading of the paraphilias or atypical sexual variations. These behaviors are sexual because, as with other sexual activities, they too incorporate, or at least partially incorporate, the basic activities of baring and caressing. Thus, masochistic and sadistic sexual practices each tend to involve a baring of the body. Here, however, the baring of the body is desired primarily not for the purposes of caressing but rather for hurting. Such instances might involve the whipping, cutting, or burning of flesh or, in cases of a male's sadistic use of sexual intercourse, perhaps using the penis, as Reich has noted, as a piercing instrument that is meant to hurt the woman. The line, however, between what might be called rough caressing and violence can be indistinct. It is this indistinctness, along with the desire for the baring of the body, that perhaps leads us to see these practices as still being instances of sexual desire.

With necrophilia, however, things are more complex. For although the necrophile might fondle and have sexual intercourse with a corpse and thus display desires for the baring of the corpse's flesh, such desires are not so clearly, as they are with other sexual practices, instances of the desire for vulnerability. This is because the flesh of a corpse is dead flesh. Hence, the baring of a corpse does not render it vulnerable in the same sense that the baring of a living person's body renders the living person's body vulnerable. For a dead body cannot be cared for or harmed in the same way that a living person's body can. This is evident from the simple fact that the dead person no longer exists. Consequently, although, in the moment of baring it is of the utmost importance to the living person how his or her body is treated, it is of no importance to the dead person. For, in the moment of baring, the dead person is not there to give importance to the treatment. This awareness would seem to lie behind the famous proclamation of Heraclitus that "corpses are more fit to be thrown out than dung" (1987, p. 59).

In another sense, however, the body of a corpse can also be vulnerable and thus cared for or harmed: as when a body is bared in order to be washed and prepared for a funeral or as when a body is mutilated. The ancient Greeks, for example, took much care in the washing, perfuming, and adorning of the dead body before committing it to the funeral pyre, which is no doubt what Heraclitus, social critic that he was, was protesting against. Still, because it is a corpse, such baring does not render it in need of care, at least not in the sense of care that will fulfill its needs, for corpses have no needs.

This ambiguity concerning the baring of a corpse is attended by the further ambiguity of the baring of the necrophile's own body in order to have sexual activity with the corpse. For although he is baring himself and therefore seems to be rendering himself physically vulnerable, what he is baring himself to is something before which he cannot really be vulnerable, namely, a corpse. For a corpse can neither care for him with caresses nor harm him. Of course, a person who is engaged in baring a corpse might merely be an opportunist who is fantasizing that the body is a living person and thus be, despite appearances to the contrary, actually desiring the physical vulnerability of a living body while desiring that he himself be similarly vulnerable before a living person. But then, such an individual would not be displaying truly necrophilious desires. He would be more engaged in what Rosman and Resnick (1989) call pseudo-necrophilia. For here the fantasy shows that where the person's real desires lie with the living, not with the dead.

However, what the person with necrophilious desires is attracted to in a corpse is precisely that it is something that is dead and, thus, is imbued with the meanings of death, destruction, and decay. This does not rule out Rosman and Resnick's claim that a common motive in true necrophilia is the desire for an unresisting and unrejecting partner. For this is quite compatible with the desire for a dead partner: one salient feature of the dead is that they are unresisting and unrejecting (Rosman and Resnick also note that necrophiles often have more than one motive). However, the fact that necrophilious acts are not infrequently accompanied by murder or mutilation and further destruction of the corpse or are performed on a mutilated or decomposing corpse (Krafft-Ebing [1886] gives various accounts) suggests that there is far more to true necrophilia than simply the desire for an unresisting and unrejecting partner.

What we have, then, is a hierarchy of orientations that begins with the desires for reciprocal love as the most complex member in the hierarchy. Removing some of the elements of this way of being in love (the desires for reciprocation), we come to the next members in the hierarchy: dependency and paternalism. Taking these two orientations, we then remove further elements (the desires for care) and, inserting in their place new elements (the desires for harm), so arrive at masochism and sadism. Canceling the final element of love (the desire for vulnerability) from sadism, we are left with necrophilia.

It must be seen, however, that each of these ways of being in love, including the reciprocal orientation, are best understood as prototypes that different persons will normally approach only more or less. And just as the atypical sexual variations tend to appear together in varying degrees, it will more often be the case that the orientations we have been considering will also manifest themselves as being blended together in varying degrees. Freud (1905) notes, for example, that sadism and masochism tend to appear to together in various amounts in the same individual (which is why the term "sadomasochism" is often used). Also, someone may have a predominantly reciprocal orientation to another person and yet lean slightly more toward, say, a dependent orientation. While having primarily reciprocal desires, such a person will desire to be vulnerable in order that she may be cared for more than she desires the other person to be vulnerable in order that she may care for him. Or, again, although someone may display a predominantly paternalistic orientation, the paternalism displayed may nonetheless be colored with shades of sadism. A person blending these two modes of being in love will be someone who nonreciprocally desires the other person's vulnerability in order to show care but will nevertheless be prone to take advantage of the other's vulnerability to control or harm the person.

LOVE'S RELATION TO SEXUAL DESIRE

It can now be seen why being in love tends to imply the existence of sexual desire. For according to the description just given, love is but one more way of wanting what sexual desire wants: mutual vulnerability and care. One difference here is that while love aims primarily at the psychological expressions of vulnerability and care, sexual desire aims at the bodily expressions, that is, at baring and caressing. Yet it might be reasonably asked why the type of desires that make up love need include the type of desires that make up sexual desire. Why, it could be asked, cannot one simply be in love, having all the constituent desires that make up that relation, and yet not engage in the desires for bodily baring and caressing? The answer here, it seems, is that because of the intense and all-encompassing nature of the desires that make up love, they will naturally tend to include more than just psychological ways of expressing themselves. In my desiring complete reciprocal vulnerability and care with the one I love, my desire does not rest content with wanting reciprocal psychological vulnerability and care but *at the same time* wants mutual physical vulnerability and care, that is, to be bare before the one I love in order to be caressed and have the beloved bare before me in order to caress her.

In this way the original ends of love—complete vulnerability and care—are achieved to the fullest extent by engaging the loved person in sexual activity. Further, love cannot, because of its intensity, stop short of desires for such engagement. Love wants vulnerability and care to the highest degree, and engaging another person sexually is one of the most powerful ways of achieving such a degree of vulnerability and care. But this does not entail that sexual engagement will necessarily take place in every instance of romantic love, only that the desires for such an engagement will, at some level of awareness, tend to be present.

Because love will tend to seek out complete vulnerability and care by also expressing itself in sexual desire, it follows that the various ways of being in love will also tend to express themselves in various related forms of sexual desire. Thus, the masochistic orientation will tend to be accompanied by masochistic sexual desires, while the sadistic orientation will tend to be accompanied by sadistic sexual desires. Likewise, a person with a dependent orientation will also express dependent or passive sexual desires, while the paternalistic orientated person will express sexual desires that aim at a paternalistic, caring but non-reciprocal form of sexual interaction. This is because all these love orientations are elements of character structure, and, as Fromm (1973) puts it, "in no sphere of behavior does the character of a person show more clearly than in the sexual act—precisely because it is the least 'learned' and patterned behavior" (p. 282).

That love wants the same thing as sexual desire is underscored by the fact that, as stated previously, the gender of the other person is as crucial to love as it is to sexual desire. Thus, just as to have sexual desire is to desire mutual (physical) vulnerability and care with a person of a specific gender, so to be in love is to desire mutual (psychological) vulnerability and care with a person of a specific gender.

It might seem, however, that in focusing on the psychological rather than physical elements of vulnerability, love is not as strongly based as sexual desire is upon the gender of the other person. However, because the intensity of the desires that make up love ensure that they will not remain with only the psychological elements but will also aim toward the body, then in the same breath that one falls in love, one also "falls" in sexual desire. As a result, love will carry with it, from its first swift appearance, the stirrings of sexual desire. If this might not appear to be so, it is, I suggest, because love is more than sexual desire. For in its essence it moves beyond desires for baring and caressing to include desires for psychological vulnerability and care as well. Consequently, sexual desire can become hidden, so to speak, in the maze of other desires that direct themselves to the psychological elements. But to be hidden is not to be absent.

Thus, in undergoing the desires of love, I direct myself to the other person's innocence, openness, laughter, kindness, and other expressions of psychological vulnerability and care. But even though it might be such elements that form the focal point of my awareness in love, these elements are permitted to hold the place they do only because they float upon a deeper phenomenological layer of gender, a layer that finds its way into my desires simply because it is an element in the object of my sexual desires. For it is the gender of the other person that stirs my cravings for mutual baring and caressing. It is this supportive layer of gender that propels the various psychological features of the loved person into my desires of love, much like the waves of a turbulent sea might lift a piece of driftwood up into view. And just as such driftwood is soaked through and through with the seawater that at once supports it and thrusts it up into view, so is the loved person's innocence, openness, laughter, kindness, and so on soaked through and through with the person's gender, a gender that supports it and thus enables it to be brought into my awareness as an element toward which I can direct my desires. Because of all this, the various dynamics of the twoness of gender discussed earlier will also tend to make their appearance in the moments of being in love.

Now although being love with someone will as a result tend to carry with it desires for mutual baring and caressing, that is, sexual desire, this should not lead us to infer that the converse is true, that is, that having sexual desire for someone will encompass being in love with that person. As is evident, sexual desire operates quite happily outside the domain of love. Someone might want to object, however, saying that sexual desire outside of love is not really sexual desire, that it is a different form of sexual desire from that experienced in love, or some such thing. Here, I think, is where the term "lust" often gets brought in. Thus, for example, a man who is sexually desirous toward a woman he does not love is sometimes said to have lust for her or to be lusting after her. This can even be said in the situation where the man *does* love the woman but, in the instance he sexually desires her, his desires are seen to be purely sexual rather than being blended with or the result of love. And this is often said as though lust were a distinct type of sexual phenomenon.

My impression, however, is that the word "lust" is usually nothing more than a pejorative term for sexual desire that does not involve love. It is interesting to note here that a similar critique used to be (and still is in some religions) aimed at those who have sexual desire without the desire to have a baby. On this view, one that in the West was much influenced by Augustine, sexual desire that is not accompanied by the desire for procreation is said to be lust. In a way, one could say that the more recent view—that sexual desire unaccompanied by the desires of love is lust—is merely the earlier view—that sexual desire unaccompanied by the desire for a baby is lust—in a new guise. Both are attempts to stigmatize or reject the idea of sexual desire as an independent phenomenon.

I see nothing, however, in the nature of sexual desire that implies that it is somehow different (or absent) when experienced independently of being in love (or the desire for a baby). In either case it is composed of essentially the same thing, namely, a complex of desires for mutual baring and caressing. What is different when sexual desire occurs in the context of being in love is simply that these desires occur simultaneously with the similar desires for psychological vulnerability and care. Of course, someone could accept all this and still want to hold that sexual desire without love is somehow immoral, socially undesirable, or some such thing. But that is another matter and has no bearing on the point being made.

Another way of trying to criticize the view that sexual desire can exist without love would be to argue that, in such cases, the simultaneous non-existence of the desires of love is only apparent. On this view it might be held that the desire for love is there in a disguised form. Kernberg (1995), for example, suggests that many people who have sexual desires outside a love relationship mistake the physical intimacy and excitement of sexual activity for the emotional intimacy and excitement of love. Consequently, although such people might think they desire only sexual interaction, what they really desire is love. It is just that they mistakenly think sexual activity is the same as being in love.

This is no doubt true in many cases, and it is easy to see how such a situation might occur. For in both love and sexual desire there exist the desires for vulnerability and care—albeit in different forms—along with the sense of excitement that being vulnerable before another person can easily give rise to. However, there is no reason to think that every time a person has sexual desire that appears independently of the desires of love that he or she must be engaged in mistaking the former for the latter. Indeed, it is obvious that many who embark on a purely sexual affair do so with the explicit purpose of being able to fulfill their sexual desires without having the extra complication of the desires that a love relation would imply. In such a situation it seems pointless to insist that the person is mistaking sexual desire for the desires of love. It therefore is unfounded to argue that sexual desire can occur only together with the desires of love.

But how is it that desires for psychological vulnerability and care will bring with them desires for baring and caressing but that desires for baring and caressing need not bring with them desires for psychological vulnerability and care? The reason for this seems best explained by the fact that since sexual desire is concerned primarily with the body, it need not make reference (as being in love does) to another person's desires. Thus, as already pointed out, my being in love with someone implies at least two things: (1) that I have certain desires directed toward the other person concerning our mutual vulnerability and care and (2) that I desire that the other person have similar desires toward me, that is, that I have desires concerning the other person's desires.

In sexual desire, however, the schema is not so complex. For although I here have certain desires directed toward a mutual baring and caressing of the other person's body, I need not also desire that the other person has desires for a mutual baring and caressing directed toward me. That is, although sexual desire contains the equivalent of (1) referred to earlier, it need not contain the equivalent of (2). So although love is the demand to be loved, sexual desire is not the demand to be sexually desired.

One could object here that sofar as I want another person to bare herself to me or to caress me, then I in fact am having desires concerning her desires. For to desire that she does such things is the same as desiring that she does them of her own accord, that is, that she is not physically forced into doing them. But to desire that she does them of her own accord is the same as desiring that she has a desire to do them.

The trouble with this objection, however, is that, as I argued in the section on the nature of desire, the fact that someone does something of her own accord does not mean that she entertains a genuine desire to do it. It simply means that she did it intentionally (and intentional acts do not have to be preceded by a genuine desire). This is a crucial distinction. For when we examine the component of sexual desire that involves the desire to have the other person bare herself or return caresses, it is apparent that nothing in these desires aims at the other person's actual desire to be bare and return caresses. What is wanted in this situation is simply that the person does bare herself and return the desired caresses, not that she genuinely wants to. That is, what sexual desire aims at here is the intentional acts of the other person's baring and caressing, making no further attempt to also direct itself to the other person's desires.

Although it is true that desires for the other person's baring and caressing are often intimately blended with the further desire that she genuinely wants to engage in these activities, the desire that she genuinely wants to do so is far from central to sexual desire itself. Sexual desire asserts itself independently of these other extrinsic desires and easily moves toward its goal without them. This is evident from the fact that, while experiencing sexual desire, many people seem unconcerned about their sexual partner's desires. A man, for example, might have a strong desire for sexual intercourse with a woman and even attempt to persuade the woman to fulfill his desires without first trying to rouse the woman's desires or without making an effort to discover if she has similar desires. Nothing in this behavior suggests that the man does not really have sexual desire. What it suggests is simply that he lacks immediate concern for the state of the woman's desires.

However, such an approach to sexual interaction, as everyone knows, severely limits and even damages the overall satisfaction that most people might gain from the encounter. It will probably make the one person feel she is being used while denying the other person the warm and sensual caresses of a truly interested participant. This is why Vatsyayana takes much time to suggest ways in which both the man and the woman should kindle each other's desires before attempting to engage in sexual intercourse. Vatsyayana was also well aware that sexual desire can easily take place without taking account of the other person's desires.

The story of a desirous individual showing little interest in the desires of the other person might well, for various reasons, be more typical of the way that male sexual desire is displayed than the way female sexual desire is displayed. Vatsyayana thought it was. But even if it is more typical of males, it does not mean that female sexual desire, in its essence, necessarily includes wanting to be sexually desired. If it did mean this, then we would have to accept that those females who do experience the desire for a mutual baring and caressing with another person, while not showing concern about being similarly desired, were not really experiencing sexual desire. We would then be left with the hopeless task of trying to explain why such desires do not count as being sexual when a woman has them but do when a man has them. This would be hopeless, I suggest, because in their basic phenomenological structure, male and female sexual desires are the exactly the same: both aspire to a mutual baring and caressing with another person of a specific gender regardless of what the other person desires. If a particular woman (or man) brings further desires to the encounter, then what she (or he) brings are no more than that, namely, further desires. They are not elements that are constitutive of sexual desire itself. The conclusion, then, is that, in its essence, sexual desire does not, like being in love, aim at the desires of the other person.

None of this implies, however, that sexual desire cannot lead to being in love. For there is nothing in the structure of sexual desire that need block the development of love, and, moreover, the structure is similar enough to that of being in love that one need not ponder too long to see how being in love could be one of the eventual results of what started as only sexual interest. Here someone might start with desiring only mutual baring and caressing with another person. However, in the midst of his desires, and especially because of his focus on the bodily expression of vulnerability and care, perhaps he notices an element of psychological vulnerability in his partner that echoes the idea of her physical vulnerability. This might stir intense desires to provide her with the emotional care that she is in need of, which again could lead to the desire that she continue to be vulnerable before him in order that he might continue to take care of her. Such intense desires could easily set in motion desires for reciprocity whereby he desires to share his vulnerabilities with her so that she might also be able to care for him.

Here, then, we would have a case where the essential core of love has arisen from what originally were purely sexual desires. This view is supported by Freud's (1922, 1930) ontogeny of love. Here love is portrayed as aim-inhibited sexual desire where the feelings of love come originally from powerful sexual desires. To become the desires of love, these sexual desires are subliminated and transformed into the more socially acceptable response of romantic desire. This is also the core of Schopenhauer's view.

The fact, however, that sexual desire does not necessarily refer to the desires of the other person should not lead us to think that, while having sexual desire, we never have desires concerning other persons' sexual desires. In most if not all cultures, a large part of a person's worth, especially a female's worth, is based upon whether she is seen to be sexually desirable. Since most people want to be valued by others, it is understandable that most people want, in some way, to be sexually desired. Since this desire might easily appear while the person is herself having sexual desire, it follows that a person can have both sexual desire and the desire to be sexually desired at the same time.

In addition, being sexually desired might even heighten the individual's own sexual desires. For in being aware that she is sexually desired by the other person, she is also aware that the possibility of fulfilling her own sexual desires with that person is within reach, or at least more in reach than if the desired person lacked all such desire. This is because a relationship between two persons in which both have sexual desire toward the other is one that has fewer barriers to fulfillment than one in which only one of the persons has such desire. As a result, with the fulfillment of her longings at hand, her desires might then begin to intensify.

But again, none of this would be basic to sexual desire in the way that the desire to be loved is basic to being in love. As Kaplan (1977) puts it, "there are many persons who feel desire for strangers, for prostitutes, for cruel and uncaring persons, for persons who look down on them and criticize them" (p. 7). What such uncaring persons have in common, or at least might have in common, is that they lack any desire for the person who is desiring them. Indeed, in many cases it seems to be just this lack of sexual desire in the uncaring person that whets the desirous person's own cravings. But it would be unwarranted to conclude from this that such things are definitive aspects of sexual desire. For they are merely, like the desires for particular positions or settings referred to previously, the limiting conditions under which certain people's sexual desires take place. In other words, to desire another person sexually, it is enough to desire mutual baring and caressing with that person. One need not also desire that the other person has these same desires toward oneself.

6

Epilogue: Sexual Desire
as an Existential Need

There remains a final question in this inquiry into the nature of sexual
desire. For even though a phenomenological analysis of sexual desire has
now been presented and its relation to romantic love subsequently disclosed, one still wants to know why sexual desire exists at all. For why is it
we desire to engage in mutual baring and caressing with another person?
This is a question that, according to one's view, might be felt to lie outside
the bounds of phenomenological inquiry. Two common views here are
those of biological essentialism and social constructionism.

According to the first view, we experience sexual desire simply because
we are biologically preprogrammed to do so. Those who take this view
often refer here to both ultimate and proximate causes (Symons, 1987). In
this case ultimate causes refer to our evolutionary history, while proximate
causes refer to the biological mechanisms that directly cause sexual desire.
The evolutionary account is one that I rejected in the earlier discussion of
the object of sexual desire. The problem with the biological mechanism
account is that, as I have argued elsewhere, there is little concrete evidence
that sexual desire is directly caused by any biological events (Giles, forthcoming, a). Of course, biological events like the release of sex hormones
affect things like erection, ejaculation, and vaginal lubrication, but none of
these events, as was shown earlier, is necessary for the occurrence of sexual desire.

Difficulties with this view have led other scholars to claim that sexual
desire is socially constructed, that is, that sexual desire exists only because

the culture in which it appears has constructed it or has, to use Simon and Gagnon's (1986) popular term, "scripted" it. Again, however, as I have also argued elsewhere, there is no evidence for this view of sexual desire, a view that is in fact fraught with confusion and inconsistencies (see Giles, 2004, forthcoming, b). Sexual desire is something that has persisted throughout all cultures at all times and whose genesis has little to do with cultural dictates. This does not mean that things like preferred positions for sexual intercourse, perceptions of homosexuality, or lesbian identities are not somehow socially constructed, only that sexual desire, which lies at the heart of all sexuality, is not in any meaningful sense a construction of culture.

But if sexual desire has its origins in neither biological events nor cultural dictates, where does it come from? The answer, I want to argue, is that sexual desire is an existential need that has its ultimate roots in specific experiential features of the human condition. This is an answer that once again returns us to the field of phenomenology. For here the wellspring of sexual desire is to be found in the center of human consciousness. The idea of an existential need is one that was first clearly formulated by Fromm. According to Fromm, specific abilities of human consciousness lie at the basis of a permanent state of disequilibrium in human existence. Thus, says Fromm,

Self-awareness, reason and imagination disrupt the "harmony" which characterizes animal existence. Their emergence has made man into an anomaly, into the freak of the universe. He is part of nature, subject to her physical laws and unable to change them, yet he transcends the rest of nature. He is set apart while being a part; he is homeless, yet chained to the home he shares with all creatures. Cast into the world at an accidental place and time, he is forced out of it, again accidentally. Being aware of himself, he realizes his powerlessness and the limitations of his existence. He visualizes his own end: death. Never is he free from the dichotomy of his own existence: he cannot rid himself of his mind, even if he should want to; he cannot rid himself of his body as long as he is alive—and his body makes him want to live. (1955, p. 24)

This harsh situation in which human beings find themselves has given rise to various needs. These are the needs that strive to overcome or at least come to terms with the sense of disequilibrium that is created by our awareness of our existential situation. Here, then, we can see how such existential needs have no basis in biological instinct. For in being founded on the nature of the human condition, there is no preprogrammed biological mechanism that gives rise to such needs. Rather, it is simply the way in which human consciousness perceives its own situation that makes us undergo these needs.

Of course, human consciousness is possible only because human bodies exist. And the body is based on biology. But that is not the same as saying that there is a biological mechanism that directly causes a specific existential need. Further, existential needs are not the product of social construction. For in contrast to socially constructed phenomena, existential needs are an inherent and universal feature of the human condition. No matter what cultural scenarios, "scripts," or dictates one lives under, one is still a human being with the same existential needs. This is because to be human is to have self-awareness, reason, and imagination. And it is the very use of these abilities that engender the need to overcome the disequilibrium that they cause.

What, then, are these needs? Fromm (1973) lists the following: the need for a frame of orientation and devotion, for rootedness, for unity, for effectiveness, the need for excitation and stimulation, and the need for character structure. Each of these needs arises in a different way from our awareness of our situation. For example, the need for rootedness is a response to the sense of separateness that comes from being "cast into the world." Being torn from my mother at birth—a tearing that deepens as I become more and more aware of my separateness from her—a need gradually appears that engenders my yearning for new emotional ties to the world and to other people, ties that give me a sense of rootedness. The need for effectiveness, on the other hand, is a response to the awareness that I am limited in my existence and powerless to choose its beginning or indefinitely extend its duration. Being aware of this I strive to overcome the resulting sense of powerlessness by being effectual in some other way. What each of the existential needs has in common is that each expresses a desire to overcome some aspect of dichotomy inherent in the human condition.

But where does sexual desire fit into this scheme? The answer is that, for Fromm, it does not. This is because Fromm shares the view—one we have just had occasion to reject—that sexual desire is essentially a biological need and therefore on par with hunger, thirst, and the need for sleep. It is peculiar that Fromm, who is in so many ways a brilliant observer of humankind, nevertheless fails to notice the crucial and non-physiological role that sexual desire plays in human interaction and thus in human existence. Had he looked closer, however, he might even have seen that sexual desire not only is far from being a physiological need but in fact comes close to what he means by an existential need. For an existential need is based on the awareness of a disequilibrium in the human condition—a state of imbalance, which is the essence of human existence.

Sexual desire is a need that is based precisely on such an awareness, namely, the awareness of having a gender, which implies a sense of incompleteness that calls out to be fulfilled by the gender of another person. Here self-awareness (together with the awareness of others) makes me see that I am gendered and consequently makes me feel the incompleteness that this implies, reason makes me see this as a problem that needs to solved, and imagination enables me to picture or fantasize ways—namely, baring and caressing of the desired gender—of trying to solve it. All this gives rise to a state of disequilibrium that sends me forward into a state of existential need, a need that is none other than sexual desire. For sexual desire is the need to deal with this problem. Further, this state of sexual desire is permanently embedded in the human condition as we know it, for to be human is to be lacking in one of the genders.

It is these specific aspects of sexual desire that also make it clear that sexual desire is an existential need unto itself, that is, that it cannot be subsumed under the other existential needs. For although sexual interaction can be used as an attempt to satisfy the need for, say, rootedness or effectiveness, the desire that lies behind such attempt is the desire for rootedness or effectiveness, not the desire for sexual fulfillment. The desire for rootedness is the desire for emotional ties to the world or other people, ties that are meant to address one's sense of separateness. But this is a need that can be dealt with by engaging in numerous activities, none of which needs to be sexual. One can, for example, attempt to feel rooted by joining a religion or a political movement.

Likewise, the desire for effectiveness is the desire to overcome a sense of powerlessness by being effectual in some way. But this need can also be addressed in numerous non-sexual ways. Here one might take to oil painting or to running a business in order to create a sense of effectiveness. To say then that sexual desire is just the desire for rootedness or effectiveness is to deny that there is any essential difference behind sexual interaction that is engaged in for sexual reasons and sexual interaction engaged in simply to feel rooted or effective. But, plainly, there is huge difference. For sexual desire is the desire for bodily vulnerability and care with someone of the desired gender, expressed through the desire for mutual baring and caressing with that person. The fundamental aspects of this desire—desires for baring, caressing, and a person of a specific gender—play no essential part in the needs for rootedness or effectiveness (or in any other of the existential needs).

But might it not be that sexual desire is simply an expression of the more general need for human interaction and thus, in this sense, not a need completely unto itself? For plainly such interaction is not desired simply as one of many possible ways of satisfying the needs for devotion and a frame of orientation, rootedness, effectiveness, and so on. For were we to have all those needs satisfied by non-human objects, we would still feel the independent need for human interaction and communication, a need that stems specifically from a sense of aloneness and separateness from other *people*.

Perhaps, then, it should be allowed that we also have the existential need for human interaction. But if we do this, then the question arises concerning the relation of the need for such interaction and the need of sexual desire. For if sexual desire is also a form of interaction, then is not sexual desire merely a form of the need for interaction? In one sense this is, of course, true. For the object of sexual desire is sexual interaction, and sexual interaction is a form of interaction.

But even here it should still be apparent that sexual desire is not merely an expression of a more general need for interaction. For the need to interact with others is a need that is not particularly concerned with the gender of the person with whom one interacts. The need for human interaction focuses simply on the fact that the object of the need is interchange and communication with another human being regardless of the human being's gender. The need of sexual desire, however, is aimed precisely at a particular gender. That is, although the need for interaction might be addressed equally well by interacting with either a male or a female, an individual's sexual desire is not.

Of course, in any particular human relationship there are numerous and diverse needs being brought into play. Consequently, in practice, it may prove next to impossible to disentangle them from each other. Thus, although a heterosexual female may be engaging her need for interaction primarily by having a conversation with a male friend, the simple fact that she is heterosexual and that he is a male will probably be enough to tempt her sexual desire to make its way secretly into the interchange, blending itself with the need for interaction. Therefore, as the conversation unfolds and the woman feels her need for mere human interaction being addressed, sexual desire might well weave its way into the fabric of her awareness and, quietly reaching out toward the man, whisper back to her, "This is something I too want." It might even be that the need for human interaction is never completely free from some level of sexual desire when the person to whom the need is directed is someone of the desired gender. Here we might find, as the woman cited earlier calls it, that "real little, small little hint of sexual that's going on." Of course, the sexual attractiveness of the other person will play a major role here, but then sexual attractiveness, like sexual desire, is a matter largely of degree. Consequently, in its mildest forms sexual desire might be barely distinguishable from the awareness that the other person displays the desired gender.

Against this the protest could be raised that sexual desire is not the only place where the need for an interaction with a specific gender makes itself heard. For although someone is, say, a heterosexual male, he nevertheless has a need for interaction or companionship with other males. Consequently, the complaint might go, he has a non-sexual need for human interaction that cannot be equally well addressed by his interacting with either gender, and, as a result, the element of gender does play a role in non-sexual needs. D. H. Lawrence seems to hold a view similar to this. Thus, in his novel *Women in Love* (1920), we find the supposedly heterosexual character Birkin arguing that female companionship is not sufficient and expressing his need for companionship specifically with males (though, suggestively enough, various of Birkin's interactions with his male companions—such as the naked wrestling match in which the two men "drive their white flesh deeper and deeper against each other"—have a definite sexual air about them).

Here it must be allowed that some people do experience a need to inter-act, and in a non-sexual way, specifically with members of their own gen-der. But then it must also be allowed that others do not have such a need. There are many people whose opposite-gender sexual partners are also their best friends and their main, if not exclusive, companions. Such people have no major need for specifically same-gender interaction. Here the need for human interaction and the need of sexual desire are being satisfied by the same person. Therefore, the need to interact non-sexually with persons of the same gender is a personal need that only some people feel, a need that has its basis in the person's particular character structure rather than in the nature of the human condition. It is, therefore, neither a universal nor an existential need.

In this way the need of sexual desire separates itself off from our other needs by holding firmly to the element of gender. This is because the need expressed by sexual desire is the need to fill the emptiness that lies at the nucleus of our experience of gender, that most primal division that sepa-rates us from each other.

With these observations enough ground has been gained to see the answer to the question that was raised in the first pages of this study, namely, the question of why the fulfillment of sexual desire is of such sig-nificance to us. The answer is that it is of such significance to us because sexual desire has in its core the human distinction that is of the utmost sig-nificance to us. Thus, since no other distinction in the human condition raises itself so powerfully before us as the distinction of gender, no other need so powerfully demands its fulfillment as the need of sexual desire. And this is true not just for the heterosexual who seeks to fulfill his or her desire through a baring and caressing of the gender that lies on the oppo-site side of the division but also for the homosexual. This is because even though the homosexual's desires are toward the same gender, the distinc-tion of gender is still of supreme significance to him or her. For just as it is of vast importance to the heterosexual that his or her sexual partner is of the opposite gender, so is it of vast importance to the homosexual that his or her sexual partner is of the same gender. And the notion of "same gen-der" is one that can be experienced only if one has an awareness of the division of gender. With the bisexual, the gender of his or her partner is, in each particular instance of sexual desire, similarly of much significance. In each case gender holds sway over the particular desires.

But still, for all its strength, for all that sexual desire rushes forward to fill the chasm of gender, in one way it seems as though such a chasm can never be filled. For, from one point of view, a male body is male and a female body is female, and uniting them in sexual interaction does not change that (just as the uniting of two bodies of the same gender does not make either of them more of the gender they already are). In other words, for all his penetration of the female, for all her receiving of the male, the male and female remain male and female, alone and isolated from each other by the chasm of gender.

It is this idea, I sense, that lies behind much of the discontentment with and even hostility toward sexual desire. These ill feelings are commonly masked as religious, moral, or even medical concerns. Thus, many religions attack sexual desire as being evil, impure, lustful, or coming from our "baser nature." Here the religious leaders and holy ones are put forward as those who lack or at least have "overcome" this "sinful" desire. Likewise, there are popular versions of morality containing the idea that there is something intrinsically wrong with sexual desire and activity and that such desire and activity must be strictly controlled (See here Nietzsche's [1889] critique in *Twilight of the Idols* of such "anti-nature" views).

Under its medical guise, hostility toward sexual desire and sexuality has taken various forms. Thus, there was the well-known belief, advocated by Krafft-Ebing and others, that masturbation and other sexual activities led to mental illness and various disorders. Although it might be thought that such dated views have now largely gone their way, in fact their ghosts continue to haunt us in the form of new pseudo-medical attacks on sexual desire. Thus, in their place we now have the new "disorders" of hypersexuality, sexual compulsivity, and sexual addiction. Although such concepts seem to have gained wide acceptance, a careful analysis of these "syndromes" will show that, as Levine and Troiden (1988) have aptly demonstrated, such terms refer not to any specific clinical entity but simply to behavior patterns that are stigmatized by our dominant institutions. That is, they too are merely hostile moral judgments.

But how might it happen that such hostility could arise from the experience of an unbridgeable gulf between genders? It will be recalled that in an earlier chapter we came upon May's observation that it was the moment of penetration rather than orgasm that bears within it "great wonder, tremendous and tremulous," a moment that, I argued, was not strictly limited to the penetration of sexual intercourse. Yet he follows this with the qualification "or disappointing and despairing, which says the same thing from the opposite point of view," a qualification that he does not, I am sorry to say, expand upon. Here, however, it can be seen how the fulfillment of this most significant of our desires could nonetheless be a moment of despair. For to arrive at the instant where one's most pressing desire is supposed to be fulfilled and yet to feel that it is somehow not really being fulfilled is to arrive at a moment of despair. Here, in the midst of overwhelming desire, in the moment of the longed-for union, the desirer suddenly sees that the desired has nonetheless escaped him. Her gender remains beyond his grasp, fleeing into the distance while he looks helplessly on.

But what has happened here to the experience of sexual fusion, the instant in which the genders are seen to commingle and lose their separateness? In other words, what has happened to the interpenetrating two-body Gestalt? Clearly, a person who cannot find this awareness has, for any of innumerable reasons—of which anxieties or guilt over baring and caressing are probably the most prevalent—refused to allow it to emerge. Here a person might respond to the first glimmerings of the Gestalt by quickly diverting his gaze to a point of view that construes his and his partner's bodies as two distinct physical objects that are merely spatially conjoined. From this point of view—which depends on a refusal to surrender to what presents itself to awareness in the sexual process—there is no mixing of genders, only two separate bodies alone and isolated from each other by the chasm of gender. In doing so, however, the person who thus diverts his awareness has chosen the road to disappointment and despair. For the sexual desire that led him to his sexual interaction—if it was sexual desire—contains within it the third appearance of gender. That is, it contains the interpenetrating two-body Gestalt as an integral element of the object of sexual desire.

The problem, then, is that upon arriving at the verge of the fulfillment of his desire, the bearer of sexual despair, as he might be called, suddenly casts off the emerging Gestalt but nevertheless proceeds with the motions of penetration and sexual interaction. It is as if he had been led by a burning desire for a glass of water to cross a desert and then, upon at last holding the glass in his hands, was to pour out the water and go through the drinking motions with the empty glass. Such dealings are the actions of despair, for they pursue the fulfillment of a desire while at the same time refusing to allow its fulfillment to take place. They consequently are the assurance of failure. It is easy to see, then, how someone entangled in such a conflict might become discontent with and even hostile toward sexual desire. Turning his dislike toward sexual desire—all the while cloaking it in religious, moral, or medical terms—might also help him avoid the pain of confronting the real source of his suffering, namely, the anxieties or guilt he has over his own desires.

To enter into such a state, however, is to abandon receptive awareness—the same awareness found in phenomenological inquiry—and look past the experience of the sexual interaction as it immediately presents itself. For in the moment of sexual interaction, what manifests itself to consciousness is an interpenetrating two-body Gestalt. This twoness of gender, which is an integral element in the object of sexual desire, appears to us from that place within, as Dogen calls it, that is beyond discriminatory thought. In this state we no longer try to reduce experience to fit preestablished opinions about what the world must be like. Rather, we merely let the world present itself to us as it will. And what presents itself to us here in all its meaningful clarity is a fusion of my gender with the gender of the other person. Here a simultaneous filling of the emptiness of each of our genders by each other's gender rushs through awareness, signaling the collapse of the barrier between us. In this moment I surrender myself to the formation of the Gestalt that arises before me, allowing myself to be swept up into its nearly unfathomable complexity. Here our genders seem to wrest themselves free as they pour into and diffuse throughout each other, transforming themselves into something beyond their mere individual expressions. For here my gender provides the basis that enables me to infiltrate and partake of hers, while her gender provides the basis that enables her to infiltrate and partake of mine. It is in this transformation that we have won each other. And it is in such a winning that sexual desire is at last fulfilled.

It is important, however, to recall what was shown earlier, namely, that a desire's fulfillment does not necessarily imply its cessation. With some desires, fulfillment brings about cessation, but with sexual desire things are otherwise. For although partaking of the Gestalt of sexual fusion will bring with it the fulfillment of sexual desire, sexual desire will continue into and beyond such fulfillment. In this sense, sexual desire sweeps forever through us like a shifting but endless wind, sending us forward while refusing to be completely stilled by its moments of fulfillment. And what sexual desire thus sends us forward to is, of course, more of its own fulfillment.

This tells us something further about the nature of sexual desire, namely, that what it searches for is continuous fulfillment, a fulfillment that, it must also be remembered, is composed of not just sexual intercourse or even genitally centered sexual activity but all forms of baring and caressing with the desired gender. And here we see something about the role of persisting relationships involving mutual sexual desire. For in these relationships one of the things that the participants normally attain is more engagement in such interaction and thus a better chance for continuous sexual fulfillment than those who lack such relationships (Laumann et al., 1994).

This should not be taken to mean, however, that merely achieving a desired amount of sexual interaction—that is, an amount of interaction that matches the strength of one's sexual desire—is a sufficient basis for sexual fulfillment. For obviously numerous other factors will come into play: the quality of the sexual interaction, the sensitivity that is shown toward each other, the addressing of each other's sexual tastes, and so on. What it does mean is that such an amount of interaction is necessary for sexual fulfillment. This is clear simply because even if one engages in sexual interactions with all the qualities just mentioned, if the instances of such interactions are well below the amount that one desires, then one will lack a general sense of sexual fulfillment.

But what is the most likely way to secure relationships wherein one can acquire continuous sexual fulfillment, especially where one's needs and specific tastes are genuinely taken into account? One likely answer is through relationships of romantic love (though this is by no means the only way). This is true if for no other reason than individuals in such relationships desire to be together. This in turn means that they will tend to be normally available to address each other's desires for continuous sexual fulfillment, something that the very structure of being in love implies that they will desire to do. Here, then, we see yet another connection between sexual desire and romantic love. For since sexual desire seeks continuous fulfillment, and since such fulfillment is usually available within the structure of a romantic love relationship, it is understandable that sexual desire often leads us on to the desires of love. The fulfillment of romantic love, as has been shown, involves more than the fulfillment of sexual desire, but without the seeds of sexual fulfillment it is doubtful that the desires of love could ever grow.

References

Addiego, F., Belzer, E. G., Comolli, J., Moger, W., Perry, J. D., and Whipple, B. (1981). Female ejaculation: A case study. *Journal of Sex Research, 17,* 13–21.

Altman, I., and Taylor, D. A. (1973). *Social penetration: The development of interpersonal relationships.* New York: Holt, Rinehart and Winston.

Alzate, H. (1985). Vaginal eroticism: A replication study. *Archives of Sexual Behavior, 14,* 529–537.

Alzate, H., and Londoño, M. L. (1984). Vaginal erotic sensitivity. *Journal of Sex and Marital Therapy, 10,* 49–56.

American Psychiatric Association. (1994). *Diagnostic and statistics manual of mental disorders.* Washington, DC: American Psychiatric Association.

Arndt, W. B. (1991). *Gender disorders and the paraphilias.* Madison, CT: International Universities Press.

Arora, R., and Solursh, L. P. (1991). Male multiple orgasm—Does it exist? In P. Kothari and R. Patel (Eds), *The first international conference of orgasm* (pp. 221–226). Bombay, India: VRP.

Averill, J. (1985). The social construction of emotion: With special reference to love. In K. J. Gergen and K. E. Davis (Eds), *The social construction of the person (pp. 89-109).* New York: Springer.

Balint, M. (1948). *Primary love and psychoanalytic technique.* London: Tavistock (1959).

Bancroft, J. (1989). *Human sexuality and its problems* (2nd ed.). Edinburgh: Churchill Livingston.

Basson, R. (2001). Using a different model for female sexual response to address womens' problematic low sexual desire. *Journal of Sex and Marital Therapy, 27,* 395–403.

Baumeister, R. F. (2000). Gender differences in erotic plasticity: The female sex drive as socially flexible and responsive. *Psychological Bulletin, 126,* 347–374.

Beauvoir, S. de. (1949). *The second sex* (H. M. Parshley, Trans. and Ed.). New York: Vintage (1989).

Beiber, I., Dain, H. J., Dince, P. R., Drellich, M. G., Grand, H. G., Gundlach, R. H., Kremer, M. W., Rifkin, A. H., Wilbur, C. B., and Bieber, T. B. (1962). *Homosexuality: A psychoanalytic study of male homosexuals.* New York: Basic Books.

Bell, R. (2002). Unconventional sexual lifestyles. In D. Miller and J. Green (Eds), *The psychology of sexual health* (pp. 292–303). Oxford: Blackwell Science.

Bem, D. J. (1996). Exotic becomes erotic: A developmental theory of sexual orientation. *Psychological Review, 103,* 320–335.

Bem, D. J. (1998). Is EBE theory supported by the evidence? Is it androcentric? A reply to Peplau et al. (1998). *Psychological Review, 105,* 395–398.

Bem, S. L. (1989). Genital knowledge and gender constancy in preschool children. *Child Development, 60,* 649–662.

Bentler, P. M., and Peeler, W. H. (1979). Models of female orgasm. *Archives of Sexual Behavior, 8,* 405–423.

Bergström-Walan, M. (1981). *Den svenska kvinnorapporten: Kvinnor I Sverige berättar om sitt sexliv.* Stockholm: Trevi.

Berliner, B. (1947). On some psychodynamics of masochism. *Psychoanalytic Quarterly, 16,* 459–471.

Berne, E. (1977). *Intuition and ego states: The origins of transactional analysis.* San Francisco: TA Press.

Bernstein, D. (1990). Female genital anxieties, conflicts and typical mastery modes. *International Journal of Psycho-Analysis, 7,* 151–165.

Berscheid, E., and Walster, E. (1974). A little bit about love. In T. L. Huston (Ed.), *Foundations of interpersonal attraction* (pp. 356–381). New York: Academic Press.

Bogart, L. M., Cecil, H., Wagstaff, D., Pinkerton, S. D., and Abramson, P. R. (2000). Is it "sex"?: College student's interpretations of sexual behavior terminology. *Journal of Sex Research, 37,* 108–116.

Bork, E. (2000, October 22). Ladyboys. *Berlingske tidende,* sec. 2, p. 7.

Bowlby, J. (1969). *Attachment and loss: Vol. 1. Attachment.* New York: Basic Books.

Bowlby, J. (1973). *Attachment and loss: Vol. 2. Separation: Anxiety and anger.* New York: Basic Books.

Bowlby, J. (1980). *Attachment and loss: Vol. 3. Loss.* New York: Basic Books.

Bringle, R. G., and Boebinger, K. L. G. (1990). Jealousy and the "third" person in the love triangle. *Journal of Social and Personal Relationships, 7,* 119–133.

Bringle, R. G., and Buunk, B. (1986). Examining the causes of and consequences of jealousy: Some recent findings and issues. In R. Gilmour and S. Duck (Eds), *The emerging field of personal relationships* (pp. 225–240). Hillsdale, NJ: Erlbaum.

Bringle, R. G., and Buunk, B. (1991). Extradyadic relationships and sexual jealousy. In K. McKinney and S. Sprecher (Eds), *Sexuality in close relationships* (pp. 135–153). Hillsdale, NJ: Erlbaum.

Bruijn, G. de. (1982a). From masturbation to orgasm with a partner: How some women bridge the gap—and why others don't. *Journal of Sex and Marital Therapy, 8,* 151–167.

Bruijn, G. de. (1982b). How women orgasm. In Z. Hoch and H.I. Lief (Eds), *Sexology: Sexual biology, behavior and therapy* (pp. 141–145). Amsterdam: Excerpta Medica.

Burgess, A.W. (1981). Physician sexual misconduct and patients' responses. *American Journal of Psychiatry, 138,* 1335–1342.

Buss, D.M. (2003). *The evolution of desire: Strategies of human mating* (Rev. ed.). New York: Basic Books.

Buss, D.M. (2000). *The dangerous passion: Why jealousy is as necessary as love and sex.* New York: Free Press.

Byer, C.O., and Shainberg, L.W. (1991). *Dimensions of human sexuality* (3rd ed.). Dubuque, IA: Wm C Brown.

Byers, E.S., and Demmons, S. (1999). Sexual satisfaction and sexual self-disclosure with dating relationships. *Journal of Sex Research, 36,* 180–189.

Byers, E.S., Demmons, S., and Lawrence, K. (1998). Sexual satisfaction within dating relationships: A test of the interpersonal exchange model of sexual satisfaction. *Journal of Social and Personal Relationships, 15,* 257–267.

Cawood, H.H., and Bancroft, J. (1996). Steroid hormones, the menopause, sexuality and the well-being of women. *Psychological Medicine, 26,* 925–936.

Chalkley, A.J., and Powell, G.E. (1983). The clinical description of forty-eight cases of clinical fetishism. *British Journal of Psychiatry, 142,* 292–295.

Chesser, E. (1969). *Love and the married woman.* New York: G.P. Putnam's Sons.

Churchill, S.D. (1990). Considerations for teaching a phenomenological approach to psychological research. *Journal of Phenomenological Psychology, 21,* 46–67.

Cleary, T. (Trans.). (1999). *Sex, health, and long life: Manuals of Taoist practice.* Boston: Shambala.

Coen, S. (1992). *The misuse of persons: Analyzing pathological dependency.* Hillsdale, NJ: Analytic Press.

Cyr, R. (2004, May 28). Personal interview with Ronald Cyr, Clinical Assistant Professor, Department of Obstetrics and Gynecology, University of Michigan.

Darling, C.A., and Davidson, J.K. (1986). Enhancing relationships: Understanding the feminine mystique of pretending orgasm. *Journal of Sex and Marital Therapy, 12,* 182–196.

Darling, C.A., Davidson, J.K., and Conway-Welch, C. (1990). Female ejaculation: Perceived origins, the Grafenberg spot/area, and sexual responsiveness. *Archives of Sexual Behavior, 9,* 29–47.

Davenport, W. (1965). Sexual patterns and their regulation in a society of the southwest Pacific. In F.A. Beach (Ed.), *Sex and behaviour* (pp. 164–207). New York: Wiley.

Davenport, W.H. (1987). An anthropological approach. In J.H. Geer and W.T. O'Donohue (Eds), *Theories of human sexuality* (pp. 197–236). New York: Plenum Press.

Diamond, L. M. (1998). Development of sexual orientation among adolescent and young women. *Developmental Psychology, 34,* 1085–1095.

Dickinson, R. L., and Beam, L. (1934). *The single woman: A medical study in sex education.* Baltimore: Williams and Wilkins.

Dickinson, R. L., and Beam L., (1932). A thousand marriages: A medical study of sex adjustment. Baltimore: Williams and Wilkins.

Dion, K. L., and Dion, K. K. (1973). Correlates of romantic love. *Journal of Consulting and Clinical Psychology, 41,* 51–56.

Docter, R. F. (1988). *Transvestites and transsexuals: Toward a theory of cross-gender behavior.* New York: Plenum.

Dogen. (1994). *Master Dogen's Shobogenzo* (Bk. 2)(G. Nishijima and C. Cross, Trans.). Woking: Windbell.

Dogen. (1996). *The shobogenzo or the treasure house of the eye of the true teachings* (H. Nearman, Trans.). Mount Shasta, CA: Shasta Abbey.

Doi, T. (1981). *The anatomy of dependence* (J. Bester, Trans.). Tokyo: Kodansha International.

Donnelly, D. A. (1993). Sexually inactive marriages. *Journal of Sex Research, 30,* 171–179.

Dossett, J. (2002). *An empirical phenomenological investigation of sexual desire.* Unpublished doctoral dissertation, Tennessee State University.

Driscoll, R., Davis, K. E., and Lipitz, M. E. (1972). Paternal interference and romantic love: the Romeo and Juliet effect. *Journal of Personality and Social Psychology, 24,* 1–10.

Dunn, M. E., and Trost, J. E. (1989). Male multiple orgasms: A descriptive study. *Archives of Sexual Behavior, 18,* 377–387.

Dutton, D. G., and Aron, A. P. (1974). Some evidence for heightened sexual attraction under conditions of high anxiety. *Journal of Personality and Social Psychology, 30,* 510–517.

Dwyer, M. (1988). Exhibitionism/voyeurism. *Journal of Social Work and Human Sexuality, 7,* 101–112.

Ellis, H. (1905). The mechanism of detumescence. In *Studies in the psychology of sex* (Vol. 5, pp. 115–200). Philadelphia: F. A. Davis.

Ellis, H. (1903). Analysis of the sexual impulse. *Studies in the psychology of sex* (Vol. 3, pp. 1–55). Philadelphia: F. A. Davis.

Emerson, J. P. (1970). Behavior in private places: Sustaining definitions of reality in gynecological examinations. In H. P. Dreitzel (Ed.), *Recent sociology: Vol. 2. Patterns of communicative behaviour* (pp. 74–97). New York: Macmillan.

Faix, A., Lapray, J. F., Courtieu, C., Maubon, A., and Lanfrey, K. (2001). Magnetic resonance imaging of sexual intercourse: Initial experience. *Journal of Sex and Marital Therapy, 27,* 475–482.

Fausto-Sterling, A. (1993, March–April). The five sexes: Why male and female are not enough. *The Sciences,* 20–24.

Fausto-Sterling, A. (2000). *Sexing the body: Gender politics and the construction of gender.* New York: Basic Books.

Festinger, L. (1957). *A theory of cognitive dissonance.* Stanford, CA: Stanford University Press.

Fisher, H. (1995). The nature and evolution of romantic love. In W. Jankowiak (Ed.), *Romantic passion: A universal experience?* (pp. 23–41). New York: Columbia University Press.

Fisher, S. (1973). *The female orgasm: Psychology, physiology, fantasy.* London: Allen Lane.

Fisher, S. (1989). *Sexual images of the self: The psychology of erotic sensations and illusions.* Hillsdale, NJ: Erlbaum.

Ford, C. S., and Beach, F. A. (1952). *Patterns of sexual behavior.* New York: Harper and Row (1972).

Foucault, M. (1979). *The history of sexuality: An introduction* (R. Hurley, Trans.). London: Allen Lane.

Francoeur, R. T., Cornog, M., Perper, T., and Scherzer, N. A. (2000). *The complete dictionary of sexology* (Rev. ed.). New York: Continuum.

Freese, M. P., and Levitt, E. E. (1984). Relationships among intervaginal pressure, orgasmic function, parity factors, and urine leakage. *Archives of Sexual Behavior, 13,* 260–268.

Freud, S. (1905). Three essays on the theory of sexuality (6th ed.). In J. Strachey (Ed.), *The standard edition of the complete psychological works of Sigmund Freud* (Vol. 7, pp. 125–243). London: Hogarth Press and the Institute of Psycho-analysis (1986).

Freud, S. (1908). On the sexual theories of children. In J. Strachey (Ed.), *The standard edition of the complete psychological works of Sigmund Freud* (Vol. 9, pp. 207–226). London: Hogarth Press and the Institute of Psychoanalysis (1986).

Freud, S. (1910). Leonardo da Vinci and a memory of his childhood. In J. Strachey (Ed.), *The standard edition of the complete psychological works of Sigmund Freud* (Vol. 9, pp. 63–137). London: Hogarth Press and the Institute of Psycho-analysis (1986).

Freud, S. (1916). Introductory lectures on psycho-analysis (Parts I and II). In J. Strachey (Ed.), *The standard edition of the complete psychological works of Sigmund Freud* (Vol. 15). London: Hogarth Press and the Institute of Psycho-analysis (1986).

Freud, S. (1922). Group psychology and the analysis of the ego. In J. Strachey (Ed.), *The standard edition of the complete psychological works of Sigmund Freud* (Vol. 18, pp. 69–143). London: Hogarth Press and the Institute of Psycho-analysis (1986).

Freud, S. (1924). The economic problem of masochism. In J. Strachey (Ed.), *The standard edition of the complete psychological works of Sigmund Freud* (Vol. 19, pp. 159–170). London: Hogarth Press and the Institute of Psycho-analysis (1986).

Freud, S. (1927). Fetishism. In J. Strachey (Ed.), *The standard edition of the complete psychological works of Sigmund Freud* (Vol. 21, pp. 149–157). London: Hogarth Press and the Institute of Psycho-analysis (1986).

Freud, S. (1930). Civilizations and its discontents. In J. Strachey (Ed.), *The standard edition of the complete psychological works of Sigmund Freud* (Vol. 21, pp. 59–145). London: Hogarth Press and the Institute of Psycho-analysis (1986).

Freund, K., and Seto, M. (1998). Preferential rape in the theory of courtship disorder. *Archives of Sexual Behavior, 27,* 433–443.

Freund, K., Watson, R., and Rienzo, D. (1988). The value of self-reports in the study of voyeurism and exhibitionism. *Annals of Sex Research, 1,* 243–262.

Friday, N. (1975). *My secret garden: Women's sexual fantasies.* London: Virago

Friday, N. (1998). *Men in love. Men's sexual fantasies: The triumph of love over rage.* New York: Delacorte Press.

Fried, E. (1960). *The ego in love and sexuality.* New York: Grune and Stratton.

Friedman, M. (1974). *The hidden human image.* New York: Dutton.

Fromm, E. (1955). *The sane society.* London: Routledge and Kegan Paul (1979).

Fromm, E. (1956). *The art of loving.* Toronto: Bantam Books (1972).

Fromm, E. (1973). *The anatomy of human destructiveness.* New York: Holt, Rinehart and Winston.

Fugate, S. R., Apodaca, C. C., and Hibbert, M. L. (2001). Gender reassignment surgery and the gynecological patient. *Primary Care Update: Obstetrics/Gynecology, 8,* 22–24.

Galenson, E., and Roiphe, H. (1974). The emergence of genital awareness during the second year of life. In R. Friedman, R. Richardt, and R. L. Van de Wiele (Eds), *Sex differences in behavior* (pp. 233–258). New York: Wiley.

Gamman, L., and Makinen, M. (1994). *Female fetishism: A new look.* London: Lawrence and Wishart.

Giffin, K., and Patton, B. R. (1976). *Fundamentals of interpersonal communication* (2nd ed.). Lanham, MD: University Press of America.

Giles, J. (1994). *A study in phenomenalism.* Aalborg, Denmark: Department of Languages and Intercultural Studies, Aalborg University.

Giles, J. (1997). *No self to be found: The search for personal identity.* Lanham, MD: University Press of America.

Giles, J. (1999). Sartre, sexual desire, and relations with others. In J. Giles (Ed.), *French existentialism: Consciousness, ethics, and relations with others* (pp. 155–174). Amsterdam and Atlanta, GA: Rodopi.

Giles, J. (2004). Review of *Sambia sexual culture: Essays from the field.* By Gilbert Herdt. *Archives of Sexual Behavior, 33,* 413–417.

Giles, J. (forthcoming, a). Sex hormones and sexual desire.

Giles, J. (forthcoming, b). Social constructionism and sexual desire.

Goldberg, D. C., Whipple, B., Fishkin, R. E., Waxman, H., Fink, P. J., and Weisberg, M. (1983). The Grafenberg spot and female ejaculation: A review of initial hypotheses. *Journal of Sex and Marital Therapy, 9,* 27–37.

Goldman, R., and Goldman, J. (1982). *Children's sexual thinking.* Boston: Routledge and Kegan Paul.

Gonsiorek, J. C., and Weinrich, J. D. (1991). The definition and scope of sexual orientation. In J. C. Gonsiorek and J. D. Weinrich (Eds), *Homosexuality: Research implications for public health policy* (pp. 1–12). Newbury Park, CA: Sage.

Grafenberg, E. (1950). The role of the urethra in female orgasm. *International Journal of Sexology, 3,* 145–148.

Grossman, W. I. (1986). Notes on masochism: A discussion of the history and development of a psychoanalytic concept. *Psychoanalytic Quarterly, 55,* 379–413.

Gulik, R. H. van. (1961). *Sexual life in ancient China*. Leiden: E. J. Brill.

Hampson, J. L., and Hampson, J. G. (1961). The ontogenesis of sexual behavior in man. In W. C. Young (Ed.), *Sex and internal secretions* (Vol. 1, pp. 1401–1432). Baltimore: Williams and Wilkins.

Harris, H. (1995). Rethinking Polynesian heterosexual relationships: A case study on Mangaia, Cook Islands. In W. Jankowiak (Ed.), *Romantic passion: A universal experience?* (pp. 95–127). New York: Columbia University Press.

Harvey, J. (1995). *Odyssey of the heart: The search for closeness, intimacy, and love*. New York: W. H. Freeman.

Hatfield, E., and Rapson, R. L. (1987). Passionate love/sexual desire: Can the same paradigm explain both? *Archives of Sexual Behavior, 16*, 259–278.

Hatfield, E., and Rapson, R. L. (1993). *Love, sex, and intimacy: Their psychology, biology, and history*. New York: HarperCollins.

Hatfield, E., and Walster, G. W. (1981). *A new look at love*. Reading, MA: Addison-Wesley.

Hazan, C., and Shaver, P. (1987). Romantic love conceptualized as an attachment process. *Journal of Personality and Social Psychology, 52*, 511–524.

Heath, D. (1984). An investigation into the origins of copious vaginal discharge during intercourse—"enough to wet the bed"—that is not urine. *Journal of Sex Research, 20*, 194–215.

Heidegger, M. (1927). *Being and time* (J. Macquarrie and E. Robinson, Trans.). New York: Harper and Row (1962).

Hendricks, C., and Hendricks, S. (1986). A theory and method of love. *Journal of Personality and Social Psychology, 50*, 392–402.

Hendricks, S. S., and Hendricks, C. (1993). *Romantic love*. Newbury Park, CA: Sage.

Heraclitus. (1987). *Fragments: A text and translation with commentary* (T. M. Robinson, Trans.). Toronto: University of Toronto Press.

Herdt, G. (1999). *Sambia sexual culture: Essays from the field*. Chicago: Chicago University Press.

Hobbes, T. (1974). *Leviathan* (C. B. MacPherson, Ed.). Harmondsworth: Penguin Books.

Hoch, Z. (1980). The sensory arm of the female orgasmic reflex. *Journal of Sex Education and Therapy, 6*, 4–7.

Hoch, Z. (1983). The G spot. *Journal of Sex and Marital Therapy, 9*, 166–167.

Hoeck, S. (2002, October). Hvad har disse kvinder til fælles? *Månedsmagasinet IN, 10*, 93–100.

Holmes, J. G., and Rempel, J. K. (1989). Trust in relationships. In C. Hendricks (Ed.), *Close relationships: Review of personality and social psychology* (Vol. 10, pp. 315–359). Newbury Park, CA: Sage.

Holt, J. C. (2002, December 8–13). *A Buddhist transformation of Visnu*. Paper given at the 13th Conference of the International Association of Buddhist Studies, Chulalongkorn University, Bangkok, Thailand.

Hunt, D. D., and Hampson, J. L. (1980). Follow-up of 17 biologic male transsexuals after sex reassignment surgery. *American Journal of Psychiatry, 137*, 432–438.

Hupka, R. (1981). Cultural determinates of jealousy. *Alternative Lifestyles, 4*, 310–315.

Husserl, E. (1913). *Ideas: General introduction to pure phenomenology* (W.R. Boyce Gibson, Trans.). New York: Collier Books (1962).

James, W. (1890). *The principles of psychology* (Vol. 1). New York: Dover (1950).

Jankowiak, W. (1995). Introduction. In W. Jankowiak (Ed.), *Romantic passion: A universal experience?* (pp. 1–19). New York: Columbia University Press.

Jankowiak, W.R., and Fisher, E.F. (1992). A cross-cultural perspective on love. *Ethnology, 31,* 149–155.

Jayadeva. (1964). The Ratimañjarī of Jayadeva. In A. Comfort (Trans.), *The Koka Shastra: Being the Ratirahasya of Kokkoka and other medieval Indian writings on love* (pp. 88–94). London: George Allen and Unwin.

Jones, J.C., and Barlow, D.H. (1990). Self-reported frequency of sexual urges, fantasies, and masturbatory fantasies in heterosexual males and females. *Archives of Sexual Behavior, 19,* 269–279.

Kalyanamalla. (1963). *The Ananga Ranga of Kalyanamalla* (R. Burton and F.F. Arbuthnot, Trans.). London: Kimber.

Kaplan, H.S. (1977). Hypoactive sexual desire. *Journal of Sex and Marital Therapy, 3,* 3–9.

Kaplan, H.S. (1987). *Sexual aversion, sexual phobia, and panic disorders.* New York: Brunner/Mazel.

Kaplan, H.S. (1995). *The sexual desire disorders: Dysfunctional regulation of sexual motivation.* New York: Brunner/Mazel.

Kardener, S.H., Fuller, M., and Mensh, I.N. (1973). A survey of physician's attitudes and practices regarding erotic and nonerotic contact with patients. *American Journal of Psychiatry, 130,* 1077–1081.

Kelly, H.H. (1983). Love and commitment. In H.H. Kelly, E. Berscheid, A. Christensen, J.H. Harvey, T.L. Huston, G. Levinger, E. McClintock, L.A. Peplau, and D.R. Peterson (Eds), *Close relationships (pp. 265-314).* San Francisco: W.H. Freeman.

Kernberg, O.F. (1995). *Love relations: Normalcy and pathology.* New Haven, CT: Yale University Press.

Kessler, S.J. (1998). *Lessons from the intersexed.* London: Rutgers University Press.

Kessler, S.J., and McKenna, W. (1978). *Gender: An ethnomethodological approach.* New York: Wiley.

Khouri, R.K., and Casoli, V.M. (1997). Reconstruction of the penis. In S.J. Aston, R.W. Beasley, and C.H.M. Thorne (Eds), *Grabb and Smith's plastic surgery* (5th ed., pp. 1111–1119). Philadelphia: Lippincott-Raven.

Kinsey, A.C., Pomeroy, W.B., and Martin, C.E. (1948). *Sexual behavior in the human male.* Philadelphia: W.B. Saunders.

Kinsey, A.C., Pomeroy, W.B., and Martin, C.E., Gebhard, P.H. (1953). *Sexual behavior in the human female.* Philadelphia: W.B. Saunders.

Klein, F., and Schwartz, T. (Eds). (2001). *Bisexual and gay husbands: Their stories, their words.* New York: Harrington Park Press.

Kokkoka. (1964). The Ratirahasya of Kokkoka. In A. Comfort (Trans.), *The Koka Shastra: Being the Ratirahasya of Kokkoka and other medieval Indian writings on love* (pp. 101–171). London: George Allen and Unwin.

Krafft-Ebing, R. von. (1886). *Psychopathia sexualis* (Domino Falls, Ed. and Trans.). London: Velvet Publications (1997).

Kronhausen, P., and Kronhausen, E. (1969). *Erotic fantasies: A study of the sexual imagination*. New York: Grove Press.

Kvale, S. (1983). The qualitative research interview: A phenomenological and a hermeneutical mode of understanding. *Journal of Phenomenological Psychology, 14,* 171–196.

Ladas, A.K., Whipple, B., and Perry, J.D. (1982). *The G spot and other recent discoveries about human sexuality*. New York: Holt, Rinehart and Winston.

Langevin, R., Paitich, D., Ramsay, G., Anderson, C., Kamrad, J., Pope, S., Geller, G., Pearl, L., and Newman, S. (1979). Experimental studies of the etiology of genital exhibitionism. *Archives of Sexual Behavior, 8,* 307–331.

Lao Tzu (or Lao-tze) (1927). *The canon of reason and virtue—Being Lao-tze's Tao Teh King. Chinese and English* (P. Carus, Trans.). Chicago: Open Court.

Laumann, E., Gagnon, J., Michael, R., and Michael, S. (1994). *The social organization of sexuality: Sexual practices in the United States*. Chicago: Chicago University Press.

Lawrence, A.A. (2003). Factors associated with satisfaction or regret following male-to-female sex reassignment surgery. *Archives of Sexual Behavior, 32,* 297–315.

Lawrence, D.H. (1920). *Women in love*. London: Penguin (1989).

Lawrence, D.H. (1922). "The Horse Dealer's Daughter." In W. Stone, N.H. Packer, and R. Hoopes (Eds), *The short story: An introduction* (pp. 318–328). New York: McGraw-Hill (1983).

Leary, T. (1957). *Interpersonal diagnosis of personality*. New York: Ronald.

Lee, J.A. (1977). A typology of styles of loving. *Personality and Social Psychology Bulletin, 3,* 173–182.

Leif, H.I., and Hubschman, L. (1993). Orgasm in the postoperative transsexual. *Archives of Sexual Behavior, 22,* 145–155.

Levinas, E. (1961). *Totality and infinity: An essay on exteriority* (A. Lingis, Trans.). The Hague: Martinus Nijhoff (1969).

Levine, M.P., and Troiden, R.R. (1988). The myth of sexual compulsivity. *Journal of Sex Research, 25,* 347–363.

Levine, R.J. (2002). Human female sexual arousal. *Archives of Sexual Behavior, 31,* 405-411.

Lips, H. (1997). *Sex and gender* (3rd ed.). Mountain View, CA: Mayfield.

Llewellyn-Jones, D. (1990). *The A-Z of women's health* (2nd ed.). Oxford: Oxford University Press.

Locke, D. (1982). Beliefs, desires, and reasons for action. *American Philosophical Quarterly, 19,* 227–242.

Mahler, M.S., Pine, F., and Bergman, A. (1975). *The psychological birth of the human infant: Symbiosis and individuation*. New York: Basic Books.

Maleson, F.G. (1984). The multiple meanings of masochism in psychoanalytic discourse. *Journal of the American Psychoanalytic Association, 32,* 325–356.

Maltz, W., and Boss, S. (1997). *In the garden of desire: The intimate world of women's sexual fantasies*. New York: Broadway Books.

Manderson, L. (1992). Public sex performances in Patpong and explorations of the edges of imagination. *Journal of Sex Research, 29,* 451–475.

Marrow, J. (1997). *Changing positions: Women speak out on sex and desire.* Holbrook, MA: Adams Media Corporation.

Marshall, D. S. (1971). Sexual behaviour among the Mangaia. In D. S. Marshall and R. C. Suggs (Eds), *Human sexual behaviour: Variations in the ethnographic spectrum* (pp. 103–162). New York: Basic Books.

Masters, W., and Johnson, V. (1966). *Human sexual response.* Boston: Little, Brown.

Masters, W., Johnson, V., and Kolodny, R. (1993). *Biological foundations of human sexuality.* New York: HarperCollins.

May, R. (1969). *Love and will.* New York: Dell.

McCarthy, B., and McCarthy, E. (1998). *Male sexual awareness: Increasing sexual satisfaction* (Rev. ed.). New York: Carroll and Graf.

McDougall. W. (1908). *An introduction to social psychology.* London: Methuen.

Mellen, S. L. W. (1981). *The evolution of love.* San Francisco: W. H. Freeman.

Menaker, E. (1979). *Masochism and the emergent ego.* New York: Human Sciences Press.

Merriam, A. (1971). Aspects of sexual behavior among the Bala (Basongye). In D. S. Marshall and R. C. Suggs (Eds), *Human sexual behaviour: Variations in the ethnographic spectrum* (pp. 71–102). New York: Basic Books.

Millet, C. (2003). *The sexual life of Catherine M* (A. Hunter, Trans.). London: Corgi.

Mills, J., and Clark, M. S. (1982). Exchange and communal relationships. In L. Wheeler (Ed.), *Review of personality and social psychology* (Vol. 3, pp. 121–144). Beverly Hills, CA: Sage.

Milsten, R., and Slowinski, J. (1999). *The sexual male: Problems and solutions.* New York: W. W. Norton.

Morris, P. T. (Trans.). (1992). *Cantonese love songs: An English translation of Jiu Ji-yung's Cantonese songs of early 19th century.* Hong Kong: Hong Kong University Press.

Morrison, T. L., Goodlin-Jones, B. L., and Urquiza, A. J. (1997). Attachment and the representation of intimate relationships in adulthood. *Journal of Psychology, 131,* 57–71.

Murphy, R. E. (1990). *The Song of Songs: A Commentary on the Book of Canticles* or *The Song of Songs.* Minneapolis: Fortress Press.

Nichiren. (1990). *Selected writings of Nichiren* (B. Watson and others, Trans.; P. B. Yampolsky, Ed.). New York: Columbia University Press.

Nietzsche, F. (1889). Twilight of the idols. In R. J. Hollingdale (Trans.), *Twilight of the idols and the anti-Christ* (pp. 21-112). Harmondsworth: Penguin (1974).

Nir, Y., and Maslin, B. (1982). *Loving men for all the right reasons: Women's patterns of intimacy,* New York: Dial.

Offit, A. (1995). *Night thoughts: Reflections of a sex therapist* (Rev. ed.). Northvale, NJ: Jason Aronson.

Perovic, S. V., Stanojevic, D. S., and Djordjevic, M. L. J. (2000). Vaginoplasty in male transsexuals using penile skin and a urethral flap. *British Journal of Urology International, 86,* 843–850.

Pinto, R. P., and Hollandsworth, J. G. (1984). A measure of possessiveness in intimate relationships. *Journal of Social and Clinical Psychology, 2,* 273–279.

Pitts, M., and Rahman, Q. (2001). Which behaviors constitute "having sex" among university students in the UK? *Archives of Sexual Behavior, 30,* 169–176.

Plato. (1973). Symposium (M. Joyce, Trans.). In E. Hamilton and C. Huntington (Eds), *The collected dialogues of Plato including the letters* (pp. 526–574). Princeton, NJ: Princeton University Press.

Rancour-Laferriere, D. (1985). *Signs of the flesh: An essay on the evolution of hominid sexuality.* Amsterdam: Mouton de Gruyter.

Rathbone, J. (2001). *The anatomy of masochism.* New York: Kluwer/Plenum.

Reich, W. (1941). *The function of the orgasm: The discovery of the orgone* (T. P. Wolfe, Trans.). New York: Meridian (1971).

Reik, T. (1940). The characteristics of masochism. *American Imago, 1,* 26–59.

Reik, T. (1957). *Of love and lust: On the psychoanalysis of romantic and sexual emotions.* New York: Condor.

Reinisch, J. M. (1990). *The Kinsey Institute new report on sex: What you must know to be sexually literate.* New York: St. Martin's Press.

Reiss, I. L. (1960). Toward a sociology of the heterosexual love relationship. *Marriage and Family Living, 22,* 139–145.

Richards, R., and Ames J. (1983). *Second serve: The René Richards story.* New York: Stein and Day.

Riley, A. J., Lees, W. R., and Riley, E. J. (1992). An ultrasound study of human coitus. In W. Bezemer, P. Cohen-Kettenis, K. Slob, and N. van Son-Schoones (Eds), *Sex matters: Proceedings of the Xth World Congress of Sexology, Amsterdam, 18–22 June, 1991* (pp. 29–36). Amsterdam: Excerpta Medica.

Rivers, W. H. R. (1906). *The Todas.* London: Macmillan.

Roach, M. E., and Eicher, J. B. (1979). The language of personal adornment. In J. M. Cordwell and R. A. Schwarz (Eds), *The fabrics of culture: The anthropology of clothing and adornment* (pp. 7–22). The Hague: Mouton Publishers.

Robinson, P. (1976). *The modernization of sex: Havelock Ellis, Alfred Kinsey, William Masters and Virginia Johnson.* New York: Harper and Row.

Rosman, J. P., and Resnick, P. J. (1989). Sexual attraction to corpses: A psychiatric review of necrophilia. *Bulletin of the American Academy of Psychiatry, 17,* 153–163.

Rougement, D. de. (1983). *Love in the western world* (M. Belgion, Trans.) (Rev. ed.). Princeton, NJ: Princeton University Press.

Rubenstein, C. (1983, July). The modern art of courtly love. *Psychology Today,* 40–49.

Rubin, Z. (1974). From liking to loving: patterns of attraction in dating relationships. In T. Huston (Ed.), *Foundations of interpersonal attraction* (pp. 383–402). New York: Academic Press.

Rubin, Z., Hill, C., Peplau, L., and Dunkel-Schetter, C. (1980). Self-disclosure in dating couples: Sex roles and the ethics of openness. *Journal of Marriage and the Family, 42,* 305–317.

Rudra. (1964). The Smaradipika. In A. Comfort (Trans.), *The Koka Shastra: Being the Ratirahasya of Kokkoka and other medieval Indian writings on love* (pp. 84–96). London: George Allen and Unwin.

Sanders, S. A., and Reinisch, J. M. (1999). Would you say you had sex if . . . ? *Journal of the American Medical Association, 281,* 275–277.

Sartre, J-P. (1943). *Being and nothingness: An essay on phenomenological ontology* (H. E. Barnes, Trans.). New York: Philosophical Library (1956).

Sax, L. (2002). How common is intersex? A response to Anne Fausto-Sterling. *Journal of Sex Research, 39,* 174–178.

Schachter, S. (1964). The interaction of cognitive and physiological determinants of emotional states. In L. Berkowitz (Ed.), *Advances in experimental social psychology* (Vol. 1, pp. 105–121). New York: Academic Press.

Schad-Somers, S. P. (1996). *Sadomasochism: Etiology and treatment.* Northvale, NJ: Jason Aronson.

Schafer, S. (2001, March 24). New gender, same job: Transsexuals slowly gaining acceptance in the workplace. *Toronto Star,* sec. M, pp. 10–11.

Schopenhauer, A. (1966). *The world as will and representation* (Vol. 2). New York: Dover.

Scruton, R. (1986). *Sexual desire: A philosophical investigation.* London: Weidenfeld and Nicolson.

Sell, R. L. (1997). Defining and measuring sexual orientation: A review. *Archives of Sexual Behaviour, 26,* 643–658.

Seneca. (1964). On benefits (J. W. Basore, Trans.). In T. E. Page (Ed.), *Seneca: Moral essays* (Vol. 3). London: William Heinemann.

Shaffer, J. A. (1978). Sexual desire. *Journal of Philosophy, 65,* 175–189.

Shively, M., and De Cecco, J. (1977). Components of sexual identity. *Journal of Homosexuality, 3,* 41–48.

Simon, W., and Gagnon, J. H. (1986). Sexual scripts: Permanence and change. *Archives of Sexual Behavior, 15,* 97–120.

Singer, J., and Singer, I. (1972). Types of female orgasms. *Journal of Sex Research, 8,* 255–267.

Sipe, A. W. R. (1995). *Sex, priests, and power: Anatomy of a crisis.* New York: Brunner/Mazel.

Skrine, R. (1997). *Blocks and freedom in sexual life: A handbook of psychosexual medicine.* Oxford: Radcliffe Medical Press.

Spinoza, B. de. (1955). *The chief works of Spinoza: On the improvement of the understanding, The ethics, Correspondence* (R. H. M. Elwes, Trans.). New York: Dover.

Sprecher, S. (1998). Social exchange theories and sexuality. *Journal of Sex Research, 35,* 32-43.

Stayton, W. R. (1980). A theory of sexual orientation: The universe as a turn on. *Topics in Nursing, 1,* 1–8.

Stayton, W. R. (1989). A theology of sexual pleasure. *American Baptist Quarterly, 8,* 94–108.

Sternberg, R. J. (1986). A triangular theory of love. *Psychological Review, 93,* 119–135.

Stoller, R. J. (1975). Sexual excitement. *Archives of General Psychiatry, 33,* 899–909.

Stoller, R. J. (1982). Erotic vomiting. *Archives of Sexual Behavior, 11,* 361–365.

Storms, M. (1980). Theories of sexual orientation. *Journal of Personality and Social Psychology, 38,* 783–792.

Storms, M. D. (1978). Sexual orientation and self-perception. In P. Pliner, K. R. Blanstein, I. Spigel, and M. Spigel (Eds), *Advances in the study of communication and affect: Vol. 5. Perception of emotion in self and others* (pp. 165–180). New York: Plenum.

Suggs, R. C. (1966). *Marquesan sexual behavior.* London: Constable and Company.

Sykes, B. (2003). *Adam's curse.* New York: Bantam Press.

Symons, D. (1987). An evolutionary approach: Can Darwin's view of life shed light on human sexuality? In J. H. Geer and W. T. O'Donohue (Eds), *Theories of human sexuality* (pp. 91–125). New York: Plenum Press.

Taylor, C. C. W. (1986). Emotions and wants. In J. Marks (Ed.), *The ways of desire: New essays in philosophical psychology on the concept of wanting* (pp. 217–231). Chicago: Precedent Publishing.

Tripp, C. A. (1988). *The homosexual matrix* (2nd ed.). New York: Meridian.

Vātsyāyana. (1994). *The complete Kāma Sūtra* (A. Daniélou, Trans.). Rochester, VT: Park Street Press.

Wålinder, J. (1967). *Transsexualism: A study of forty-three cases.* Göteborg, Sweden: Akademiforlaget.

Walsh, A. (1991). *The science of love.* Buffalo, NY: Prometheus Books.

Walster, E., and Berscheid, E. (1971). Adrenaline makes the heart grow fonder. *Psychology Today, 5,* 47–62.

Watts, A. W. (1958). *Nature, man and woman: A new approach to sexual experience.* London: Thames and Hudson.

Westheimer, R. K., and Lopater, C. (2002). *Human sexuality: A psychosexual perspective.* Philadelphia: Lippincott Williams and Wilkins.

White, G. L., and Mullen, P. E. (1989). *Jealousy: Theory, research, and clinical strategies.* New York: Guilford.

Williams, C. J., and Weinberg, M. S. (2003). Zoophilia in men: A study of sexual interest in animals. *Archives of Sexual Behavior, 32,* 523–535.

Yashodhara. (1994). *Jayamangalā* Commentary. In Vātsyāyana, *The complete Kāma Sūtra* (A. Daniélou, Trans.). Rochester, VT: Park Street Press.

Yoshimoto, B. (1993). *Kitchen* (M. Backus, Trans.). London: Faber and Faber.

Zgourides, G. (1996). *Human sexuality: Contemporary perspectives.* New York: HarperCollins.

Zilbergeld, B. (1978). *Male sexuality: A guide to sexual fulfillment.* Boston: Little, Brown.

Zilbergeld, B. (1999). *The new male sexuality* (Rev. ed.). New York: Bantam.

Index

active role, 32, 46; male in full view, 128; meaning of events, 43; phenomenological account, 45; phenomenology, 44–50; preferred term, 32; relation to human sexual activity, 17; relation to sexual desire, 13, 35–44

sexual response cycle, 30–35; early extensive criticism, 32; neglect of sexual desire, 33–35; suggests passive and automatic reactions, 32–33; voyeur, 87

sexual strategy/strategies, 53–55

sexual taste/tastes, 5, 187

Shaffer, J. A., 65–66

Shively, M., and De Cecco, J., 117

sho, 8

Simon, W., and Gagnon, J. H., 180

Singer, J. and Singer, I., 34

Sipe, A. W. R., 116

Siriono of eastern Bolivia, 78

skin, 62, 69 (*see also* caress/caressing, bare skin; caress/caressing, bare skin by bare skin; hair, roots penetrate the skin): color, 92; contact, 74–75; grafts, 106; mottling, 31; object caressing, 91; smoothness, 40; stroking, 83; surface congestion, 19; tingling, 133

Skrine, R., 78

sleep (*see also* post-coital behavoir, sleep): biological need for, 181

"Smaradipika" ("Light of Love"), 3

smell, 132. *See also* hair, smell; perfume; vaginal fluid, perfumed

sneezing. *See* orgasm, sneezing

social constructionism, 179–180

sociobiology, 51–52

Solomon, 138

"Song of Songs, The," 138

Sorge, 148

space. *See* awareness of space

spermatic cord, 44

Spinoza, B. de., 10

spirit, 122

spiritual satisfaction, 17

spreading outward and into body, 133; sense of softness, 133

stalking, 143

stargazing. *See* post coital behavior, stargazing

state of fusion with other gender, 133

Stayton, W. R., 111–112, 114–116

Sternberg, R. J., 145

Stoller, R., 41, 92

stomach, 70, 126

Storms, M., 117–119

strangers; sexual desire, 177

stroking, 46, 71, 84 (*see also* hair, stroking; skin, stroking): legs, 64, 120

Studies in the Psychology of Sex, 18

sucking, 84. *See also* finger sucking; toe and finger sucking; vagina, sucking in penis

suffusion of warmth, 31–32

suppression, 39

suspension or stoppage; feeling, 31

Symposium, 137

taboo, vii. *See also,* incest, taboo

Talk on Supreme Guidence for the World, 17

Tao Te Ching, 134

Tao, 135

Taoist philosophy/thinking, 122, 134

Taoist sex manuals, 135

Taoist thinkers, 17

Taylor, C. C. W., 14

teeth, 126. *See also* biting

testes, 31. *See also* testicles

testicles, 100, 103, 106, 126 (*see also* erotogenic region/zone, testicles): elevate of own accord, 106; fundamental to being male, 99–102

thirst; biological need, 181

Three Essays on Sexuality, 20, 21

throat, 17, 25

thrusting upward; awareness, 31

time. *See* awareness of time

tingle/tingles, 59, 69. *See also* skin, tingling

to the things themselves. *See* Husserl, E.

Toda culture (*see also* sexual intercourse, Toda approach): jealousy virtually non-existent, 159; polyandrous culture, 159

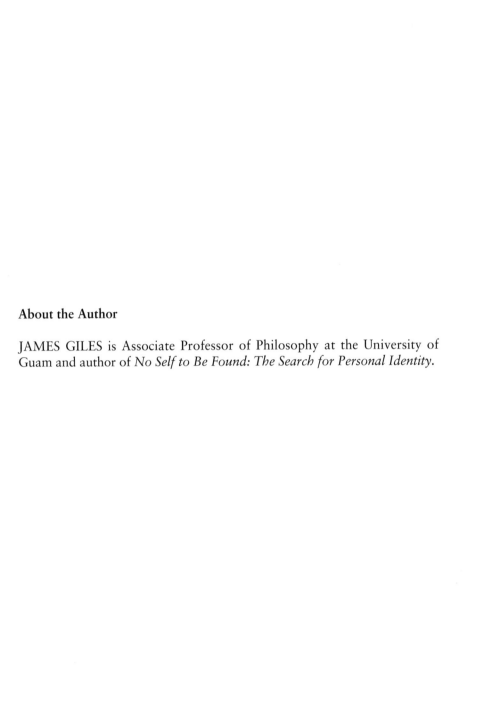

About the Author

JAMES GILES is Associate Professor of Philosophy at the University of Guam and author of *No Self to Be Found: The Search for Personal Identity.*